Long Mile Home

continued . . .

LONG MILE HOME

Boston Under Attack,
the City's Courageous Recovery,
and the Epic Hunt for Justice

SCOTT HELMAN *and* JENNA RUSSELL

Reporters for The Boston Globe

 NEW AMERICAN LIBRARY

New American Library
Published by the Penguin Group
Penguin Group (USA) LLC, 375 Hudson Street,
New York, New York 10014

USA | Canada | UK | Ireland | Australia | New Zealand | India | South Africa | China
penguin.com
A Penguin Random House Company

Published by New American Library, a division of Penguin Group (USA) LLC. Previously
published in a Dutton edition.

First New American Library Printing, April 2015

REGISTERED TRADEMARK—MARCA REGISTRADA

NEW AMERICAN LIBRARY TRADE PAPERBACK ISBN: 978-0-451-46942-7

THE LIBRARY OF CONGRESS HAS CATALOGUED
THE DUTTON HARDCOVER EDITION AS FOLLOWS:
Helman, Scott.
Long mile home: Boston under attack, the city's courageous recovery, and the epic hunt for
justice/Scott Helman and Jenna Russell, reporters for the Boston Globe.
p. cm.
Includes bibliographical references and index.
ISBN 978-0-525-95448-4 (hardcover)
1. Boston Marathon Bombing, Boston, Mass., 2013.
2. Terrorism—Massachusetts—Boston—Case studies.
3. Bombing investigation—Massachusetts—Case studies.
I. Russell, Jenna, 1970– II. Title.
HV6432.8.H45 2014
363.32509744'61090512—dc23   2014000091

Printed in the United States of America
1 3 5 7 9 10 8 6 4 2

Set in Times Ten LT Std
Designed by Amy Hill

*To those who lost their lives on April 15, 2013,
and those whose lives were forever altered*

Contents

CONTENTS

CONTENTS

PART 2

About This Book

Long Mile Home is the product of an enormous team effort by the *Boston Globe* staff to capture the full magnitude of the Boston Marathon attack on April 15, 2013, and its many repercussions. The authors are indebted to each and every colleague who contributed to the paper's coverage, an extraordinary body of work in which this book is grounded.

As of this writing in late 2013, the surviving bombing suspect, Dzhokhar Tsarnaev, had not been convicted of any crimes in the case. The accounts and descriptions, in *Long Mile Home*, of his alleged acts during Marathon Week are based on the criminal indictment against him; interviews with witnesses, law enforcement officials, and other sources; and news reports.

Long Mile Home

PROLOGUE

Laced up and pointed toward the sea

What you see first, after the starting gun's crack, is a column of bobbing runners, thousands of them, surging downhill on a twisting two-lane road, a kinetic rainbow of tank tops, radiant T-shirts, race-day costumes, visors, headbands, and hats. It is a thrilling sight every year, these opening moments of the Boston Marathon, in a part of Hopkinton, Massachusetts, known as Cookie's Corner, named for a longtime townie who used to man the starting line. Here, the fast and the slow, the agile and the aging, the big names and the also-rans all begin their unison descent to Boston's Copley Square, 26.2 miles away in the heart of the city.

Runners have assembled at this spot for decades, carrying their hopes, their mettle, and their anxieties under the bib numbers on their chests. Each has imagined that exultant moment at the finish, muscles aching, arms thrust skyward, a sweet sensation of relief and satisfaction. But those visions begin here, 490 feet above sea level, with a dash over the letters that say, simply, START, hand-stenciled across a road just thirty-nine feet wide, nestled between a tranquil town green and a weathered cemetery. Hopkinton's small-town charm signals just how far away the finish line lies, on Boylston Street, a crowded thoroughfare at the feet of Boston's tallest skyscrapers. Indeed, it's easy to forget, at the start, the hard realities of running 26.2 miles, the difficult hours that always come. Adrenaline throbs beneath the skin. The crowd is expectant, its enthusiasm infectious. All this excitement, this unique sensation of participating in the world's most storied road race, puts air under your feet: For the first few miles, you feel as though you're floating.

The Boston Marathon, for many runners, is the crown jewel of road races, difficult to qualify for but a joy to run once you're in. It is not, however, just the province of elites. The magic of the Boston Marathon is the breadth of participation, its invitation to both top athletes and recreational runners competing for charity. There is room for both Shalane Flanagan, one of the country's leading woman runners, and Orange Man, aka Alain Ferry, a Boston Web entrepreneur who sometimes runs in his gleaming, full-body spandex suit, stopping along the way to take pictures with friends, dance, and high-five spectators, downing beers as he goes. The race is at once a collective and deeply personal endeavor, the confluence of thousands of individual goals, stories, causes, experiences, triumphs, and disappointments.

At heart, the Boston Marathon honors something very simple. It celebrates life's constructive forces: good health, fellowship, hard work, discipline, philanthropy, and a belief that we can push ourselves to greater heights, especially alongside others reaching for them, too. In the words of Olympic champion Frank Shorter, "Running is an affirmative act." To line up in Hopkinton is to put your hand up and say: *Me, too.*

Some run to raise money for causes close to their hearts—cancer, Alzheimer's, autism—often competing in the name or memory of a loved one. Some hope to crack the top spots, to cement their status in the running hierarchy. Some aspire just to make it to the finish, a feat they will brag about to friends and relatives over backyard beers, or with an oval 26.2 sticker on the bumper of their car. Most approach the start knowing that out there, along the snaking course, are spouses, children, parents, neighbors, cousins, siblings, coworkers. They know much of Greater Boston will be out there, too, with cheers, whistles, bongo drums, homemade signs, kelly green Boston Celtics T-shirts, high fives, water bottles, orange slices, Gatorade, energy gel, dogs, babies, singing, and beer. In a sense, there are no spectators; everyone is a participant, part of a time-tested ritual on the most cherished day of the Boston calendar.

Every April, Massachusetts halts to mark Patriot's Day, as it has for more than a century, in part to commemorate the opening battles of the Revolutionary War. The whiff of revolution has long faded, but the spirit of the old town endures—plucky, proudly independent, and fiercely protective of tradition. And there is hardly a bigger tradition than Marathon Monday. The day typically kicks off spring break for public school students statewide. It heralds the arrival of a hard-earned spring. It brings a special morning game for the beloved Boston Red Sox at Fenway Park. It's a chance to breathe in a place that defines high-strung, a chance for Boston to put aside, at least for a moment, its tribalism and fractiousness, to welcome outsiders to a town not always known for its hospitality. To celebrate the top runners but also the stragglers, the strivers, and the hobbyists, all of them laced up and pointed toward the sea.

As runners make their way eastward, the landmarks begin to unfold: the old train depot in Framingham Center, around the six-mile mark, its more urban setting a hint of the big city that lies ahead; the tidy brick façades of Natick's town center, where the crowds begin to build; the women of Wellesley College, perched like birds on a long stone wall, their invigorating roar audible from hundreds of feet away; the unwelcome incline of Heartbreak Hill, the last of seven slopes in suburban Newton that test runners' endurance of mind and body; the ebullience of Boston College students at the crest, eager to tempt with a cold brew; the iconic CITGO sign in Kenmore Square, lit up like the city's year-round Christmas tree, beckoning runners toward the homestretch; and then the bulging crowds toward the finish line. As runners cross the finish, a blue-and-yellow adhesive laid on Boylston Street, there by the Boston Public Library, their names are read individually over a public address system. They complete the race alone, on their own power. But in running Boston, these men and women share a fraternity unlike anything else in American sport.

On April 15, 2013, the rituals renew for the 117th year. Veteran runners come prepared with their superstitions, their traditions, their routines. First-timers forge their own. In Hopkinton on this morning, among some 23,000 other competitors, is Vicma Lamarche, a thirty-two-year-old marketing specialist from Boston running her first Boston Marathon. She nibbles on boiled eggs and a sweet potato she has brought in a Glad container, on the advice of a nutritionist. Tom Mitchell, a forty-eight-year-old software engineer from nearby Lexington, is also running his first Boston. The charity team he belongs to gathers at a house near the starting line, where Mitchell trades jokes with other runners and eats his customary prerun meal: a banana, a honey wheat bagel from Price Chopper, and Peanut Butter & Co.'s Smooth Operator peanut butter. Amy Formica, a thirty-nine-year-old ultramarathoner from Pennsylvania, arms herself for the morning cold, putting on gloves, arm warmers, and a jacket for the early miles.

The runners these days all have timing tags in their bibs, allowing anyone to track their progress electronically. When Vicma Lamarche stomps across the first checkpoint, knowing her family will get an automated message, she says aloud, "This is for you, Victoria!" dedicating the milestone to her four-year-old daughter waiting down the course. Amy Formica wants to be home in bed. Through the early miles, she feels horrible. *Why am I doing this?* she thinks to herself. She fights on, finally finding her rhythm about twenty miles in. At Kenmore Square, steps from Fenway, Joann Kwah, a thirty-six-year-old doctor-in-training at Boston Medical Center, grows euphoric, believing she has passed a critical threshold: Having made it this far, nothing will stop her from finishing her first-ever marathon. *Bucket list: check.* The theme from *Rocky* blares in her head, her smile a mile wide.

Michelle Hall, who is fifty-three and owns a science education company in Los Alamos, New Mexico, is running with a banner to honor a friend with brain cancer, who had qualified for Boston but was unable to come because of recent surgery. About halfway through, Hall puts her foot down and tears a muscle in her hip, screaming in agony. She tries to continue. People in the crowd around her catch sight of her name on a label stuck to her shirt. "Michelle, you look awesome!" they yell. "You look great, girl!" She starts to cry and keeps going, making it to mile nineteen, where a physical therapist she knows only as John gives her a massage. (In keeping with the spirit of the marathon, she doesn't flinch when he pulls her shorts down a bit to find the trouble spot; she tells him she loves him.) A mile later, Hall leans against a display table to ease the pain. She looks up and notices a red Solo cup six inches from her face. She glances at a man standing nearby.

"Is that cold beer?" Hall asks him.

"Yes," he says. "Do you want it?"

"Yes."

"Go ahead."

She hoists the cup to her lips. The crowd gives an encouraging cheer. She chugs it. *What the heck*, she thinks. *This is either going to do me in or get me to the finish line.*

Tom Mitchell's left knee is giving him hell, but he tries to run through the pain, gaining momentum into the homestretch. He passes his kids before the final turn, high-fiving them, and then rounds onto Boylston, his arms raised in victory. He approaches the twenty-six-mile marker, which this year has a special flag that pays tribute, with twenty-six gold stars, to the victims of the December 2012 school shooting in Newtown, Connecticut. He veers over to the flag and touches it with his right hand. Then he starts back toward the center of the road. The finish line is mere blocks away.

Oh my gosh—she must be mentally ill, Nicole McGurin thinks. *Why does she have a number?* McGurin, a forty-year-old from west of

Boston who works for the local chapter of the Alzheimer's Association, is on Beacon Street in Brookline, about to enter Boston, eager to complete her second Boston Marathon. A woman on the course, another runner, begins yelling about a bomb going off, shouting to anyone willing to listen. No one pays her much heed. Everyone races by her: a crazy person on the corner, that's all. A little ways behind McGurin, Vicma Lamarche turns to her right and sees a group of people watching TV in front of an apartment building. Images of an explosion fill the screen, but she only catches a glimpse. She can't tell what she's seeing. Whatever it is, she thinks, it must be happening somewhere else. *Maybe there has been a bombing in Iraq. Maybe there's a big forest fire in California.*

Tom Mitchell's wife, Christine, forty-eight, a freelance marketer running her fourth consecutive Boston, is less than a mile from the finish. She hears sirens wailing, more than usual, but she assumes this just means lots of runners are battling injuries. That makes sense — she herself has suffered leg cramps today. She begins to see people in street clothes coming toward her, intruding on the race. *The Sox game must be over and Fenway is letting out*, she thinks. Suddenly Lamarche sees police cars race by the runners, recklessly close. "Wow, that's rude," she says to herself. "They could totally hit someone." *Maybe someone fainted*, she thinks. She reaches the twenty-four-mile marker and race officials are pulling up the mat. She hears someone say, "The race is over." She wonders, *Am I running that slowly?* This must be how it is, she figures. And yet the people streaming out of Fenway, many with a beer or two in them, are cheering her and other runners on. She keeps going.

Michelle Hall looks up to see a gray plume of smoke. A platoon of police, bright vests over their dark uniforms, rush in the direction of the finish line. Tom Mitchell, up ahead of his wife, is just steps from the finish when he hears a tremendous boom. It sounds like a cannon. He thinks perhaps someone special has just crossed — maybe it's Dick Hoyt, who has pushed his son, Rick, a quadriplegic with cerebral palsy, through the course in a wheelchair for more than three decades, their unique bond an inspiration every year. *Maybe this is part of the tradition*, Mitchell thinks. *Maybe this always happens.* Alain Ferry, the Orange Man, has promenaded now through nearly the whole course, posting pictures to Facebook and drinking beer along the way, and is approaching Massachusetts Avenue when he sees his friend Stephen, who is waving him over. Ferry is having a ball. It's clear that Stephen isn't, by the stony look on his face. "Something's wrong," Stephen tells him. "You can't keep running." Stephen's wife grabs Ferry's arm. She urges him: "Please don't run any farther until we know what happened."

Just up the road, police and race officials establish a barricade, stopping runners at the 25.5-mile marker, less than a mile from the end. "Stay here!" police are yelling. Some 5,752 of the more than twenty-three thousand runners have yet to finish, nearly all of them competing for charity. "Stay right here!" A mass of runners gathers, more and more arriving every second, all of them forced to halt at the bottleneck. They are confused, frustrated, angry. They have nearly finished a marathon. Now they're being told to go no farther. And they don't know why. *You cannot do this*, Eduardo Kelly, a fifty-three-year-old physician and marathoner from south of Boston, thinks to himself. *You cannot do this to me.* Their brains are fried, their bodies empty, their legs spent. All they can hear are sirens.

A runner near Joann Kwah pulls out her phone and checks Twitter. "Oh my God," the woman says, reading aloud reports of explosions at the finish line. The news spreads through the crowd. The details are sketchy but terrifying. Many runners have family at the finish line. They begin sharing cell phones, furiously looking for news about friends and relatives. *My wife is at the finish line*, they're saying. *My husband. My father. My kids.* It is hard to get through to anyone, the lines are down, communication cut off. A few text messages break through: *There have been explosions; people are hurt.* The runners fear the worst. Some are crying, hysterical. Rumors begin flying. Is this another 9/11? Is this war? No one knows. *All the buildings downtown are still standing*, Nicole McGurin thinks. *How bad can it be?*

A chilly afternoon wind is blowing through the city. The stopped runners, after only a few minutes, are getting cold. They begin to huddle together like bees in a hive. All respect for personal space evaporates. Staying close is the only way to keep warm. Michelle Hall, carrying the brain cancer banner for her friend, wraps it around a skinny older runner, maybe in his seventies, who is standing next to her. He appears to be suffering from hypothermia. A woman on his other side wraps herself around him, too. The man is shaking uncontrollably from head to toe. A spectator brings him hot coffee. He tries to drink it, but it makes him vomit. Hall walks him to the apartments along Commonwealth Avenue, searching for help. Someone inside the building comes down with blankets. Two men help the man up to a woman's apartment, out of the cold.

Runners take refuge wherever they can—in the vestibules of brownstones, in campus buildings at Boston University, in a Bank of America branch, on nearby stoops. No one knows what to do, where to go. So they wait, the cold now stiffening their muscles, seeping into their bones. Residents of nearby apartments bring them water, food, blankets, garbage bags to cut the wind, and armfuls of clothing—yoga pants, exercise jackets, sweatshirts. They offer use of their cell phones. Some bring runners into their homes. All of these small gifts of humanity and generosity will add up to something much larger in the days ahead. They will not be forgotten.

The Boston Marathon, for the first time ever, has come to a halt. The race, begun in 1897, has survived brutal heat waves, unforgiving April nor'easters, wheelchair collisions, fraudulent victors, a freight train blocking the route, a legendary scuffle over women's participation, and much more. But it has never just stopped. Until now. Some runners start to walk away, hoping to reconnect with their families, or get home, or to their hotels. Locals shepherd the out-of-towners, guiding them through uncertain moments in an unfamiliar place. No one knows much about the tragedy unfolding up ahead. No one even knows which streets are open, which ones are closed. They are walking a block at a time, trying to navigate a changed city, the sounds of emergency vehicles ringing out over the darkening streets.

As runners gradually disperse, the day's gravity reveals itself in individual moments. For some, it's a text message or phone call from the finish line. For others, it's a radio report in a girlfriend's car after finally arranging a pickup. It's a breaking-news flash on a TV in a desolate downtown shopping mall. A glorious day has been corrupted by evil, horror, sadness.

The blow is inconceivable and all too real, the shock and grief touching so many, the damage at once widespread and devastatingly precise. Underneath it all, a difficult question presents itself: Why? *Why!* The answer will prove elusive: the illogic of it all, the cowardly calculus, the random cruelty, immune to analysis. In the hours and days ahead, panic and anger will settle over Boston, the city's vulnerability—*every* city's vulnerability—exposed. Strength and courage will follow. Hundreds of families will be tested in ways they never imagined. The city, its people, and its marathon, irrevocably changed.

PART 1

CHAPTER 1

APRIL

Five lives, one race

t was spring, and change was on the way. Heather Abbott didn't know what kind of change it would be, but she could feel momentum gathering. She had felt it before, and she knew what it meant. It was almost time for her to move on.

April marked the end of the winter off-season in Newport, Rhode Island, when the seaside bars and restaurants belonged to year-round residents like Heather and her friends. In another month tourists would descend, crowding the brick sidewalks and the mansions along Bellevue Avenue. This final quiet moment was one to savor. Heather had grown to love Newport in her four years there. She loved the house she lived in, tucked into the historic district right behind the Elms, one of the city's opulent turn-of-the-century summer estates. She loved her close-knit group of friends, Tommy and Jason and Jess and Michelle and the rest, who were like the siblings she never had. It was comfortable and sociable and fun, dressing up and frequenting their favorite places every weekend. But Heather had begun to feel restless with the routine. The world outside was waiting, and she was ready for it.

At thirty-eight, the good-natured blonde with the warm brown eyes and the calm, capable manner had built a life on seeing opportunities and stepping out to meet them. She was driven, and in many ways, she was bold. She liked the idea of landing a new job and moving to a new city. She had fallen in love with Charleston, South Carolina, on a short trip south the previous fall, and now she wondered if that small historic city should be her next destination. Closer to home, just seventy miles to the north, Boston was a more obvious choice, near her family and friends. The company she worked for in Rhode Island, Raytheon, was headquartered near Boston; if she wanted to, she could pursue a new job there. Early in April, talking with a friend over dinner in Boston, Heather had contemplated where she might live if she moved to the city. The South End, with its vibrant restaurant scene and beautifully renovated brownstones, was one possibility, but she was also intrigued by the North End, Boston's historically Italian neighborhood, where elements of the old-world culture persisted amid tourists and newer, upscale hotspots. Sitting across from her, Heather's friend Steve picked up his phone and typed out a text message to a woman he knew who lived there, inquiring about rents.

Heather knew the woman he was asking. Her name was Roseann Sdoia; they had met through him, and saw each other occasionally at outings with friends. Heather and Roseann usually ran into each other on Patriot's Day, at the Boston Marathon. Both of them liked to go to the same place near the finish line, a bar and restaurant on Boylston Street called Forum. The marathon was about ten days away, and Heather figured maybe she would see Roseann then. They could talk about the North End and life in Boston. One more step toward figuring out where she would go next.

There was nothing like running a marathon in your own city. That was what Boston was to him now, Dr. David King realized—his city. It had taken a long time for him to feel that way. The attachment to the place, the sense of belonging, was still tentative and new to the thirty-nine-year-old doctor. He had gone to college in Tampa and medical school in Miami, and it was there, during long overnights at the Ryder Trauma Center, facing an endless parade of stabbings, gunshot wounds, speedboat accidents, and motorcycle crashes, that he had honed his skills as a trauma surgeon. He had loved Miami, its vibrancy and energy and its work-hard-play-hard mentality. King had met his wife, Anne, a scientist, in college, and she shared his appreciation for the laid-back Floridian lifestyle.

Still, both of them had lasting ties to New England. David had grown up in Rhode Island and his mom and dad were still there. Anne's parents had retired in New Hampshire, after years of moving around in the military. After King and his wife graduated, it seemed to make sense to look for jobs in Boston. He accepted an internship at Beth Israel Deaconess Medical Center. They moved north—and soon discovered that they did not like Boston one bit. Partly it was the ratty apartment that was all they could afford. The lack of parking didn't help. Nor did the cold, or the fact that King was working around the clock. He often fell asleep at the table while eating his dinner. They wondered if they could ever fit in, in a medical community where a Harvard degree could seem like a prerequisite. Strangest of all, Bostonians seemed to do nothing but work, or talk about work. The Kings escaped back to Miami as soon as they could.

Six years passed. David had volunteered as an army reserve surgeon while he was in Boston, and in 2008 he was called to serve for several months in Iraq. The couple had a daughter now, and they had seen the bond develop between her and her grandparents in New England. Then an offer came for David from Massachusetts General Hospital—the perfect job, at one of the best hospitals in the country—and they asked themselves, was it worth another try? If they went back, they had to do it with gusto and make the place their own. And so King made it his mission: to import his own attitude and style to a foreign and perhaps unreceptive territory. He bought a big red jacket and an orange hat, a declaration of rebellion in the face of winter's drabness. Moving through the hospital at high speed but with a gentle touch, he met everyone in his path, from his patients to the janitors mopping the hallways, with an openness and warmth. "How's your day?" the wiry, blue-eyed doctor would ask the woman handing out clean scrubs from a supply room window. "How are you feeling, my friend?" he asked the injured in their beds.

Still, that first year was hard. He took some calls about jobs back in Florida, toying with the notion of surrender. The second year, he and Anne felt a growing connection to Boston. By the third year, it had deepened to attachment. They had two daughters now, giving them new appreciation for the city's museums and parks. They lived in Cambridge, just across the river from Mass General, and he walked to work every day, while Anne went to nearby Kendall Square, near MIT, to a start-up company where she helped develop more effective cancer drugs. He had a lab at the hospital and a little time for the research he loved, trying to solve problems related to his work, like how to control bleeding better after trauma. It was still hard being on call for twenty-four hours at a stretch, sleeping at the hospital and missing his kids, but life was good. The marathon in Boston was a day to celebrate that. A few weeks earlier, he had feared he would have to miss the hometown race because of back problems, and the thought had pained him more than he once could have imagined. But as April 15 approached, King felt his confidence growing. This Boston Marathon—*his* marathon—would be his fastest yet.

She was a Boston girl through and through. And she was proud of it. There wasn't a professional sports jersey Krystle Campbell didn't own—Red Sox, Patriots, Bruins, Celtics, even the Revolution, the Major League Soccer franchise—and she wore them like badges of honor. Occasionally, she would get game tickets, and invite her father, Billy Jr., along. *Take a friend*, he would often say. *Don't waste the ticket on silly old Dad*. She lit up inside those stadiums and arenas, throwing herself into the role of New England sports partisan. She loved tailgating, too. And it wasn't just sports that drew her out. The twenty-nine-year-old was game for almost anything—hitting a new bar in Boston, Fourth of July fireworks on the banks of the Charles

River, a night at the symphony. "She loved the life of the city," her father said.

On Patriot's Day, the holiday that celebrated Boston's unique character more than any other, Krystle often joined the throngs along the sidelines of the marathon. The race was just her kind of thing, a perfect marriage of sport, party, and civic pride. Plus, if anyone deserved a little respite, a chance to get off the clock and decompress, it was Krystle. In recent years, she'd worked relentlessly, unable to say no, to let things go slack, to see a job done halfway. She couldn't help it. That was her nature, and the way she'd been raised. After watching Mom and Dad put in long hours, working hard was all she knew.

For much of the previous decade, Krystle had been a trusted deputy at Jasper White's Summer Shack, a seafood-oriented restaurant company with outposts around the Boston area. Managing, waitressing, serving drinks, setting up tables, washing dishes, loading trucks—she had done it all. From the moment she started working there, in 2005, she announced herself as a competent leader. Her work ethic was almost freakish. Nowhere was that more evident than on Spectacle and Georges Islands in Boston Harbor, where Summer Shack had established seasonal eateries and a bustling business catering corporate events, clambakes, and weddings. In the warmer months, she put in eighty-hour weeks on the islands, often stepping onto the first boat out and the last boat back—and that was only if she wasn't sleeping over. With her maternal instincts, she became the de facto leader of a motley crew of people who worked on and around the islands, employed by the city, state, private vendors, and nonprofits. By the force of her personality, they grew into a kind of family. The community became known, simply, as the islands. Krystle was the island girl.

She had an easy class about her. After the hard physical work of setting up for a big event, she would effortlessly slip into a cocktail dress to play hostess, as if she had looked like that forever. Then once the guests were gone, she would immediately throw on her shorts, tank top, and flip-flops. When an especially demanding function was over, she was known to say, "How did we pull that off?" The answer, to everyone else, was clear: It was her—her energy, savvy, and attention to detail. That wasn't how she saw it, though. It was always the team that made it happen. Her refrain, once the lights came on and the VIPs had left, was often this: "My fucking guys are awesome." When it was finally time to clock out, she could play as hard as she worked. She liked to have fun. She wouldn't turn down a shot of Jack Daniel's. "She lived all the way through," said Tim Getchell, a close friend who helped manage the islands for the state.

When things went wrong, Krystle could hit the curveballs. On June 9, 2011, she was dealt a big one. Every year, the Boston Harbor Island Alliance, the nonprofit organization that promotes use of the islands, throws a huge fund-raising gala for several hundred donors and bigwigs. They come out from the city on boats, enjoy an evening overlooking the ocean, and then head back. On this Thursday night, the weather had seemed fine. Krystle and her crew were setting up on Georges Island for a party of five hundred. But just as guests began arriving, a storm system rolled in. The sky opened up. Thunder clapped overhead. The lightning was so treacherous they couldn't use the metal docks for a time. The wind blew hard. The power went out. Water came pouring off a hill in front of Fort Warren, the island's Civil War–era fortress, flooding the tent where they had set up the dinner tables. A disaster, plain and simple. Then Krystle took command.

She hiked up her dress, ditched her shoes, and began, with her team, bailing out the tent with buckets. With Getchell's help, they spread gravel and sand. They laid function tables down like bridges over the rivers that had formed. They powered up the generators. As the guests—many of them in evening dresses and tailored suits—began coming to the tent, Krystle and her staff made an announcement. They wanted everyone to go barefoot; the high heels, flats, and formal shoes just weren't going to cut it in the mud. She didn't care if the guests were big-shot CEOs or wealthy philanthropists. This was how it was going to be. They would have to make the best of it. And they did. The VIPs embraced the soggy atmosphere. The gala became a mud party for the ages, an unforgettable event that was, at the time, the alliance's highest-grossing fund-raiser ever. That night, Krystle and a colleague stayed on the island to break everything down, sleeping, in their dresses, in the cab of a Ryder truck. When they crawled out the next morning their feet were still caked in mud. And they were smiling.

This year's marathon had to be better than the last. How could it be worse? The temperature on race day in 2012 had reached 89 degrees. Great for the beach, disastrous for a marathon. Some 2,200 people required medical attention, and more than 150 were brought to hospitals. No, that marathon experience was one nobody wanted to repeat, especially not Dave McGillivray, fifty-eight, the longtime director of the race. Weather was the one thing out of his control. No amount of preparation, or contingency planning, could change it. No irate phone call could fix it. No army of volunteers could make it right. Every year, it was Mother Nature's little game, and it drove McGillivray crazy.

The Boston Marathon had been his baby since 1988, after the Boston Athletic Association, which put the whole thing on, first brought him in to professionalize the race. Over that quarter century, McGillivray's name had become synonymous with the event. He was its public face, its spirit guide, its minute-by-minute micromanager, intimately involved in everything from where the portable restrooms go at the starting line to getting all the runners and wheelchair racers safely across the finish. Every year, the marathon seemed to get more complex and more popular, a bigger test of his chops. He loved it, though. The pressure, he always said, was a privilege. McGillivray staged other road races and delivered motivational speeches. But the Boston Marathon was the sun in his solar system. April in Boston was unimaginable without him.

He'd come from Medford, not far from where Krystle Campbell would grow up years later. He was the youngest of five in a working-class household that prized faith, honored commitments to the point of obsession, and taught that hard work could overcome anything. His father, a master electrician for a can company, kept a checklist inside the medicine cabinet where his children had to record their toothbrushing. When he was young, all McGillivray ever wanted to do was be an athlete. His genes had other ideas. He was short: five four by the time he was finished growing. It was a disqualifier, as a kid, on the courts and fields. He was chosen last for pickup games and cut from the high school basketball team. Right after the coach delivered the bad news, he challenged the team's center to a game of one-on-one and beat him. He went home, found a black permanent marker, and wrote PLEASE GOD MAKE ME GROW on a piece of cardboard, which he hung above his bed with masking tape.

McGillivray had difficulty accepting his perceived deficiency, but the adversity lit a fire inside him. He decided he would never be outworked, never accept that he couldn't do something. The feelings of helpless anger became his fuel, which he soon funneled into running. It was the perfect sport, the ideal antidote to his experience with coaches and teams. As he would explain decades later, "No one can cut you from running." In 1972, as a seventeen-year-old, he decided cockily that he would run the Boston Marathon. He informed his grandfather, Fred Eaton, with whom he was very close, and Eaton said he would be out on the course, near mile twenty-four, to watch for him. But McGillivray hadn't bothered to train. He had no idea what he was doing, and he collapsed about two-thirds of the way through. Eaton waited for hours before going home. When they finally talked by phone, his grandfather told him to make this day a lesson: If you're going to do something, do it correctly. He hadn't earned the right to run the Boston Marathon. They made a pact. "You train for next year," his grandfather told him. "And I'll be there, too."

Two months later, his grandfather died of a heart attack on his way home from the grocery. McGillivray endeavored to keep his end of the bargain. He trained hard for the 1973 marathon. The day before, he came down with a brutal stomach virus. He entered the race but felt miserable. He was a sorry sight. His mother, seeing his condition, had tears streaming down her face when he passed her at the halfway point. He pushed on until he was near mile twenty-one. Then his body gave out. Defeated, he leaned against a wrought-iron fence. As it happened, the fence surrounded Boston's Evergreen Cemetery, the very place they had buried his grandfather. McGillivray realized his grandfather had been right—he was there to watch him after all. McGillivray knew that he had to make good on their deal, so he picked himself up and finished the race. It was the first of what would be forty-one consecutive completed Boston Marathons, many of them coming hours after the official finish, after he had honored his race-directing duties.

Over his life, McGillivray had worked in the toy department of a local discount store. He had been an actuary for a benefits firm. Once he had even interviewed to be a flight attendant, stuffing his platform shoes with tissues in an attempt to reach the minimum height requirement. But he had been right as a kid: He was destined for sports. After opening an athletic shoe and apparel store in Medford, he got into the race-management business, and that became his calling. His own athletic exploits were legion—running his age in miles every year around his birthday, trying to swim across the English Channel, and participating, with his son Ryan, in what was then, according to Guinness World Records, the largest-ever game of Duck, Duck, Goose, on the field of the Lowell Spinners, a single-A affiliate of the Red Sox. Often his wild endeavors had a charity component—he had helped raise millions for cancer research and other causes over the years. They were also about self-esteem, about pushing himself as far as he could. His unrelenting drive was a marvel to everyone around him. He had long outrun those teenage feelings of inadequacy, but he would never stop trying. As his mother wrote in her diary, "Once Dave starts running, maybe he'll finally be able to get some rest."

She was in the best shape, physically and mentally, of her life. Shana Cottone had stopped drinking five months earlier, in the fall. It had not been easy, over the long winter, to adapt her life to fit the decision.

It still seemed impossible, at times, for the twenty-seven-year-old to find new ways to socialize. That was partly a hazard of her job: Shana was a police officer in Boston, and so were a lot of her friends, and they liked to go to bars together when they were off duty. In one way, it was a kind of therapy. They saw a lot of hard things at work, things that other people didn't understand and didn't really want to hear about. It could be isolating. Sorting through the craziness with other cops was a ritual of healing and of bonding, and alcohol had seemed an essential part of the process.

Shana had been on the job five years. Her first assignment was in West Roxbury, but it hadn't really clicked; the neighborhood on Boston's outer edge had one of the lowest crime rates in the city, and it felt like people didn't really need her there. When her probation period ended, she had asked to be transferred to Roxbury, an inner-city neighborhood with a similar name but a lot more trouble on its streets. When she got there, the district was beginning an innovative project aimed at bringing psychiatric help to troubled residents through policing. Some officers were wary of the assignment, which demanded that they respond to calls in tandem with a civilian, a social worker trained in crisis intervention. Shana was intrigued. Paired up with the clinician, she quickly found her niche. They roamed the neighborhood together, stepping in to defuse domestic conflicts, suicide threats, out-of-control teenagers. Shana loved the sense of potential in the work, the promise of making things better. She thrived in the role, assisting in more than three hundred incidents. One involved a six-year-old boy in a Spider-Man costume who had pulled a butter knife on his foster parent. Shana talked to him as she loaded his booster seat into the back of her cruiser, trying to keep the mood light so he wouldn't be afraid. Before she dropped him off for a mental health evaluation, the little boy gave her a sticker shaped like a heart. Shana stuck it to the back of her badge, where it remained—an invisible reminder, worn over her own heart, of what mattered most to her about her work.

She cared about her job, and she knew she was making a difference. When the day came that her drinking affected her work, it was a slap in the face, and the shock of it brought instant clarity. It had happened back in the fall. She had gotten angry about something on a day off, and before she thought about it, she had acted on the anger. Word of what had happened made it to her supervisors, and the fall-out had gotten in her way at work. It was the first time that had ever happened, and she knew it had to be the last. So she had made her decision and never looked back. On the first day of October 2012, Shana had gone to Western Massachusetts, to a residential treatment program for first responders. She hadn't had a drink since.

Coming back from treatment was scarier than going. She was moving to a new assignment in East Boston, where she didn't know the place or people well. She figured they had heard where she had been, and she didn't know if they would judge her for it. She focused on the parts of her life that were stable—the house she had purchased on a quiet street in Hyde Park, at Boston's southern tip; the pet beagle named Monkey she adored. The winter passed. She found ways to bring the skills she had developed in Roxbury to her new beat, developing relationships with homeless people and addicts, earning their trust, and talking to them about getting sober.

In time, something unexpected happened. People started coming to her—friends, colleagues—telling her that they, too, wanted to stop drinking. In quiet conversations, one-on-one, they confessed that they didn't know how to go about it, and asked for her help. Shana did what she could. People had gone out on a limb for her in her darkest moments, and she wanted to repay the debt.

"No—*K-R-Y*," she would say, quick to correct the assumption that her name began more conventionally, with a *C*.

"Oh, excuse me; I've never heard it spelled like that," the chastened adult would reply.

"Well, you have now," young Krystle Campbell would say back.

That was Krystle—self-assured, outspoken, and in charge. She was born in Somerville and grew up in Medford, a solidly middle-class city north of Boston that her parents had chosen for the schools.

Her grandmother always put her in dresses and loved to curl her hair. Krystle would then try to straighten it. In the summers, her parents, Billy Jr. and Patty, took Krystle and her brother, Billy III, up to New Hampshire. One year they bought a twenty-eight-foot camping trailer, which they kept parked at a campground. It became their summer home. They put down white rock around it, planted flowers, and built a platform, where they kept a tent for toys and Nintendo. Patty and the kids stayed up there full-time after school let out, and Billy Jr. drove up on weekends and sometimes during the week. The setting, with swimming, a waterslide, dances, races, and activities for kids all season long, was ideal for families, many of whom came back year after year. Those sweet, slow summer days lasted until Krystle and her brother were teenagers, and then adolescent concerns back home—friends, young love, sports schedules—made it harder to get away.

As Krystle got older, her father still called her princess. She took up the clarinet, played softball, and began waitressing as a teenager. She graduated from Medford High School in 2001 and went on to community college, eventually earning an associate's degree and transferring to the University of Massachusetts Boston, where she got close to a bachelor's degree but didn't finish. Together with her reddish hair, big blue eyes, and mile-wide smile, Krystle's animated personality and authenticity gave her a presence that wasn't easily forgotten. "You're not supposed to have favorites, but you do," said Tony Szykniej, who taught her in middle school band. "She definitely was one."

Her forceful disposition, though, did not make her self-centered. She was conscientious to a fault, often putting herself last. When her nana, her dad's mother, got sick, Krystle moved in with her for eighteen months. It wasn't a decision most twentysomethings would make. When friends asked her why, her answer was simple: "Because she needs me." While working for Summer Shack, she took notice of one kid, an immigrant from Liberia, who worked for the state out on the islands. It was evident he didn't have much money, so she regularly sent him home with leftovers—hamburgers, hot dogs, whatever was there. Wanting to preserve his dignity, she was careful not to call it a handout. *Hey, we've got some extra food*, she'd say. *Why don't you take it?* She wrote letters to another islands employee when he was in jail for drunk driving, and then helped him try to find work when he got out. She knew the ferry crews often didn't have time to get off the boat for lunch, so she'd bring burgers down to the docks.

And she would do just about anything for her friends. Tim Getchell and his fiancée had both grown up poor. He came from the projects in Boston's Charlestown section; she was from South Carolina. They wanted a wedding but didn't have the money. Krystle told them not to worry. She took care of the whole thing at a seaside pub: tent, alcohol, pasta with red sauce, chicken parmesan. The night before the wedding, Getchell and his fiancée brought their families together for a small, modest celebration. They had bought simple cheese plates from the grocery. Then Krystle showed up with fifteen lobsters, steamers, and other seafood. She wanted to give the South Carolinians a proper taste of New England. "It was like she had you under her wing," said Sean McLaughlin, a forest and park supervisor for the state who worked closely with her on the islands. "She had you."

In the waning days of her twenties, Krystle arrived at a crossroads. She needed to slow down, both at work and after work. The pace wasn't sustainable. She had quit Summer Shack for a saner job at Jimmy's Steer House, a restaurant close to her apartment in Arlington, a suburb northwest of Boston. It was meant to be a stepping stone. Her next jump would be to something grander, perhaps something high-end like the Ritz, or something she could make her own. She and Getchell used to daydream about starting their own floating tiki bar. Maybe it would pick revelers up near Logan Airport. Maybe it would bob around Boston Harbor, lit up like a tropical paradise. Whatever form it took, Krystle was ready to run something, to have her own gig. She was growing up. She had a serious boyfriend now, too. He was going to meet her parents, for the first time, on her upcoming birthday. It was a big one. She would be thirty years old.

. . .

The day before the Boston Marathon was almost as good as Marathon Monday, David King thought. It was a day off from his demanding job at the hospital, and he could spend it with his family. Best of all, they were going to the John Hancock Sports & Fitness Expo, the giant runners' trade show that attracted eighty thousand people to a convention center every year in the days before the marathon. King was an admitted expo junkie, capable of wandering for hours through its dizzying maze of high-tech shoes, free energy bar samples, and other exhibits. He knew that standing on his feet all day was not the ideal way to spend the day before the marathon. But he couldn't help himself. It was part of the buildup, part of the fun, and at this point, it was tradition—even if his wife, Anne, did not share his passion, and would spend much of her time at the expo asking when they could go home.

They headed to the convention center on the train Sunday morning. King brought along his two young daughters, a large Starbucks coffee, and a couple of runner friends. Talk turned to King's grueling race schedule. He had run the Miami Marathon in January, and in March he had traveled to New Zealand for his first IRONMAN triathlon, which included a full marathon as well as swimming and biking races. His friends wondered if something had to give, and if in running Boston he was being too ambitious. "Do you think you'll finish?" one of them asked. King brushed aside the worry; the back pain he had felt after the triathlon was gone. Going all in was his nature; his leap from marathons to triathlons had been no surprise to those who knew him well. When his wife had trained for her first marathon, in Miami in 2007, King had watched her running ten, fifteen, or twenty miles and couldn't understand the impulse. It seemed excessive, even ridiculous—who had time to run that far? Then he stood at the finish line of her race and felt excitement coursing through the crowd. The next day he signed up for his first marathon.

His intensity and drive had been evident since he was a boy growing up in Woonsocket, Rhode Island, a small blue-collar city on the Massachusetts border. Drawn to the idea of firefighting, he started volunteering at the fire department as a teenager and signed up for EMT classes at night. He earned an EMT license as a junior in high school, and started working night shifts; instead of going home after school to do his homework, King would go out on calls with the local ambulance. In retrospect, his interest in medicine was obvious. Yet King never once imagined becoming a doctor. His father worked for the city as a laborer; his mother was a secretary. No one in his family had gone to college, let alone medical school. It wasn't until he abandoned his plan to study engineering and transferred to the University of Tampa that he first considered becoming a doctor. Then he failed a botany class. *Well, that's it*, someone told him. *You'll never get into medical school now, with an F on your transcript.* As soon as King heard the word "never," that was it. "Once they told me I couldn't," he recalled, "I said, okay, I'm definitely going."

Getting in was not easy—it looked, for a time, like no school would give him a chance. In a last-ditch effort to keep his dream alive, he applied outside the country, to a school in Grenada. Accepted, he excelled; then, against the odds, he applied for a transfer to the University of Miami and was accepted. Finally on his way to becoming a doctor, King decided to join the army reserve. He had been given a chance to learn lifesaving skills that very few people possessed; bringing those skills to American soldiers at risk seemed like the right thing to do. He was an intern in Boston, working long hours for terrible pay, when a recruiter came to his living room and commissioned him. Weary from a long on-call shift, King raised his right hand and recited the oath of enlistment, swearing to defend the Constitution, while his yellow Labrador retriever, Rachel, looked on, his only witness. The year was 2000. In 2001 America would go to war; King's decision would put him on the front lines of two conflicts. After being sent to Iraq for four months in 2008, he went to Haiti after the earthquake in 2010, and to Afghanistan for three months in 2011. He saw terrible things and survived close calls. When a massive truck bomb injured dozens of American soldiers in Sayed Abad, Afghanistan, on the tenth anniversary of 9/11, he dealt with the carnage. Another time an IED blew up people standing near him. He learned what fear really felt like, what true vigilance was.

And he gained new reverence for his life at home. A lazy, simple day like this was more precious to King now: wandering around the convention center with his wife and daughters; buying a new BOSTON MARATHON 2013 baseball hat to wear in the race tomorrow. The hat purchase was one of his marathon traditions. His runner friends objected; it was bad luck, some said, to wear a hat bearing the logo of the same race you were running in. You were supposed to wear a seasoned hat, one that had been with you in training or at other races. King dismissed the superstition. He always bought a new hat—the women's version, to fit his small head. He had made it his ritual, and he wasn't changing it now.

Heather Abbott had taken the day off from work, as she always did, so she could go to Boston with her friends on Marathon Monday. That was their tradition: They went to the Red Sox game in the morning, then to the finish line of the race. It meant getting up early and driving to Providence to take the train, but they laughed a lot along the way, swept up in the festive mood and the welcome break from routine.

Heather was a runner, too—short distances, not marathons. Running was just one of her active pursuits, along with paddleboarding and Zumba dance fitness classes. She had a good time doing it, but she was also disciplined. It was like that with everything she did; her fun-loving side disguised a steely ambition. In high school, in the small town of Lincoln, Rhode Island, near Providence, she had thought about applying to the University of North Carolina. Her parents were baffled and resistant. She attended a small college in Massachusetts instead, but always felt she had been meant for a bigger place. She studied accounting—her mother had encouraged her to learn a skill—but she soon discovered a more engaging field: human resources, otherwise known as HR. Plunging into it, she learned on her feet, building an HR operation from scratch as the start-up she worked for grew from a dozen to one hundred employees. After going to work for a bigger company, with thirty-three thousand workers, in 2003, she traveled constantly, supervising HR departments in eight states. She had purchased her first condo, in North Providence, at twenty-four; a year and a half later, she sold it on her own and traded up to a bigger, better one.

By 2003 she had earned an MBA from Providence College, attending school at night while working full-time. When she went looking for a new job in 2007, Raytheon and Dunkin' Donuts both made offers. A global defense and aeronautics firm with more than seventy thousand employees, Raytheon won her allegiance. It offered her more money, and its HR department was bigger. She became an expert in compliance, handling large, randomly scheduled government audits. She specialized in discrimination claims, defending the company's managers when they were accused of wrongful treatment of employees. It was the work no one else wanted to do, yet Heather liked it. She liked problem solving—untangling thorny conflicts and guiding them toward resolution.

A decade of advancement had left no doubt: She had what it took to be successful. Now she had to figure out what to conquer next. When she decided, in 2009, to move from North Providence to Newport to be closer to her job, she had thought she'd try it for a year. She wasn't sure if she would like it—insular and privileged, a historic resort town and a party destination, Newport was its own world in more ways than one. She hadn't counted on the closeness of the friendships she would find there, the kinship and belonging that would cast a spell. She wanted to step beyond the bars and parties to see what else there was, but she knew she would miss those things, and especially the people, after she moved on. The summer ahead could be her last in Newport, and Heather intended to make the most of it. Tomorrow's trip to Boston would help kick the season off.

He was out in Boston's Copley Square by 5:00 A.M. It was Sunday, the day before the 2013 Boston Marathon. Dave McGillivray walked the course of the 5K he would put on in a few hours for some 6,500 runners, one in a series of races and fitness events that always preceded the big one. He would record a critique of the day into his iPhone as he went, planning to write it up later. There were always lessons for next time, and he didn't want to forget them. In his memoir, *The Last Pick*, he had quoted a Chinese proverb: "The palest ink is better than the best memory." McGillivray was the kind of guy who had lots of credos, but that one he had followed faithfully.

Thirty-five years earlier, he recorded a verbal diary of what was surely the craziest of all his crazy ventures. He arranged, in 1978, to run clear across the country, a stunt he had devised to raise money for the Jimmy Fund, a Boston charity that supported adult and pediatric cancer care and research. He wanted to start in Medford, Oregon, and finish in his hometown of Medford, Massachusetts. The first night on the road, he stayed at a campsite. A stranger gave him a portion of his fresh catch of fish. Over the next seventy-nine days, he ran across deserts, through the mountains, and into the plains, some 3,452 miles in all, a member of his support crew blasting music from a trailing moped. He and his team adopted a six-week-old puppy. McGillivray ran through rattlesnakes, nosebleeds, and grasshopper swarms. He lived on junk food, downing a six-pack of Coke after each day's run. Outside Lincoln, Nebraska, he jumped aboard a moving coal train and off the other side because he didn't want to wait for it to pass. His family, through phone calls and news reports, charted his progress as he went. On the night of August 29, he ran into Fenway Park to a boisterous welcome, taking two laps around the field before the baseball game, showered with cheers and proudly donning a Red Sox cap tossed to him by relief pitcher Bill Campbell.

If that was a high point, almost twenty years later McGillivray would find himself at his lowest, when he and his first wife divorced. Here was something he couldn't remedy with preparation and training. Hard work wouldn't just push it away. He was devastated. He hated subjecting their two young sons to the breakup. He prayed, sometimes by the hour, that he could get through another day. At one point, near rock bottom, he called his sister Susan and said maybe he should just end it all. Susan was his lifeline, and she helped him bounce back. He eventually remarried and had three more children. McGillivray, in his memoir, described marathons as an apt metaphor for his life. He had run through heartache, and also through joy. "There are hills and valleys. The weather changes from year to year," he wrote. "Mostly, though, at the end of the day, it's up to me to get the job done."

The job, on this Sunday, was to make sure the day's fitness events all went well, and that everyone was geared up for tomorrow. Later on, he stopped by the runners' expo. He checked in with his marathon team. The day felt slow, which was how he liked it. There was little to report, little that required his urgent attention. The copious planning of the organizers was paying off. They were going to have a good race.

Shana worked on Sunday, her regular shift in East Boston. It would have been nice to have the next day free—Marathon Monday had been her day off on the schedule—but she had volunteered to work an extra shift. Patriot's Day might not be a big deal anywhere else, but in Boston it was a holiday, and that meant double pay. The extra money in her check would make it worth it. She had worked the marathon before; the crowds were laid-back, and the mood would be festive. Boston could be a cranky place. If there was one day when the old city felt carefree, it was Marathon Monday.

Shana had warmed to Boston the moment she arrived, a decade before, in the spring of 2003, on a visit to Northeastern University. She was a junior in high school on Long Island, getting ready to apply to colleges. She had never been to Boston; that was part of its appeal. She knew she wanted to go someplace new, and her love for the city was instant and complete. "Something clicked and I knew I wanted to be here," she said. "I loved how old it was and how safe it felt. . . . Even the air smelled right." She was seventeen that spring. The memory of September 11, 2001, a year and a half earlier, was still fresh; the fear the attack had inspired had been imprinted on Shana and everyone else in New York. Her father was working a construction job in Manhattan that day, and for several terrifying hours, her mother was unable to reach him. New York City never felt the same to her again. In Boston, even after she left the cocoon of college life to join the police department, she never felt vulnerable the way she had in New York. She experienced moments of chaos—a suspect resisting arrest, a victim sobbing in her arms—but they were only moments. It never felt like the world was unraveling.

The residue of 9/11, the fear and the desire to take back some kind of control, was part of what drew her to law enforcement. Another driving force was her childhood. On her street, in her Long Island town, Shana's house had been *that* house: the one with the parents who fought, where the police sometimes were called. Not that many years had passed since she was a kid, and Shana vividly remembered how it felt to face the cops in her living room—the crippling sense of her own powerlessness, the certainty that nobody was hearing what she said. Becoming a police officer herself gave her some control over such chaotic moments. Now, when the kids she met in troubled homes turned away and told her that she didn't understand, Shana explained to them that she really did. Mostly, though, she listened. She focused on the kids in the middle of bad situations, because they still had time to turn out differently.

Shana had used the tension in her childhood home as motivation. It drove her to get good grades, to get out and go to college. By the time she was nearly done at Northeastern, she knew what she wanted to do. With a handful of classes left before graduation, she left school to enter the police academy. It was time to move her education to the streets. Now it was five years later, and with the turmoil of last fall behind her, she felt like she had been given a second chance. She had done good work before, but now that she was sober, she felt a sense of limitless potential. She was more and more convinced that things had happened for a reason. She had made her decision to stop drinking and stuck to it, and hard as it had been, it had made her stronger.

Shana felt clearheaded, fit, optimistic. Ready for anything. And her day tomorrow at the marathon should be easy. Her friends would be at the finish line, and they would stop by to see her. It promised to be a fine day in her favorite city.

. . .

Krystle made her plans for Monday. She seemed to have friends everywhere. A group of them arranged to meet downtown. Some would be going to the Red Sox game. Then they would gather together near the finish line, maybe hit a bar along Boylston. The weather looked promising. The boyfriend of one of her close friends was running. Maybe they would get to see him cross.

David King laid out everything he would need in the morning: his Newton running shoes; his race bib, number 2594; the Vaseline to put between his toes. He took a picture of the pile and posted it on Facebook. Then he made himself a dry gin martini. The only thing left to do was sleep, and that was easy. King was used to sleeping in fits and starts on call at the hospital. He had once napped on the tarmac at Baghdad International Airport during a firefight, lifting his head occasionally at the snap-snap-snap of the gunfire, and lying back down when he decided it wasn't that close. Sleeping at home was a luxury. Once his head hit the pillow, nothing could get in his way.

Shana was almost religious about wearing her bulletproof vest. It wasn't required after the first year on the job, but she wore it anyway. You never knew when you were going to need it. But for a shift near Copley Square on Marathon Monday, the vest was overkill—even Shana could see that. It was heavy, and she would be on her feet all day. The streets would be full of police; she would be surrounded by backup. Tomorrow was one day when she would feel safe without it.

By Sunday night, the forecast had assured cooler weather for this year's marathon. For Heather, that meant resigning herself to wearing her brown leather boots—again. By April, she was ready to break out some lighter shoes. This was New England, though. Patience was required. Spring was close, but not yet in full bloom. Plenty of warm days were coming; plenty of time for open-toed shoes and bare ankles.

. . .

Dave McGillivray observed his typical rituals on the eve of the marathon, grabbing a quiet dinner and then returning early to the solitude of his hotel room. He kept the radio and TV off, to focus. He went through his mental checklist, visualizing, over and over, the next day's events in minute detail. He sat at the table with his laptop open, reviewing the notes he'd made from prior marathons. He kept his phone and two-way radio close, to field any reports of trouble. By 9:30, he was in bed. He put his phone on vibrate and went to sleep with it in his hand, so he wouldn't miss a critical call or text. He felt a calmness. *We got this*, he thought.

CHAPTER 2

DIMMED FUTURES, VIOLENT TURN

Two brothers in descent

The voice had begun speaking to him again.

It was 2012, almost a full decade after Tamerlan Tsarnaev had arrived in the United States with his family. He was about twenty-six and living in Cambridge, an unemployed immigrant from southern Russia with an intensifying interest in Islam. He was going nowhere. And the voice inside his head—the one that had first spoken to him years earlier—was growing more adamant. He never knew when it would come, but when it did, he alone was privy to its commands. As a young man, he had felt like there were two people inside his head, or so he told his mother. The voice, Tamerlan explained to a friend, had become more demanding with age, ordering him to do things, though he never said what. "He was torn between those two people," said Donald Larking, sixty-seven, who attended mosque with him and spoke to the *Boston Globe* about a side of Tamerlan never previously reported. "He said that several times."

Once, Tamerlan had embodied the hopes of his immigrant parents. He'd been a gifted boxer with Olympic dreams. His mother had doted on her older son, convinced he would bring honor to the family. That was all buried in the past. The family had collapsed. His parents had split and fled the country. Tamerlan had been unsuccessful at virtually every one of his endeavors in America. He had been blocked from participating in national Golden Gloves boxing events. He hadn't found work. He'd dropped out of college before earning a degree. With thirty not too far in the distance, the tall, muscular young man who once seemed confident and focused now looked increasingly angry and unmoored, spending hours watching Islamic YouTube videos on his computer.

In November 2012, a few weeks before Thanksgiving, Tamerlan sat listening to a guest imam at the family's Cambridge mosque. The imam said that Muslims were permitted to celebrate certain secular holidays, including Thanksgiving and the Fourth of July. Tamerlan was outraged. He leapt to his feet, angrily denouncing the imam. After the service, mosque elders sat with him. "He was listening, but he was pretty emotional," said one of the men, Ismail Fenni. "He was standing by his views." Not long after that, Tamerlan reacted with similar outrage to a sign posted at the nearby Al-Hoda Market, a Middle Eastern grocery that specializes in halal meats, which are prepared according to Islamic law. The sign advertised halal turkeys for Thanksgiving; Tamerlan demanded to know why Muslims were being encouraged to participate in an American holiday. A few months later, in January 2013, he erupted again at the mosque. At a Friday prayer service shortly before Martin Luther King Jr. Day, he shouted at the imam for holding up the late civil rights icon as a worthy example to follow. Others in the room told Tamerlan to stop. "Leave," they ordered the angry young man. "Leave now." Tamerlan stormed out of the building.

More instability loomed. The family's landlady, Joanna Herlihy, had decided, after long giving the Tsarnaevs a break on the rent, that she needed to charge a higher rate for their third-floor apartment in Inman Square. The apartment had been the one constant in the Tsarnaevs' ten turbulent years in America, and now Tamerlan was on the verge of losing it. Herlihy told him that he needed to move out by June. He was shaken, but he understood. The apartment had once hummed with the noisy, crowded ambitions of his volatile family. By this point, in early 2013, it was a shell of what it had been, long emptied of any constructive aspirations. When Tamerlan went there now, there was only a computer screen to keep him company. Losing the place was all but a formality. The home the Tsarnaevs had built—or had tried to build—was already gone. In its wake, one lost, isolated young man remained. Or perhaps there were two.

He joined the crowd near Copley Square on that April afternoon, another youthful face among the happy masses. He was there to hang out with a friend and cheer on the runners like everyone else. The Boston Marathon was one of Boston's signature public events, and in the spring of 2012, Dzhokhar Tsarnaev wanted to be part of it. On a typical April Monday, Dzhokhar, whom friends knew as Jahar, would be in one of his freshman classes at the University of Massachusetts Dartmouth. But this was Patriot's Day, which meant no school. So he and his best friend, Steve, had headed up to Boston. They had arrived too late to see the top finishers, but in plenty of time to cheer on the rest, grab some pizza, savor the sunshine, and, as was often the case with Dzhokhar, smoke a joint. He had two essays due by noon the next day, but those could wait. "We were just chilling," Steve said.

Dzhokhar's soft features and mop of hair only added to his relaxed aura. But it was a façade. He was no ordinary, aimless college boy. He was a young man who, like his older brother Tamerlan, was in the midst of a troubling transformation. Dzhokhar, eighteen, a former high school honor student and wrestling team captain, was foundering in his studies and losing his sense of direction. He had, soon after arriving on the Dartmouth campus, become the leader of a small group of friends who shared interests in global affairs, thrill-seeking, and getting stoned. He had also established himself as a high-volume pot dealer, pulling in about $1,000 a week, and sometimes more, according to several college friends. The money helped pay for luxuries previously out of his reach—designer shoes, trips to New York clubs, Cîroc vodka, and psychedelic drugs. He liked to court danger, and occasionally carried a gun to protect his valuable stash. He sold drugs out of his dorm room with the door propped open. He was as brazen as he was charming. He was the one friends relied on to sweet-talk campus police out of getting them in trouble. He was beginning to skid in college, but he seemed nonchalant, or perhaps in denial. If his future held any promise, it was hard to discern. It was not yet too late for him to right his life's wayward course. But he seemed to lean into his downward slide instead, picking up dangerous momentum as he went.

New Jersey was their first stop in America. They landed on a raw spring day in 2002, just the Tsarnaev parents and their younger son, a quiet boy of eight named Dzhokhar. The other three children, for the time being, stayed behind with relatives. In his pocket, the father, Anzor, carried the phone number of Khassan Baiev, a prominent Chechen surgeon who lived in Needham, west of Boston. "He called me and said, 'Please, can you help me. There is no one here to meet us,'" Baiev said. The Tsarnaevs stayed with the Baievs for a month and then moved into the apartment in Cambridge. Anzor started fixing cars, building himself a livelihood. Cruising around town in his battered van, he befriended both merchants and customers. He soon developed his own clients, many of whom were drawn to his competitive prices and spirited nature. "Anzor was tough as they come," said Joe Timko, a supervisor at Webster Auto Body in Somerville, where Anzor did body work for several months. "He'd change a transmission right there on the street. I mean, he was a stone. But he was also very emotional. He always came right up and gave you a hug."

The Tsarnaevs joined a loose-knit social scene made up of the few Chechen families in the Boston area. They'd arrive at picnics in their humble used Hyundai, the gaggle of children in the back. But the appearances of the two parents, Anzor and Zubeidat, spoke of grander visions. "She was very glamorous, very fancy, like she was going to walk down the red carpet," said Anna Nikaeva, a Chechen who runs a senior care facility outside Boston with her husband. "Anzor was also dressed finely and he was most handsome. They had big plans for their kids in America."

Their American dreams had taken root years earlier in the chaos of Anzor's homeland of Kyrgyzstan. The Tsarnaev clan had lived for generations in the foothills of the Caucasus in Chechnya, but they were forced out in 1944 when Soviet dictator Joseph Stalin viciously exiled the Chechen people to Central Asia and Siberia. Tens of thousands starved or froze to death along the journey. Anzor's father, Zaindy, just eleven years old at the time, was one of those who made it. He built a life in Tokmok, a rambling provincial city in what is now Kyrgyzstan. Like many others trying to scrape by, Zaindy scavenged in a local dump nicknamed the "Golden Pit" for items or scrap to sell. One day in 1988, he threw some promising metal objects into his car, unaware that live ordnance was among them. The car exploded, killing the father of seven—Tamerlan and Dzhokhar's grandfather.

Like his father, Anzor learned to work with other people's wreckage and fix junked cars. It gave him a way to make a living, and to support his wife, Zubeidat, whom he had met in the mid-1980s, and their four children. Theirs was an unlikely union: the exotic, dark-haired young woman was an ethnic Avar; her people, from Chechnya's neighbor to the east, Dagestan, historically had a tense relationship with the Chechens. Zubeidat had already fled an arranged marriage, a shockingly unconventional act in that tradition-bound time and culture. But Anzor and Zubeidat both were strong-willed, and they paid no attention to gossip. She was a dramatic beauty, prone to excess. He was a strapping former boxer and talented raconteur. More than a few envied their seemingly passionate marriage.

In the early 1990s, Anzor took the family to Chechnya, a province of Russia that had declared its independence. In late 1994, the Kremlin sent in Russian troops, in an attempt to put down the rebellion. Tens of thousands died and hundreds of thousands fled. The Tsarnaevs were among them, landing back in Tokmok, Kyrgyzstan. Anzor returned to the business of refurbishing cars. His three sisters and one of his brothers earned law degrees at a university in the capital,

Bishkek, according to school records. Anzor would later say that he, too, earned a law degree, but the university had no record of it. He did work in a district prosecutor's office in Bishkek, likely in a role akin to an unpaid internship. The connection provided Anzor with something perhaps more valuable than a law degree—an ID card from the prosecutor's office. This credential helped him evade corrupt officials and extortion gangs who sought to muscle in on his true livelihood: "shuttle trading" (moving consumer goods in the ruins of the Communist economy). Anzor and his uncle transported tobacco from a factory in southern Kyrgyzstan to buyers elsewhere in the former Soviet Union. It was a good but risky business.

Their primary motivation for leaving their homeland for America remains murky, but according to a story his wife would tell an associate years later, Anzor had drawn the wrath of the Russian mob. She said her husband had played a role in the prosecution of some mafia members involved in illegal trading. After the case was over, according to Zubeidat's account, the mob kidnapped Anzor for a week, tortured him to the brink of death, and then dumped him from a truck in the middle of nowhere. Zubeidat said she knew, when she went to the hospital and saw how badly he'd been beaten, that it was time to leave the country. But the mob's henchmen weren't finished yet. Before Anzor could leave the hospital, she said, someone took the family's German shepherd, cut off its head, and left it on the Tsarnaevs' doorstep. A longtime family friend would later say that Anzor, to win escape from Kyrgyzstan, concocted false stories about persecution of the Chechen people. That would give him political asylum—the status he needed to stay in the United States, a place the Tsarnaevs had idealized from afar. They had watched their share of Hollywood movies. The country looked so beautiful, the life there so promising. "Let's go to America," Anzor once told a friend, Bakhtiar Nurmenov. "Why should we sit here and rust?"

Their building stood out for the noise. By 2008, five years after the family of six—Anzor and Zubeidat, along with their sons, Tamerlan and Dzhokhar, and two daughters, Bella and Ailina—had reunited in the United States, the Tsarnaevs were an even larger clan. Their apartment, in a multifamily house packed in among many others on Norfolk Street in Cambridge, near Inman Square, was now as loud as it was cramped. At varying times there were one or two babies— the children of the Tsarnaevs' two teenage daughters—in the apartment as well, all of them occupying eight hundred square feet of living space. Their shoes spilled down the stairway; their voices rang out from the windows. The babies cried day and night. When the older children were around, the place got even louder, especially when Tamerlan practiced his favorite hip-hop riffs on his keyboard. None of them, however, could match the sheer volume of Zubeidat, the matriarch of the household and a woman not known for restraint. Neighbors had to cover their ears at times to find peace.

In their early years in America, the family had plunged into their new life with gusto. Tamerlan, Bella, Ailina, and Dzhokhar attended local public schools. Dzhokhar thrived at his elementary school, the Cambridgeport School. Initially held back because of his deficiencies in English, he was reading so proficiently by the end of third grade that he was bumped up to fifth grade. His parents had deemed him the brains of the family, destined to be the first to earn a diploma from an American college. Anzor would boast to friends that Dzhokhar was Ivy League material.

It was their firstborn son, Tamerlan, though, who carried the family's hopes for athletic distinction. Zubeidat was forever musing about his brilliant prospects as he became an accomplished amateur boxer. "Tamerlan was idolized," Anna Nikaeva said. "Anything he said was right. He was perfect." Except that he wasn't. One day when the two women were talking, Zubeidat shared a disturbing secret with Nikaeva, something that Tamerlan had said. "He had told his mother that he felt there were two people living inside of him," Nikaeva said in an interview with the *Globe.* "I told her, 'You should get that checked out.' But she just said, 'No, he's fine.' She couldn't accept the tiniest criticism of him." If they never sought mental health care for their son, the Tsarnaevs regularly saw a psychiatrist themselves, a

decision motivated by Anzor's troubles. Alexander Niss, a psychiatrist now based outside Los Angeles, saw Anzor and Zubeidat during
his residency at St. Elizabeth's Medical Center in Boston. Anzor told
Niss that he had been captured by federal troops in Chechnya and
repeatedly tortured. He told the doctor that his experience "was in-
terfering with his daily life," Niss said. "He had trouble sleeping,
things like that. He was really a sick person."

Anzor and Zubeidat both scaled back their professional ambitions as they struggled to build a life in the United States. Although
Zubeidat said to many that she had trained as a lawyer, she began
providing home health care and would eventually switch to cosme-
tology, providing facials and skin care at a nearby spa and then in
her apartment. Chris Walter, owner of Yayla Tribal Rugs in Cambridge, allowed Anzor to work on cars in a space behind his shop.
Able to earn up to $100 a day—ten times what he said he could make
back home—Anzor was thrilled at first. As time went on, though, he
lost affection for his adopted country. "Life here was tough," Walter
said. "Anzor always said, 'America, America is a great country.' But
it was sort of a joke. You had to work so hard here."

After a couple of years in America, Tamerlan had pounded out a
steady record of wins in the ring, becoming one of the better boxers
in the region. Among other nicknames, he was known as "The Russian." A gifted athlete and sought-after sparring partner, he had an
unorthodox style. He did handstands and cartwheels in the ring.
Sometimes he showed up with his keyboard and performed an elegant sonata. Then there were the clothes, which were anything but
the typical gym-rat wardrobe: silver high-tops, skintight jeans, a
white scarf, and his trademark furry hat. He drove a sleek white
Mercedes, apparently a perk of his father's side business in used cars.
On special occasions, he was known to sport snakeskin pants and a
shirt unbuttoned to the waist. At a Boston gym where he trained, he
was teased about his flashy garb. One training partner jokingly called
him "Eurotrash." Tamerlan joked right back.

Tamerlan's boxing prowess was one of the few bright spots for the Tsarnaev family. With all of them, at times, under one roof, the household began sagging under its own weight. Anzor developed more health problems. His stomach and head hurt constantly. He sought out acupuncture, consulted with a Chinese herbalist, and even swore off his beloved cognac. Both of his daughters' marriages, meanwhile, ended in divorce. The one thing that buoyed Anzor's spirits was seeing Tamerlan in the boxing ring.

Both Tamerlan and his father were hopeful that Tamerlan's boxing skill would take him to the big time, possibly even the Olympics. His prospects were otherwise cloudy. After graduating from high school in 2006, Tamerlan had enrolled at two community colleges but attended fitfully. Eventually he had dropped out. Although he was a voracious reader—his personal library included Sherlock Holmes and the writings of Gandhi—school did not come easy. Much of the time he spent smoking pot and listening to music with friends. Dzhokhar, meanwhile, was increasingly left to make his own way. He found community in the social scene at his high school, Cambridge Rindge and Latin, developing a diverse group of friends who seemed destined for good things. Cambridge was a famously welcoming environment. Immigrant success stories were many. One of the few cracks came around his junior year, when he was sitting with friends at a local restaurant. They were talking about religion, Islam, and the 9/11 terrorist attacks. Dzhokhar suggested that acts like that were sometimes justified by US actions around the world. Cambridge harbored plenty of dissenting views of American foreign policy, but Dzhokhar's more extreme opinions stood out. In school, he took honors classes and worked hard at wrestling. At home, he was largely an obedient child and often agreed to watch his sisters' babies. Underneath, however, Dzhokhar was a freewheeling teenager, smoking marijuana regularly and drinking more than ever.

Concerned about her children, Zubeidat decided to act. She confronted Tamerlan first, the Koran in her hand. As with many Muslims from the former Soviet Union, the Tsarnaevs had practiced a relaxed form of their Muslim faith at home and attended mosque only occasionally. But as the stress of life in their adopted country began to take its toll, the family turned to religion with mounting fervor, Zubeidat the most forcefully. Only Anzor, the patriarch, remained stubbornly secular. Tamerlan, sometimes accompanied by his brother, occasionally attended the Friday service at the Islamic Society of Boston's small blue-and-silver mosque in Cambridge, a short walk from their house. Tamerlan eventually gave up drinking alcohol, although he continued to smoke weed. He also began poring over Islamic websites, and began to moralize to his brother. If Dzhokhar announced that he was going out, Tamerlan would get on his case, insisting that he stop drinking and come home early.

It was Team New England's last fight of the night. Tamerlan had just landed a crushing blow in the first round of his bout. His opponent, Lamar Fenner, fell to the ground as the crowd let out a roar of approval. But Fenner rose to fight on, and when it was all over, the judges at the 2009 national Golden Gloves boxing tournament delivered a stunning verdict: They named Fenner the victor in his division. After a moment of shocked silence in the Salt Palace Convention Center, the crowd booed loudly. A year later, Tamerlan would become the New England Golden Gloves heavyweight champion of the year for the second time. It should have earned him a second chance at the national title he had been denied a year before in Salt Lake City. But because of a change of rules that prohibited noncitizens from participating in the Golden Gloves national tournament, Tamerlan was blocked from continuing. With that, another door slammed shut. Tamerlan's once-promising boxing career had come to an abrupt halt, and with it the family's hopes for his Olympic success. Rudderless and uncertain what was next, Tamerlan sought grounding in his faith. It would not, however, set him back on course.

The family's downward spiral accelerated. Tamerlan had been charged with assaulting a girlfriend. During a separate altercation with patrons at a Boston restaurant, Anzor was severely injured when he was struck in the head with a steel pole. With Anzor unable to work full-time because of his health problems, the family was granted food stamps for the next couple of years and, for ten months, cash assistance from the government. Even with that, money was always tight. A bright spot was Katherine Russell, a young woman from Rhode Island whom Tamerlan had met at a downtown club. Raised a Catholic, Katie was already questioning her faith in light of the clergy sex abuse scandals; she found herself intrigued by Tamerlan's commitment to Islam. For Tamerlan, dating a woman who was neither Chechen nor Muslim was problematic. When he decided to move in with her, it caused considerable distress in the family. But when Katie became pregnant, Anzor and Zubeidat warmed to their son's mild-mannered girlfriend. The family was pleased when Katie agreed to convert to Islam and take the name Karima. In June 2010, the couple married in a brief ceremony at the Masjid Al-Qur'aan mosque in Boston's Dorchester neighborhood. Not long afterward, their daughter, Zahira, was born. The young family moved into the Norfolk Street apartment. Katie supported them with her work as a home health aide. Tamerlan's job was to care for Zahira.

Like her husband's, Zubeidat's romance with America had soured. Her chaotic household became even more unsettled as her husband's health problems worsened. Anzor's stomach pain had been diagnosed as possible cancer, and his anxiety provoked night terrors. Many nights he screamed into the darkness, making sleep impossible for everyone. In August 2011, the Tsarnaevs began divorce proceedings. A few months later, Anzor departed for Dagestan. With his father gone and both Zubeidat and Katie working long hours, Tamerlan often found himself alone. He spent hours cruising the Internet for websites associated with Islamic militants in his homeland. Around this time, Tamerlan posted, on Facebook, a link to an article from an online Chechen news agency, which claimed that US leaders were engaged in an "all-out war against Islam" and urged Muslims to fight against America. By this point, Tamerlan's apparent radicalization had drawn the attention of the FBI, whose agents had probed his Internet activity, investigated potential associations with militants, and interviewed him and his parents. Investigators concluded that he posed only a minimal threat.

For his part, Dzhokhar had graduated from Cambridge Rindge and Latin in June 2011, one of forty-five students granted a $2,500 city scholarship for college. He was named to the National Honor Society. He was also awarded the MVP trophy by his high school wrestling team. While each of the other team members who received awards was accompanied by a family member or friend, Dzhokhar had neither. His coach was not surprised. During the three years that Dzhokhar had wrestled, his family members had not come to watch him compete. Nearly a decade after they had arrived in the United States, the Tsarnaev family had come apart, adrift in a culture to which they never fully adapted.

In January 2012, Tamerlan traveled to Dagestan, where his father and other close relatives lived. But his true purpose seemed to be more personal: He was looking to immerse himself further in his faith—and possibly to make contact with its radical followers. He found the southern Russian republic in the midst of an Islamic revival. Friday prayers drew crowds of worshippers, which spilled out into the street from dozens of new mosques. The revival had its violent side, too. The Islamic insurgency that failed in neighboring Chechnya had moved to Dagestan, where a jihadist underground was staging deadly raids on police and the secular government they protect. Police responded, at times, with summary executions of suspects, human rights advocates charged. The clash of cultures was apparent in the frenetic capital, Makhachkala, where Tamerlan stayed. Heavily armed police checkpoints separate streets dotted with wireless cafes, sushi bars, and glistening shopping hubs. Everyone knows someone, or knows *of* someone, who has been shot passing through these checkpoints on suspicion of being part of the underground. Young women in dark veils walk the city hand in hand with friends in short skirts and designer sunglasses, past walls with warnings scrawled in red paint:

Fear Allah, cover yourselves!
Allah sees all!
Know, you dogs, there will be jihad before judgment day!

Tamerlan hooked up with members of the Union of the Just, an organization of young Muslims led by a third cousin on his mother's side. Some members follow a strict interpretation of Islam, believing in the establishment of an Islamic state governed by sharia law that would span the region. They are sharply critical of US interventions in Muslim countries and believe the US government condones the burning of Korans. They do not openly espouse violence, but their beliefs have drawn accusations from Russian authorities that they belong to an outlawed Islamic group. Tamerlan arrived with many questions about Islam; he wanted to learn how to better express his faith. He spent time praying, studying the Koran, and playing soccer with Union of the Just members. "He was at the beginning of his path," said Mukhamad Magomedov, deputy leader of the group. "He was mostly a listener, a searcher. He was looking for answers."

But if Tamerlan was hoping to fit in, he did not succeed. Part of it was, yet again, his curious appearance. He wore a long shirt of the type favored by Pakistanis. He combed his hair with olive oil and darkened his eyes with kohl shadow, practices of devout Sunnis in some cultures, but not in Dagestan. He also began praying at a mosque attended by Salafi Muslims, a strict, orthodox Sunni sect whose members, authorities believe, often aid the armed insurgency. It was there, Russian authorities would later contend, that Tamerlan met with the insurgents he had come seeking, though that assertion would be questioned and a *Globe* investigation found strong reason to doubt such a connection ever occurred. Tamerlan left Dagestan in the summer of 2012, just as two members of the insurgency were killed by security forces. He promised to come back.

On his return to Cambridge, Tamerlan was a changed man. His face was covered by a thick beard. Gone were the silver boots and fur hat. In their place were dark clothing and a woven white prayer cap worn by Muslims. His prayers in the corner of the Wai Kru gym,

47

which once took minutes, now lasted up to half an hour. "He had really dialed up the religion thing," his training partner recalled. "The days of joking about his appearance, the Eurotrash—that kid was gone. In his place was a quiet, intense individual." Tamerlan's anger over American military actions in Afghanistan and Iraq had also escalated. He railed about Muslims being killed overseas. He launched a YouTube account with a username that combined a name given him by his Union of the Just comrades and the phrase "the sword of God." In one video in his playlist, called "Terrorists," a speaker wearing camouflage, flanked by armed men wearing masks, holds an assault rifle and says in Russian, "There will always be a group of people who will stick to the truth, fight for that truth . . . and those who won't support them will not win."

As their relationship grew closer, Tamerlan confided in Donald Larking, his friend from the mosque, about the voice inside his head, which he said he had been hearing for some time. "He believed in majestic mind control, which is a way of breaking down a person and creating an alternative personality with which they must coexist," Larking said. "You can give a signal, a phrase or a gesture, and bring out the alternate personality and make them do things. Tamerlan thought someone might have done that to him." Just as he had once described it to his mother, Tamerlan told Larking that it was like having two people inside him.

Dzhokhar, meanwhile, had begun his freshman year at the University of Massachusetts Dartmouth in the fall of 2011. He joined an intramural soccer group, made other acquaintances playing video games and watching TV, and posted jokes on a newly opened Twitter account. He was generous with favors. Mostly, though, he was recognized for a different venture—selling notably strong marijuana. "He was known for having the best bud on campus," said one longtime friend. He also took his reckless tendencies to new limits. A lit cigarette in hand, Dzhokhar loved to imitate race-car drivers, pushing his 1999 green Honda Civic up to nearly 120 miles an hour, according to several close friends. Other times he would turn corners with the steering wheel between his knees, leaving his hands free to roll a joint. If partying was a priority, schoolwork was not. As Dzhokhar's wallet thickened with cash and his sense of invincibility grew, he was rarely spotted studying at the library or student lounges.

In the spring of his freshman year, another crack appeared in his easygoing manner. The young man who had seemingly assimilated more successfully than the rest of his family claimed that he was done with his adopted country. *A decade in America already*, he wrote on Twitter. *I want out.* After a summer back in Cambridge, working as a lifeguard at Harvard University's Blodgett Pool, he returned to campus in the fall of 2012. It was a much lonelier place. His closest friends had left or moved off campus. His grades sunk further. The future looked bleak. His country, though, was ready to accept him anyway. On September 11, 2012, in a ceremony at Boston's TD Garden, Dzhokhar Tsarnaev became a US citizen.

One day in early 2013, Dzhokhar showed up at his former high school with his wrestling shoes, looking to get on the mats again with the old team. "We're all laughing; everyone's pulling his hair and saying, 'You ought to do cornrows,'" said Peter Payack, one of his coaches. It was the same old Dzhokhar—or so it seemed. Even as he continued to display his charms and party with friends, he was spending more time at his family's Cambridge apartment, where his brother lived. Tamerlan at this point was an unemployed husband and father, devoting countless hours to his Muslim faith and watching over his toddler daughter. Together the two brothers, both of their once-bright futures dimmed, began orchestrating a deadly scheme against the country that had welcomed them.

In early February 2013, Tamerlan drove up to Phantom Fireworks in Seabrook, New Hampshire, and paid $200 in cash for forty-eight mortars containing eight pounds of explosive powder. The next month, the two brothers went to a firing range in Manchester, New Hampshire. Dzhokhar spent $160 to rent two 9mm handguns, buy two hundred rounds of ammunition, and, with Tamerlan, shoot at targets for an hour. A few weeks later, Tamerlan ordered electronic components over the Internet, arranging delivery to their Cambridge apartment. At some point he used his laptop to download an article from the summer 2010 issue of *Inspire*, an English-language Al-Qaeda publication. The article was called "Make a Bomb in The Kitchen of Your Mom." It provided detailed instruction on how to make a bomb in a pressure cooker using commonly available flammables like the powder from fireworks and homemade shrapnel fashioned from nails or steel pellets. "Put your trust in Allah and pray for the success of your operation," the article instructed. "This is the most important rule."

Their Cambridge kitchen was no longer the kitchen of their mom. Zubeidat had returned to Russia months earlier after being caught shoplifting at a mall in suburban Boston. Tamerlan and Dzhokhar were on their own, with few positive influences, no direction, and little to lose, a tandem of failure whose descent had brought them lower than anyone could have imagined. The two brothers set to work on their violent plot. They readied their homemade bombs. Now it was just a question of targets. *If you have the knowledge and the inspiration,* Dzhokhar wrote cryptically on Twitter on April 7, 2013, *all that's left is to take action.* They considered public events with big crowds, like Boston's Fourth of July celebration. They considered attacking police stations. But they were impatient now, ready to go. Once the devices were finished, Monday, April 15, presented an immediate opportunity to unleash the destruction they sought. It was Patriot's Day, which would bring thousands to downtown for the 117th Boston Marathon. As night fell on Sunday, the eve of the marathon, Dzhokhar and Tamerlan walked down their street carrying a pizza box. A neighbor, Malisha Pitt, was sitting on her stoop. One of her relatives asked them for a slice, and Pitt admonished him. "Stop harassing my neighbors," she said. The two brothers laughed and kept on walking.

CHAPTER 3

STARTING LINE

Perfect day for a marathon

The volume on his alarm was set as low as it could go, but David King was instantly awake when the first faint beats of techno music reached him in the darkness. In the kitchen, his coffee was already steaming, the machine having been set to start ten minutes before his alarm. It was 4:00 A.M. on Marathon Monday. The sun would not be up for two more hours. The long-awaited day had arrived, and King rose swiftly to meet it.

He was almost always up this early. His work schedule at the hospital could be unpredictable and merciless. These quiet predawn hours were his training time, the only time he could count on to test and retest his endurance. His training had grown more rigorous in recent years, as King—the once-reluctant marathoner who had only lately tapped the rapture of distance running—had pushed himself further. Just six weeks earlier, in Taupo, New Zealand, he had completed his first IRONMAN triathlon: a 2.4-mile swim, followed by a 112-mile bike ride, topped off by a complete twenty-six-mile marathon. He had finished in eleven hours and fifty-eight minutes. Running through pain at the end, he felt buoyed by waves of bliss, a happiness so overwhelming he had to fight back tears. It was, he said, one of the purest joys he had ever felt.

Today's run would take him just over three hours, if all went as planned. He had run faster marathons elsewhere—he had run the relatively flat course in Miami in under three hours—but Boston was tougher. If he hit his goal of 3:10, it would make this, his third time running Boston, his fastest ever. Reaching for his coffee mug on the kitchen counter—the sugar cubes were already inside, where he had dropped them the night before—the doctor felt certain the race would go well. Only two weeks ago, troubled by his nagging back pain, he had not been sure if he could run Boston at all. Just in time, those doubts had lifted, like storm clouds parting to reveal the sun. Now he was ready. He couldn't wait to start. First, though, he needed to eat breakfast.

For years, King had eaten the same thing on marathon mornings: three packets of instant oatmeal, two bananas. A year ago, though, he had discovered chocolate chip pancakes, and now nothing else would do. Skilled as he was in the operating room, where he presided over hundreds of urgent, often lifesaving surgeries every year, King had yet to master the art of pancake preparation. So he relied on the kindness of his wife, Anne. She would soon be getting up to mix the batter. Later in the day, near the end of the marathon, she would be waiting on the course with their two young children just before the turn from Commonwealth Avenue onto Hereford Street, less than a mile from the finish. His parents would be there, too, cheering him on, his dad making sure the family was pressed up against the barriers when he came along, as close to the street as spectators could get. It was never hard to find them. They were always right there. That familiarity and ease of planning were part of what made it so comfortable and so much fun to run Boston, now his hometown marathon, every April.

King's informal running club, the Beacon Hill Runners, had space on a bus to the starting line in Hopkinton, so after finishing his pancakes he caught a cab across Cambridge to MIT, where the motor coach was idling. He settled into his seat, his earphones chirping more techno beats. The doctor, who had double majored in music and biology in college, favored a type of electronic dance music called dubstep. Its sound features heavy, driving bass lines and bass "drops," when the percussion stops short and plunges the song into silence before resuming with increased intensity. He used it for motivation before workouts. Other runners on the bus might have tried to shut out the world on this ride, marshaling their energy for the grueling day ahead. King was too much of a multitasker for that. It was Marathon Day, but it was also income tax day, and he had a few loose ends to tie up with his accountant. *Forgot to send you this*, he tapped on his iPhone screen as the sun rose higher and the bus rolled west. *Sorry so last minute.* Much of the city might have been enjoying a lazy Patriot's Day morning, but on April 15, tax accountants were working, even in Boston. The accountant had news for him, and it wasn't what King hoped to hear: She had calculated how much he owed the government, and it was a lot more than he had expected. He felt himself getting upset. Then, browsing through news stories on his phone, he stumbled across a fact that irked him further: President Obama had paid an effective federal income tax rate of 18.4 percent in 2012, a rate lower than King's own. *What is that guy doing that I'm not?* he messaged his accountant. *I want a deal like that.*

It was not the ideal state of mind for the start of the race. But as he stepped off the bus into the morning sun, he felt the promise of the day start to sweep everything else away.

Dave McGillivray rose alone around 3:30 A.M., greeted by the quiet of his hotel room. His family used to stay with him. Not anymore. He'd come to realize that he needed the solitude, needed the peace, to focus. This was, after all, the biggest day of his year. Outside, Copley Square lay dark and still. In a few short hours, the sun would rise on another Marathon Monday. Hundreds of thousands of runners, spectators, volunteers, police—the whole city, really—would be counting on him to again deliver a flawless race, to make it all go right. As he got up, he spoke to his pillow, as he did every year. He said the words out loud: "When I come back and lay my head on this pillow, boy, am I going to have some stories to tell."

After a shower, McGillivray pulled his gear together, separating it into two piles. In the first, he assembled everything he would need to direct the race—two-way radios, credentials, a list of colleagues' cell phone numbers, an energy bar and banana for sustenance. In the second, he laid out his running clothes. At some point that afternoon, he would return to his hotel room for a quick change, part of his Marathon Monday ritual of running the course once everyone else was done. By 6:00 A.M., McGillivray was in Hopkinton, his game face on, with a long mental list of things to inspect. He began at the athletes' village at the local high school, then surveyed the volunteer check-in, the water stations, the portable restrooms, the staging area for the lead vehicles, the local elementary school where the wheelchair athletes gathered, and the Korean Presbyterian church, home base for the elite runners. He consulted with a mobile unit of the Massachusetts State Police, made sure the school buses of runners were on their way from Boston, kept an eye on the weather, and gave interviews to the media. Then he walked up and down the starting line to see that the race marshals were in place, the ropes up, the course ready to accept the cascade of competitors, always shadowed by a volunteer with a ham radio, allowing him to communicate with his team.

After twenty-five years as race director, McGillivray had it down to a science, his wisdom an accumulation of so many Marathon Mondays, so many notes carefully logged on a voice recorder he always carried with him. Over all these years, he hadn't quite seen it all, but just about. He knew every nook and cranny of the course—every hill, every turn, every mile marker, every landmark. He could see the whole operation in his sleep, from the oasis of water cups and restrooms in the parking lot of a Hopkinton supermarket to the grandstands and expectant crowds in Copley Square. He had learned, too, how the slightest aberration could threaten the whole day—an unfortunate pile of manure from a policeman's mount, a car parked on the course, rowdy fans infringing on the runners. His task largely consisted of managing an event he couldn't even see. "We're not in an arena," McGillivray said. "This isn't beach volleyball."

The margin of error was precariously slim. Getting more than twenty-three thousand runners through a narrow chute at the start, and then safely down the course, required a careful staging of who started when, and how much space to leave between the waves of competitors. You couldn't have the elite male runners overtaking the elite women en masse. You couldn't have the leading women bumping up against the wheelchair racers. You couldn't have official race vehicles trying to pass one another on the narrow route. The wheelchair racers would roll out at 9:17 A.M.; the elite women would follow fifteen minutes later. At 10:00 A.M. came the elite men and the first wave of ordinary runners. Twenty minutes later, a second wave would follow, and twenty minutes after that, at 10:40, the final group would set off. By the time the last batch crossed the starting line, the leaders would be miles down the course. Over the years, McGillivray and his colleagues at the Boston Athletic Association had learned how critical it was that the field be spaced just right. Once the runners leave the starting line, it's too late to fix anything. Momentum takes charge, a herd of thousands of runners stampeding toward Boston with one goal in mind, everyone straining for the best time their bodies will allow. "Everything has to be perfect," McGillivray said. On this morning, as on all marathon mornings, he lived by his motto: *It isn't about putting out fires. It's about preventing them.*

King lay down on the cool gray Hopkinton pavement and gazed up at the blue sky, looking to coax forth the elation he always felt at the start of a marathon. As he lay there on the ground, though, he realized that he felt a pressing need—he had to go. This was always a problem, for King and countless other marathoners: where to relieve themselves during the tedious wait for the starting gun. It was an even bigger problem for Hopkinton residents, some of whom cordoned off their yards with yellow CAUTION tape to try to repel desperate runners heeding nature's call. King made his way to a row of portable toilets, but after waiting a few minutes in an endless line, he decided he wasn't going to make it. He would have to go into the woods. Looking around, he saw plenty of runners ducking into the brush and trees along the road; most stepped in no more than a few feet. King decided he would seek better cover. He hiked into the brush some forty feet, well off the road, with a righteous sense of having been more thoughtful than the masses. When he emerged, feeling much relieved, a police officer on a bicycle was waiting.

"What were you doing in there?" the officer demanded.

King smirked. "Farming corn," he answered. "What do you think I was doing?"

The young policeman on the bike was not amused. "You know I can give you a ticket for public indecency," he warned. The two men stared each other down, each indignant at the other's challenge.

"Fine," King told him. "Go ahead. Give me a ticket."

The officer hesitated and then waved King on. "Fine, go," he told him. "Don't let me catch you again."

King had won the standoff, but it had been close. And it hadn't done a thing to focus him before the race.

It was always hard to decide when to get into position for the start. Committing oneself to the starting corral meant giving up one's bag and phone and snacks and sweatshirt and embracing the stripped-down aesthetic needed for the race itself. Some runners held off until the last minute, but King was a fan of the opening ceremonies, and he liked to get close enough to listen. His starting position had moved up over the years as his qualifying times had improved, from the back of the pack when he was a newer, slower marathoner, running four hours or more, into the first wave of racers, starting just behind the elite runners. Moving into place there, King felt the exhilaration that had eluded him earlier start to kick in. He felt the same way every time, standing at the starting line with the familiar course spread out before him—almost giddy, he said, "like a five-year-old sneaking downstairs to see his Christmas presents." He waited, reveling in the electric charge of the countdown, and listened for the national anthem. That was the emotional highlight for him. Once he heard it, he was ready to run.

The roots of the Boston Marathon reach back to the first modern Olympic Games, held in Athens in 1896. Most of the delegation representing the United States came from the Boston Athletic Association, a sports and leisure organization the city's heavy hitters had established almost a decade earlier. In those days, the ornate, Gilded Age BAA clubhouse on Boylston Street had a gym, a bowling alley, tennis courts, and Turkish baths. Boxing, fencing, and water polo were among the most popular sports. Inspired by the marathon in Athens, the BAA decided to stage its own race closer to home. On April 19, 1897, fifteen men competed in the first Boston Marathon, then called the BAA Road Race. New Yorker John J. McDermott took the inaugural crown in 2:55, despite walking at various points during the final miles. Initially the course was 24.5 miles long, later stretching to 26.2 miles in accordance with the standard distance set by the 1908 London Olympics.

In the century that followed, the Boston Marathon became one of the premier road races in the world. It made folk heroes out of American runners like Bill Kennedy, a New York bricklayer who won the 1917 race despite sleeping the night before on a pool table in Boston's South End; as he sprinted toward the finish, fellow "brickies" working on a building along the route clapped their bricks together to cheer him on. Or Johnny "the Elder" Kelley, who competed in no fewer than sixty-one Boston Marathons, winning two of them. Or Ellison "Tarzan" Brown, a member of the Narragansett tribe who rarely trained but won the race twice on his natural athleticism. After World War II, the marathon became an international draw, with runners from countries like Japan, Finland, and Kenya asserting their dominance in different eras. Later, the American running boom of the 1970s created a surge in interest, fueling exponential growth in the size of the field. The 1975 Boston Marathon had 2,365 entrants. Thirty years later, it had 20,405. The race's popularity grew to the point that getting a bib number became a sport unto itself—the registration window for the 2011 marathon closed in just eight hours and three minutes. Qualifying for Boston hadn't been easy, exactly—noncharity runners had to achieve competitive times to even enter—but race organizers ultimately had to tighten eligibility requirements further. A few thousand runners, no matter how slow, still get bib numbers every year after committing to raising healthy sums for charitable causes.

Once upon a time, the *Boston Globe* printed the names of all Boston Marathon entrants prior to the race. Spectators would then bring the paper to the course as a guide, calling out to each runner as he passed. "When you ran Boston, you felt a respect and admiration that runners garnered nowhere else," 1968 men's champion Amby Burfoot wrote in a 2013 essay for *Runner's World*. "In other races, we were often mocked. Boston welcomed us, honored us." Plenty of cities—Chicago and New York, to name two prominent ones—have developed their own marathon traditions. But the spirit of the Boston Marathon has remained distinct, its hold on runners—and on the city's soul—lasting and exceptional.

April in New England was famously fickle. Runners had faced winter-like conditions in some years and unforgiving heat in others. The prospects for this Monday, April 15, 2013, had seemed tailor-made, as if McGillivray had ordered it up: pleasantly cool, a high near 50 degrees, a mix of sun and clouds. As he walked the starting line, he saw smiles on runners' faces. He saw the gears of his machine turning, all the pieces moving as designed. His year-long planning and relentless attention were paying off. The 117th Boston Marathon was poised to go off as well as could be.

The only break from routine came just before the 10:00 A.M. start. The race organizers asked everyone to pause for twenty-six seconds of silence, one second for every victim of the mass shooting at Sandy Hook Elementary School in Newtown, Connecticut, four months earlier. McGillivray and his team had scripted a brief ceremony and arranged it so runners across Hopkinton could take part. In the midst of a noisy morning, a blanket of quiet settled over the area. Runners put their heads down or looked to the sky. McGillivray joined the silent gathering, right at the starting line, moved by how still thousands of runners could be. After it was over, he recorded his emotions on his iPhone: *That was one of the most amazing moments in forty years of my involvement with the Boston Marathon.*

The power of it struck David King, too. One of his daughters was a first grader, like the twenty children killed in the school shooting. As the silence deepened around him at the starting line, he thought about the randomness of what had happened in Newtown, how it could have been anyone's kids. King had worried more about his children since going to Iraq as an army surgeon—the experience of war had fundamentally altered his sense of his own and his family's vulnerability—but now he felt humbled by horrors he couldn't imagine. Flooded with gratitude for his family, he felt lucky to know they were safe. As the opening ceremonies wound to a close, King began to focus on his race. He needed to figure out when to turn on his GPS tracker, the device he wore around his wrist to tell him how fast he was running and whether he was on pace. The trick was to activate the tracker just before the gun, giving it sufficient time to find his position but not enough time to needlessly drain the battery. Everyone else in the corral around him was attempting the same feat, the chirps from their gadgets filling the air as if they stood in a summer meadow full of crickets. King pushed the On button. The starting gun cracked and the elite runners took off. Moving slowly toward the starting line behind them, he saw that his tracker was still searching. *Come on*, he thought. *Almost there; come on!* Just as he crossed the line, the bars popped up on the screen. It was a satisfying way to kick things off: stepping onto the storied course in perfect sync with distant satellites circling the Earth.

In the first four miles of the marathon, the elevation of the course drops some three hundred feet, creating the illusion that the race is all downhill. That's partly why in 1990, the national governing body for track and field sports ruled that Boston's marathon could not be the source of world or national records. The downhill start has long troubled elite runners, because it speeds the pack of amateurs along; four-time winner Bill Rodgers once said it allowed runners "who aren't necessarily world-class" to stick around long enough to be "bothersome." When he first ran Boston, King had felt the same annoyance as inexperienced runners bolted down the hill behind him, nipping at his heels. It took half a mile before the swarm would thin enough that he could start running with his normal stride length. In time, though, he had come to embrace the madness of the start, the distinctively careening, jammed-in, jostling movement forward. It was crazy and uncomfortable, and it felt like home.

McGillivray was also in his accustomed spot, well out ahead on the course. He had hopped on the back of a motorcycle that would take him to Boston, always several paces ahead of the leading runners. This was how he kept tabs on everything: whether the green wax paper cups of Gatorade and Poland Spring water were stacked correctly, whether the volunteers were at their posts, how spectators were behaving. He scanned the course for trouble—an errant car, a bicyclist riding where he shouldn't be. But once he was out there on the road, he began to feel like he had handed the race off, giving it to the runners and volunteers and police and everyone else strategically positioned all the way into downtown. It was like a relay. McGillivray had run the initial legs. Now he was passing the baton.

The first few miles went quickly for King. The runners passed from Hopkinton into Ashland just before the two-mile mark; around mile four, as the surrounding landscape changed from rural to suburban to commercial, the pack had to navigate around "three-mile island," a cement island and dreaded tripping hazard in the middle of the road. At mile five in Ashland they passed the Sri Lakshmi Temple, with its fifty-foot tower and ornate statues of Hindu gods. It was near this spot in 1967, when the marathon was officially for men only, that outraged race official Jock Semple chased runner Kathrine Switzer through fat snowflakes, yelling at her to "get out of my race!" The confrontation—which ended with Semple being knocked down by Switzer's boyfriend, and Switzer being banned from amateur running—helped bring about the inauguration of a coed marathon five years later. It became one of the most famous chapters in marathon history.

King passed the Framingham bars and their patrons' inevitable offers of swigs of beer, and the spot near mile seven where a local Dixieland band used to play on the roof of R. H. Long's Cadillac dealership every year, serenading runners below with "When the Saints Go Marching In." Around the halfway point, King arrived at one of his favorite places in the race, the mile-thirteen stretch past Wellesley College, where students at one of New England's best-known women's schools come out to watch in droves. Yelling at top volume for everyone who passes—a tradition almost as old as the marathon itself—the students create a "scream tunnel" that some marathoners find obnoxious or distracting but that King loved and drew on for renewed enthusiasm. He slowed down enough to slap high fives along the roadside, and scattered a few sweaty kisses on eager recipients waving signs like KISS ME, I'M A SENIOR and KISSES MAKE YOU RUN FASTER. The noisy uplift of support always tempted him to speed ahead. But he told himself to hold steady, to stick to his plan: every mile at exactly the same pace.

As he finished miles seventeen, eighteen, and nineteen, passing graceful Georgian mansions and the highway rumble of Route 128, King was on track to achieve his goal: a three-hour, ten-minute race. Then came the exhaustion, settling in at mile twenty, deeper, sooner, and more threatening than he had expected. Afraid that cramps might cripple him, the doctor slowed just slightly. Now he was in his own box, his own lonely struggle, in the midst of all the other runners doing the same thing. He hit mile twenty-two—the "haunted mile," as marathon legend Johnny Kelley called it—the point where the body's reserves of fuel and energy are depleted and a runner's focus narrows to survival. He came to Cleveland Circle, and more clusters of college students. He kept going onto Beacon Street and into Brookline and on to Coolidge Corner. He was almost in Boston now, entering the final miles of the race. He crossed over the Massachusetts Turnpike and descended into Kenmore Square. This was the homestretch, with less than two miles to the finish. His family was up ahead, waiting for him. He turned his gaze toward the left side of Commonwealth Avenue, scanning the crowd as he fought through the pain, closer and closer to the turn onto Hereford Street. And then he saw them, his mother and father and Anne and their two little girls, screaming for Daddy.

King veered toward them. He always stopped here to hug his children; he always somehow found the breath to tell them how glad he was to see them. He knew some other runners might not sacrifice the time—after all, he would see them soon at the finish line. But he meant to send a message, that his girls were more important to him than anything—certainly more important than the marathon clock. The meeting was a high point, and it would carry him to the finish.

Turning left onto Boylston Street, he had run twenty-six miles. That left about 350 yards, or 1,050 feet, to the finish line. The crowd here was dense and deafening, thousands of people packed in so close together beneath the skyscrapers they looked like the colored dots of a pointillist painting. In the street, between the barricades containing the twin rivers of spectators, the pace of the race was quickening. Runners who had walked up Heartbreak Hill or walked through Kenmore Square—none of them were walking now. The finish line up ahead was the same one the winners had crossed just an hour earlier. The crowd was screaming now just as it had for the winners. It was the same race, and they were all in it together. King took the time to register the magic of that. He thought about the time, in 2009, that he had fallen down in the street after crossing the finish line, his face contorted in pain, and how another runner had come to him beaming, asking how he felt. King had mumbled something about cramps. "You should feel great," the other man had told him with conviction. "We just finished the Boston Marathon!"

King crossed the finish line and slowed to a walk. Then, as he always did, he stopped and turned around to face the runners coming in behind him. Standing there a minute, looking back down Boylston

Street, he listened to the roar of the enormous crowd and watched the runners' faces as they finished. He considered the magnitude of what they had accomplished. He tried, for just one moment, to consider what it meant. Then he turned back into the natural flow of traffic, away from the finish and back toward his regular life, the search for water and bananas and his family. They would be coming to find him in their designated meeting place, by the sign marked *K*, the first letter of his last name.

Around the same time, at 1:45 P.M., McGillivray sent a text message to Tom Grilk, the executive director of the Boston Athletic Association. With everything appearing okay at the finish line—with the winners long done, and thousands more having already crossed behind them—McGillivray thought the time had come to put on his Adidas and begin his own run. *Hi Tom*, he wrote. *All seems fine so may head out soon. Okay? Great job!*

Beat it, Grilk replied.

The words from Grilk—unequivocal, assured—meant a lot. McGillivray sometimes felt trepidation seeking this permission. He was the race director, after all. Asking to leave the scene always felt like a big thing, a little part of him believing he was abandoning his troops, even though he ran with his phone in his hand. At the same time, running the course was a deeply personal obligation, one he did not intend to break. Ever since 1973, he had kept the promise to his grandfather to finish. His start time varied year to year, depending on how things were going. In 2012, he didn't begin running until 8:30 P.M. because the crippling heat had sent so many runners to medical tents and hospitals. That year he crossed the finish line just shy of midnight. Sometimes when he ran, people along the course, not knowing who he was, would shout words of encouragement like "Hey, you slug, the race is over!" or "The eighty-year-old guy went by hours ago. Pick it up." With Grilk's reply this year, McGillivray began preparing for his cherished routine—the ride to the starting line from longtime friend Ron Kramer, the state troopers' escort through the course, the companionship of running buddy Josh Nemzer, and McGillivray's brother Bob shadowing them in his car, ready with water, Gatorade, and food, including a batch of chocolate chip cookies made from their mother's recipe. The heavy responsibility having largely fallen away, McGillivray could now allow himself the privilege of worrying only about pushing his body through 26.2 miles. It would be the capstone to another successful year, another satisfying feat. "Beat it" were just the words he wanted to hear.

CHAPTER 4

FINISH LINE

Gathering on the sidelines

Shana Cottone reported to roll call before 9:00 A.M. The spot where cops assembled, the Boston Police Department's District 4 station in the South End, was directly behind the massive stone Cathedral of the Holy Cross. The bosses handed out assignments for the marathon: Shana was to be stationed on Boston Common, the oldest public park in America, five or six blocks beyond the finish line. After roll call, though, another officer approached her and asked if she would swap assignments so he could work the Common with a friend of his. Shana agreed without hesitating. She would gladly go to Boylston Street to patrol the finish line itself. It made no difference to her. She parked beside the library and got to work.

A rare holiday spirit swept the city on this day each year; everyone seemed to be wound a little less tightly. The party-like atmosphere could present its own headaches for police, however. Shana figured she would deserve it if a pack of drunk, obnoxious college students came her way. Not so long ago, the twenty-seven-year-old police officer had been a college kid herself. She and her Northeastern friends had not always been on their best behavior when they came to the finish line, sipping wine out of plastic cups and climbing on the chain-link fence by Lord & Taylor until the cops yelled at them to get down. Now the tables were turned; any rowdiness would be, for her, a kind of karmic payback. The street, though, remained fairly quiet at 10:00 A.M. Most college students were probably just getting out of bed.

Marathon Monday began early for Heather Abbott. It was barely light outside when her friend Jason Geremia picked her up in Newport for the drive to Providence, where they would catch a train to Boston. Jason was like an older brother to Heather, a little bit bossy and overprotective. In the car, he talked about being single; Heather was newly single, too. "I'll be your date anytime," Heather told him. They were friends, nothing more, but they were close. People often mistook them for a couple; people who knew them well understood why they weren't. It worked the way it was, and neither one wanted to change it. Sitting on the train to Boston, laughing with their friends, was like a scene out of high school. When the conductor kicked them out of the quiet car for being too noisy, it only made them laugh harder. They got to the city at 9:30, stopped for coffee, and headed to Fenway Park for the Red Sox game. The first pitch was at 11:05.

The crowds at the finish line built quickly and steadily through the morning. The marathon winners came across around noon—Lelisa Desisa of Ethiopia for the men, with a time of 2:10, and Kenya's Rita Jeptoo for the women, in 2:26. Governor Deval Patrick crowned them with the traditional wreaths, made of olive leaves that came all the way from Greece. Typically, the governor crowns the women's winner and the mayor crowns the men's. But Boston mayor Thomas Menino was in the hospital, recovering from surgery two days earlier on a broken leg. With great reluctance, he had called Patrick to ask him to do the honors. It pained Menino to miss out on a day he loved. Just two weeks earlier, he had announced he would not run for office again, after a record twenty years in power. He had never missed a marathon, and he would not get another chance to be there in his ceremonial role. The mayor's favorite part came later, though, after all the dignitaries had departed. He often stayed for hours, watching the waves of average people cross the finish line.

Around lunchtime, Shana ate a sandwich in a suite at the Lenox Hotel that was being used as a break room by police. It was fancier than her usual workday digs, with plush armchairs and complimentary shoulder massages. Then she returned to her post in the street. In front of her, a row of flags flapped gently in the breeze, their bold blocks of color representing the runners' many countries. Police officers in bright yellow vests were lined up there with gaps between them, facing the sidewalk in front of the Marathon Sports store, a final barrier between the runners and the crowd.

The mass of spectators was like a giant hive of bees, its constant, seemingly random movements revealing more predictable patterns upon close study. College and high school students, families with children, coworkers and spouses, Bostonians and out-of-towners were all bunched up together. They remained in constant flux, bodies replacing bodies in a continuous cycle. Friends and family members tracking particular runners timed their arrival at the finish line to coincide with their loved one's approach. They pushed their way to the front to see and cheer and photograph the magical moment of fulfillment, and then retreated, setting off to find their runner. Fresh faces flowed in to replace them. Today, the hive was peaceful. Shana couldn't find much to worry about.

Deval Patrick never had days like this. It was a state holiday, so technically he was off the clock—as much as a governor can be. Plus his wife was in New York. That left him alone for a warmish April afternoon. After greeting the marathon winners, he offered hugs and thanks to race volunteers, and then headed out around 1:00 P.M. He went to get a buzz cut at the Summer Street Barber Shop, at the edge of the Financial District. Afterward he played squash across the street at the Boston Racquet Club. Then he went to his home in Milton, a town just south of Boston, to putter in the garden, preparing it for the spring planting season. Maybe clean the fountain. A little manual labor to clear the head. "It's slow, it's quiet," he said of the yard work. "You don't have to talk to anybody."

Around the same time, Boston Police superintendent William Evans finished his eighteenth Boston Marathon. Evans was usually the guy in charge of the street for any big event in the city, but on Marathon Monday he was a runner first. He was thrilled at his time, 3:34; he knew being under 3:40 would qualify him for next year's race. He saw his wife, Terry, and son Will in the grandstand waving as he came in. He grabbed some water in the recovery area and hoped for a free massage near the finish line, but the wait was longer than he wanted. He and his family went home to South Boston, and then Evans hit the nearby Boston Athletic Club, where cops usually met after the race. He sank into the whirlpool.

Boston Police commissioner Edward Davis left the marathon for home close to 1:30. Everything was going well, and he had a conference call with the White House at 2:00—Vice President Joe Biden was marshaling support among police chiefs for a gun control bill. Before he left, Davis spoke to his lieutenants, urging them not to let their guard down. Stay vigilant, he told them.

Around 2:00, Krystle Campbell got a text message from John Colombo and Liz Jenkins, friends whom she knew from her days working at Summer Shack. They were in Arlington, buying motorcycle gear at a store across the street from Jimmy's, the restaurant where Krystle now worked. They wanted to see if she was on duty, so they could come see her.

Krystle had the day off, though. She was downtown with her friend Karen Rand, another member of the Summer Shack crew.

They had strolled through the Public Garden and were going to the marathon to watch Karen's boyfriend, who was running. At 2:01, Krystle texted back to tell Colombo and Jenkins she wouldn't see them in Arlington.

Miss you, she wrote.

The Red Sox game at Fenway Park ended eight minutes after 2:00. The Sox had won 3 to 2 over Tampa Bay, a fierce rival in the American League East. They had been within a run of each other for most of the game, before the Sox took it with a walk-off double. After the final out, the capacity crowd of 37,449 flooded into the streets, many of them planning to check out the marathon in nearby Kenmore Square or several blocks away, at the finish line on Boylston Street.

Heather Abbott and her friends had split up at Fenway. Four of them had paid extra for good seats behind home plate, but Heather and Jason and Michelle had settled for less expensive tickets in right field. Their friends in front mocked their cheap seats, text messaging Jason during the game to ask him if he could even see the game. Soon enough, as the crowd started to thin, empty seats became available. Heather and her seatmates joined the group down by home plate. By the seventh inning, though, Heather and two of her girlfriends were getting cold. They went to the restroom, wandered up to the stadium gate to wait for the others, then decided to head for Game On!, a large sports pub steps from the ballpark. Before too long, Jason and the others were ready to join them, but the line outside the bar was long and slow-moving. *We'll meet you at Forum*, Jason texted, as he and his group started out for the bar on Boylston Street. Around 2:30, Heather texted Jason that she was on her way to Forum, too.

The brothers from Cambridge were already on Boylston. At 2:37 P.M., Dzhokhar and Tamerlan Tsarnaev were captured by a surveillance camera rounding the corner from Gloucester Street. Tamerlan led the way with his hands in his pockets, his backpack firmly strapped onto both shoulders. Dzhokhar followed a short distance behind, weaving slightly to avoid oncoming pedestrians. His pack was loosely slung over one shoulder, swinging slightly side to side with every step. They paused then, photographs taken from across the street would later show, loitering and talking for several minutes in a doorway next to Whiskey's Steakhouse. A couple of minutes later they were in motion again, still carrying their backpacks, heading up the sidewalk toward the finish line.

Firefighter Sean O'Brien was working the south side of Boylston, across the street from Forum. The crowd size had been building since 2:00, as people coming from the Red Sox game flowed onto the street. Many of them wanted to know how to get across Boylston, to the bars on the other side. "You can't," O'Brien told them, half joking. "Give up." As 2:30 came and went, he considered when to go and find the captain to discuss the 4:00 P.M. shift change. He didn't want to move down the street too soon, in case an emergency happened and he had to get back to his post. It was a pessimistic thought on a day that was going perfectly smoothly.

Across the street, Pat Foley, another firefighter, reminded himself that he was off at 4:00. The cowbells were getting to him. Every time a runner finished, the clanging swept through the crowd. He was glad he wouldn't have to listen to the noise much longer. About 2:45, as he passed by Fairfield Street, he sent his wife a text message, asking if she wanted him to buy her a marathon T-shirt. *Why don't you swing by Tiffany*, she texted back, referring to the upscale jewelry store nearby. The sassy quip made Foley smile. *Details don't pay THAT good*, he texted back. Then he started walking back toward the finish line.

Frederick Lorenz, a Boston fire lieutenant leading the city's emergency medical team, was patrolling the finish area in a golf cart. The medics had hip pouches with all kinds of antiterrorism gear, like masks and kits to use in case of a chemical attack. They felt prepared, but they didn't expect to need any of that stuff. After a while, as it got colder, Lorenz decided to get some hot soup at Shaw's, a supermarket just around the corner. He parked the golf cart down the street and walked into the store.

Nearby, an army of volunteers staffed the main medical tent, a makeshift but elaborate operation just beyond the finish line; in all, some 1,400 medical volunteers were on duty throughout the marathon course. Typically, the doctors and nurses working in the tent treated conditions associated with running—things like sprains, hypothermia, heat stroke, and hyponatremia, a dangerous sodium deficiency. If anyone required more intensive care, several top-tier hospitals were only a mile or two away. The unseasonable heat at the 2012 marathon had kept the medical tent exceptionally busy, with hundreds of runners needing treatment. So far in 2013, things seemed to be much calmer. And for that everyone was thankful.

Brighid and Brendan Wall had miscalculated. With three young children in tow—their own, ages four and six, plus their five-year-old nephew—they had hoped to avoid a long wait at the finish line. So they postponed their arrival, riding the Swan Boats in the Public Garden, lingering over lunch, aiming to get there just before Brighid's sister raced down the homestretch. Still, despite their efforts, they got there too soon. The children grew restless. The parents promised ice cream in exchange for patience. They were on the sidewalk outside Starbucks, next to Forum. The kids were pressed up against the barricade, next to the street, high-fiving the occasional runner who ventured near. It was her sister's tenth time running Boston; Brighid had wanted to surprise her, so she had not told Siobhan that they were coming. Siobhan thought all of them, her own son included, were at home in Duxbury, thirty-five miles away. Brighid imagined her sister sprinting over, grabbing her son's hand, and running with him to the finish. They would remember a moment like that forever. She checked her phone again, tracking Siobhan's progress. By 2:40 the wait was almost over. She tried to refocus the children's attention: The moment they had waited for all day was almost here. "Watch for her; keep your eyes open," she told them. "Look for her red shirt—she's coming, any minute."

A short distance to her right, closer to Forum, another family was waiting, too. Bill and Denise Richard had their three children with them; their son Martin, eight, and daughter, Jane, seven, were also standing up against the barricade between the sidewalk and the street. The family had been watching a few blocks away, where the runners turn onto Boylston at Hereford Street, when they decided to take a break for ice cream. Returning to the race about 2:30, they opted to move closer to the finish line. They were watching for some runners they knew from their Dorchester neighborhood. Jane and Martin stepped up onto the metal fence in front of them to get a better view.

Along with the families and young children, college students jammed the Boylston sidewalks. Standing near the Richards out in front of Forum, Lingzi Lu was one of them. She was twenty-three years old, a graduate student from China studying statistics at Boston University. She had just learned on Sunday that she had passed an important exam, and it had put her in a happy mood. Monday morning, over breakfast with her roommate at their Arlington apartment, Lingzi had toyed with the idea of going to the marathon. She decided that she would, after doing some work on a project; her friend Zhou Danling wanted to go, too. They had made their way to the finish line. Now they stood close to the runners bearing down on the finish, the day's great drama unfolding an arm's length away.

She wasn't in the marathon, but Alma Bocaletti was still running. Running along the sidelines. She and six others had gone to support another friend, Natalie, who had entered the race. They'd made matching black-and-white T-shirts with the image of a sunflower. They'd drawn up posters. They'd bought a bouquet of yellow balloons, so Natalie could find them in the crowd. After seeing Natalie pass at mile seventeen, they hopped on the train to Boston hoping to see her at the end, too. Bocaletti wanted to go all the way to the finish line but was worried she wouldn't make it before Natalie crossed. So she took off running, figuring she'd reconnect with her friends later. She dashed up to a spot in the crowd near Marathon Sports, where the flags of all the countries stood. The freckled face of a stranger turned around.

"Who are you waiting for?" Krystle Campbell asked her with a smile.

"I'm waiting for a friend," Bocaletti said, explaining that Natalie had crossed the thirty-kilometer mark a little while ago. "How about you?"

Krystle pointed to her friend Karen, standing nearby. "Her boyfriend just crossed the thirty-K, too," she said.

Bocaletti's friends then caught up with her. One of them had Bocaletti's phone. Using the tracking system, she could see now that Natalie was nearing the finish. She went back up to Krystle to show her Natalie's location on the phone. Krystle smiled.

"Oh, yours is coming any moment now," she said.

"Yes, if my calculations are correct, any moment," Bocaletti said.

It was about 2:45. A woman in front of both of them, who was right up against the barricade, took a phone call and walked away. That left open a prime spot in the front row, a perfect spot for viewing. Krystle had as much right to it as anyone. But she didn't move forward. She smiled, shifted over, and let Bocaletti go up front.

Heather finally made it to Boylston Street. Crossing over from Fenway Park, she and her friends had gotten lost in the marathon street closures, just like last year, but they were having a good time, and the slight delay didn't bother them. They walked up the sidewalk on the same side as Forum, approaching with the restaurant to their left. The door to the bar was open. A bouncer was checking IDs. Moving closer to the door, her friends in front of her, Heather peered into the bar. It didn't look as crowded as she had expected. She didn't see anyone she knew, not yet. In a minute, when they were inside, she would get a better look.

On his own now, Tamerlan Tsarnaev continued walking eastbound toward the finish line. Dzhokhar moved a little farther east, too, then stopped on the sidewalk in front of Forum, a few feet behind eight-year-old Martin Richard. Lingzi Lu was nearby, too. He eased his heavy backpack to the ground, letting go of the straps. A block away, close to where Krystle Campbell was standing, Tamerlan did the same. As Tamerlan waited in the crowd outside Marathon Sports, something about him—a lone man in a black baseball hat and dark sunglasses—drew the attention of Jeff Bauman, a twenty-seven-year-old who was at the race to watch his girlfriend run. The man with the backpack wasn't cheering or clapping for the runners; he seemed out of place, Bauman thought. For an instant, the two young men locked eyes. At 2:48, Dzhokhar called Tamerlan from a prepaid cell phone. They spoke for several seconds, then hung up. Each one then started moving down the sidewalk, leaving their packs on the ground behind them, their remote detonators close at hand. Tamerlan walked away from Jeff Bauman and Krystle Campbell and the other spectators standing near Marathon Sports. Dzhokhar walked away from Jane and Martin Richard and the rest of the children perched on the metal barrier, away from Heather Abbott and the others waiting outside Forum to get in. The brothers had made their commitment; there was no going back. The time was 2:49 P.M.

CHAPTER 5

2:50 P.M.

Agony on Boylston Street

Carlos Arredondo made the sign of the cross with one hand. "God protect us," he said. Then the man in the cowboy hat ran across the street, toward the spot where a ball of white fire had just erupted. He began tearing down the fencing in his way. He could see people in a pile on the sidewalk, some of them missing legs. Arredondo knew trauma, more than any man should. He'd lost one son to combat in Iraq in 2004; he had been so distraught when the marine detail came to tell him the news that he lit himself on fire. Seven years later, his surviving son committed suicide. In the mayhem on Boylston Street, Arredondo dropped the American flag he'd been carrying, leaned over a gravely injured young man, and asked him his name. He could feel his sons' presence protecting him. "It's okay," he told the man at his feet, trying to calm him.

Twenty yards from the finish line, Bill Iffrig was running down the left side of the course, on pace, at age seventy-eight, to complete his third Boston Marathon. The thundering force of an explosion hit him hard, a massive wall of noise. He knew it was a bomb. His legs collapsed beneath him and he crumpled to the ground. *This might be it*, he thought. *This will be the end of me.* Lying on the pavement in his orange tank top and black shorts, he looked up to see three police officers running at him, drawing their weapons. "Are you okay?" one of them asked.

Perched near the finish line with her grandchildren, Ana Victoria was eager to see her daughter, Vicma Lamarche, make it across, having traveled all the way from the Dominican Republic for the marathon. When the explosion rocked the sidelines, she frantically gave the children to Vicma's husband and ran toward the smoke. Victoria knew that Vicma, given her pace, was unlikely to have reached the finish yet. But she didn't care. *I'm going to find my daughter,* she said to herself. Quickly overwhelmed by the scene, by the blood, by the vast needs of the wounded, she felt helpless and scared. She dropped to her knees, eyes closed, mouth open, hands pressed together at her lips. *Make it stop*, she prayed. *Please don't let these people die.*

Inside Marathon Sports, Shane O'Hara had just popped open a Guinness and poured it into a coffee mug. This was a workday, but it was a celebration, too, a day-long toast to the running community. There, inside the tidy storefront, O'Hara was helping a former employee try on a pair of running shoes when he felt a massive boom rattle through him. The building shook. The front window went white with smoke. O'Hara ran to the door, alarms, screaming, panic ringing in his ears. He found a dazed woman shrouded in smoke and helped her into the store. He noticed blood running down her lower leg, under her black jeans, and onto the tile. He got down and put his hand gingerly on her calf, feeling for the wound. Blood covered his fingers, its warmth reminding him of the fresh cow's milk he used to handle on the farm where he grew up. His Adidas sales rep, standing nearby, grabbed some shorts off a rack and pressed them tight against the woman's leg.

O'Hara ran back outside. He started ripping away the metal scaffolding that separated the sidewalk from the street. It had become a lethal barrier, blocking emergency responders from reaching the wounded. He ran in and out of the store, delivering clothes from the racks to bleeding victims and the people helping them. All around him he saw overwhelming damage. "Stay with me," somebody said to one woman, her head resting on a helper's lap. "Stay with me."

Out there on the sidewalk, just for one still moment, O'Hara felt everything fall away. A calm came over him, the world slowing to a crawl. He didn't know what was next, if another explosion would follow, if he and everyone around him were about to die. Was he satisfied with what his life had been? He decided that he was. His mind was at peace. He was willing to accept whatever came. And then just like that, the sensation passed. He threw himself back into the pressing work of trying to save lives.

It was there, right outside the store O'Hara managed, that Krystle Campbell had stood seconds before, watching the runners finish, hanging with her friends, taking part in one of the Boston sports traditions she so loved. Now she was on the ground, her head tipped back to the sky. She had suffered devastating wounds to her torso and lower extremities, worse than those of anyone around her. A Georgia emergency room physician and other rescuers tried desperately to save her. They rushed her to the medical tent, but it was too late. Her pulse had slipped away.

That's not a cannon, Boston firefighter Sean O'Brien thought when he heard the first explosion. *Maybe a transformer?* He was standing in front of the Mandarin Oriental Hotel, a couple blocks before the finish line. "Obie, that's a bomb," the firefighter next to him said. Right then, a second explosion tore through the sidewalk across the street. The first blast had happened in front of Marathon Sports, at 671 Boylston Street. The second explosion, just twelve seconds later, detonated one block to the west, in front of Forum restaurant, at 755 Boylston. Both spots were packed with afternoon crowds. Those who could ran for their lives, away from whatever might happen next—a third bomb? A fourth? Many, like O'Brien, thought the first blast was some kind of accident. When the second echoed, they knew it was something much worse.

O'Brien's thoughts raced first to his wife and his four daughters. In an instant, he sorted through his recent interactions with them and found them acceptable. No fights, no harsh words would stand among their final memories of him. Then he moved forward, over the barricade toward the bomb scene, the wounded walking toward him in a daze. He could smell the burning. He looked back across the street, near the spot where he'd just been standing, and saw a little girl's bag, pink with flowers, abandoned on the sidewalk. *That one's next*, he thought. *I know it*. He waited for the pink bag to blow up.

The first explosion had rippled the surface of Jason Geremia's drink as he stood near the bar inside Forum. Conversations around him stopped midsentence. Smiles faded, replaced by looks of confusion. "What was that?" the bartender asked. The sound was loud, but far enough away that it wasn't clear what had caused it. Jason turned to look at the front entrance and saw his friends Michelle and Jess standing in the doorway. He didn't see Heather Abbott, who was supposed to be with them. Just then the second blast blew his friends into the bar. They were stumbling forward, falling, as he grabbed them and pulled them to the back, away from Boylston Street and whatever had just happened. Everyone else was stampeding the same way.

Brighid Wall threw her six-year-old son onto the ground when the second bomb exploded some ten feet away to their right. She lay across him on the sidewalk, her pregnant belly beneath her, and looked back over her left shoulder at the dazed people covered with black soot. She saw a man struggling to stand up; she realized he was struggling because he was missing a leg. The urge to flee seized her then, pushing away shock and fear, and she scanned the ground, looking for the bag that held her car keys. She stood up. Her husband grabbed their son and nephew. A stranger picked up her four-year-old daughter and they all ran into the Starbucks next door to Forum, blood and broken glass and spilled coffee under their feet. People were screaming but the children were silent—waiting, she realized, for someone to make them safe.

Searching in the smoke for one of his friends, Mike Chase came across a man holding seven-year-old Jane Richard in his arms. "We gotta do something here," said the man, an off-duty firefighter named Matt Patterson. Chase, a high school soccer coach who had been watching the race, grabbed the belt Patterson had wrapped around the child's thigh and pulled it tight. Her leg was in bad shape. Jane's father, Bill Richard, was nearby, holding on to his oldest son, Henry, who was not badly hurt. Chase looked down and saw his missing friend, Dan Marshall, kneeling on the ground over another little boy. Others bent to join him, trying to help Martin. "My son, my son," the stricken father said. There was nothing anyone could do.

Allison Byrne was so eager to finish the race that she was sprinting down Boylston. She saw the first explosion and veered away from the left side of the street. She felt the second bomb's impact before she heard it. Something black hurtled toward her legs. It was an iPhone-sized piece of shrapnel, and it lodged in the meat of her left calf. With her good leg, she dove to the right, somehow crashing through the metal barricades on the opposite side of the street. Alone and scared, she lay bleeding on the sidewalk.

"Oh my God, I can't die!" she screamed. People trampled over her, desperate to escape. "Please don't leave me," she pleaded, making eye contact with some as they ran over her.

Then she heard a voice: "I'm not going to leave you." The voice came from Nancy Shorter, who appeared like an angel as ash fell all around them. Shorter was a spectator, there with her husband and stepsons. But she was much more than that. A retired nurse, she had spent years working in the ER at one of Boston's best hospitals. She quickly elevated Byrne's leg, grabbed her husband's jacket, and applied pressure to the wound. Byrne rested her head against the window of a bank. Shorter sat with her, then helped her into the backseat of a police car.

After he heard the deafening explosions, Dr. Sushrut Jangi walked out the back of the marathon's block-long medical tent and looked down Boylston Street toward the finish line. He saw smoke and a crowd of people running. "There are bombs," a woman whispered at his side. Jangi, a medical volunteer who had spent the day treating chilled and dehydrated runners, felt the urge to flee. His hands began to shake, and he thought about slipping away. Inside the tent, someone in charge was speaking into a microphone, asking everybody to stay calm and remain with their patients. Jangi turned around and went back in. A nurse standing between two cots began to cry.

Heather Abbott lay on the floor inside Forum watching her friends disappear, running with the crowd into the back of the restaurant. She had been just outside the door, waiting to get in, when she heard the first explosion; she had turned her head at the sound and seen smoke rising. Her first thought was of 9/11: some dislodged memory of TV coverage from that day, surfacing before she knew what was happening. Then, before she could think of anything else, the second explosion blew her through the door and into the restaurant. Her left foot felt like it was on fire. She tried to get up and couldn't, and thought to herself, *I might die here. Everyone is running away. Who is going to help me?* She sat up and called out for help. It was hard to tell in the din if her voice was a scream or a whisper. She took care not to look at her foot, fearful that she might faint at the sight of it. She had to keep her focus on finding a way out. All at once a woman appeared beside her, a stranger asking for her name and praying out loud: "Hail Mary, full of grace, the Lord is with thee." The woman's husband bent down, lifted Heather up, and carried her in his arms out the back door into daylight. Her foot was still burning, but she wasn't alone anymore.

Shana Cottone reached for her gun when the first bomb exploded. Something had gone wrong and she didn't know what it was. Twelve seconds passed, the second bomb went off, and then, like so many others, Shana understood. They were being attacked and she was going to die. Fighting off the overwhelming urge to run away, she started ripping down the barricades along the sidewalk, moving into the drifting smoke in front of Forum. She picked up strollers, the babies still strapped inside, and carried them into the middle of the street, where it seemed like they might be safer, as stunned parents followed her blindly. She put one stroller down on the open pavement and saw a woman lying nearby, on the pavement in the middle of the street. She was covered with abrasions, her blonde hair singed to black around her face. Shana knelt and looked into her eyes. The woman was awake. Shana took her hand and started talking.

"Talk to me," she told the woman in the street. "Who did you come to watch? Where do you live?"

"I can't feel my leg," the woman said. She was bleeding heavily, one of her legs nearly severed. Shana looked down the street. Where were the ambulances? Why weren't they coming?

"Your leg is there," Shana said.

"I can't feel it," the woman insisted.

Shana wanted to call her by her name, to reach her through the fog of shock and pain and hold her there. She searched for one of the woman's ID cards and found it: "I swear on my life, Roseann, your leg is there."

Around them was a churning sea of chaos: terrified spectators running away; police and firefighters running in; bystanders whipping off belts and handing them to first responders. Across the bloodstained pavement, small desperate clusters formed around the most gravely wounded victims. Within each knot of kneeling people in the street, the focus narrowed to one face, one broken body, one makeshift tourniquet. Time seemed to slow down. The motions of people trying to help were frantic, video clips from the scene would later show, but in the moment, every action seemed to unfold as if underwater. Even to those who worked there every day, Boylston Street in those first minutes was utterly foreign, a place that looked and felt completely unfamiliar. Seconds felt like minutes; death hovered close. They would not be able to fend it off for long.

Lingzi Lu, the graduate student from China, was already gone. She had been standing in the crowd near Forum; now she lay still and silent on the ground, her lower body ravaged by the explosion. Firefighters tried to revive her, but it was futile. They determined she was dead and covered her body.

Standing where the second bomb had just blown up in front of Forum, Boston fire lieutenant Fred Lorenz surveyed the carnage. He saw two people who looked like they didn't have long to live. Those who weren't making any noise were the ones who needed help the most. Looking up Boylston toward the scene of the first blast, he could see ambulances. On his radio, he called for help—*755 Boylston, we need ambulances!*—but all the other crackling voices drowned him out. The police and firefighters at the site of the first explosion, just a block away, were consumed with their own tangle of casualties; their focus had narrowed so tightly they did not yet realize a second deadly scene lay a short distance down the street.

Firefighter Pat Foley was rushing toward the site of the first blast when the second bomb exploded just fifty feet away. Two or three more steps and he stood in the middle of the smoke and wreckage, surrounded by bodies and body parts on the ground. Foley was a thirty-four-year veteran of the fire department; as the assistant chief of the city's dive team, he routinely rescued and recovered bodies from the water. As he began barking orders at the hysterical people around him, his authoritative tone silenced some of the screaming. "Gimme the belt," he told a woman standing at his side. Other people turned toward the sound of his voice—people who were unscathed;

people with shredded clothes and holes in their legs—seeking the small comfort of direction. "I need more belts," he ordered, and people obediently fumbled to comply. Foley knelt beside a critically wounded man and cinched a belt tight around his leg, cutting off the blood flow. "Go get every towel in the restaurant," he told a young man nearby, who sprang into action. Then Foley looked closer at the injured man whose tourniquet he gripped, and realized that his legs were still on fire. Grabbing his knife, he sawed at the man's burning pants. The man, whose name was Marc Fucarile, lay not far away from Roseann, the woman with the singed blonde hair whom Shana was trying to comfort.

Finally, an ambulance was coming toward them. "Here it comes; it's almost here," Foley assured the two victims. Roseann heard the sirens and thought, *This one must be for me.* But as the vehicle approached it showed no sign of stopping. Frantic bystanders and police rushed forward, screaming and waving, trying to flag down the driver. All at once their nightmare felt like a prison: There was no way out and no way to end it. "We're full, we're full!" the driver yelled as he passed them. Another ambulance approached and it, too, kept on rolling. Shana could not believe what was happening. What did the driver mean "full"? Was there any space at all, on the floor, in the front seat? Were these people going to bleed to death here on the street? *We've got to get them out of here right now*, she thought with mounting desperation. *There are a million hospitals, but we've got to get them there.*

A van pulled up beside them in the middle of the street. It was a Boston Police Department prisoner transport vehicle—otherwise known as the "paddy wagon"—a white truck with a blue stripe down the side and a big metal box to carry passengers on the back. It was typically stationed near big events like the marathon, mostly to send a sobering message to any rowdies in the crowd. The driver, Jim Davis, was a large, imposing man with the tattoos of a biker and decades on the force. He could see and hear the desperation in Roseann's eyes and in Marc's voice, pleading with the first responders not to let him die. "I'll get you to the hospital," Davis said. People were already struggling to wrench open the truck's rear doors, yelling about which victims needed to go first. To Fred Lorenz, in charge of the day's EMS operation, it was perfectly clear who would go. But with the clamor in the street, no one seemed to hear him. Looking at Roseann and Marc, he spoke again, this time with a clarity that ended the debate: "These two people need to go now or they're going to die."

Shana Cottone, Pat Foley, and another firefighter, Mike Materia, helped load Roseann and Marc into the back of the van. Each of the victims lay across a backboard; the firefighters propped the boards on the bare metal benches along the sides of the cab. Foley and Materia knelt on the van's metal floor back to back, each cradling a victim in his arms as they tried to hold the man and woman steady on the benches. Up front, Shana leapt into the passenger seat of the wagon. The metal doors slammed shut, plunging the four passengers in the back into blackness.

In the alley between Boylston and Newbury Streets, Jason Geremia had discovered that his friend Heather was missing. Seven of them had come to the marathon together; now six were gathered behind Forum restaurant, in the frightened, confused sea of people who had fled through the back doors of businesses on Boylston. "Where is she?" Jason urgently asked their friend Michelle. She had been standing next to Heather at the front door when the bomb exploded, when everyone started running, but now she had no idea where Heather was.

"What do you mean you don't know?" Jason demanded. He moved back toward the metal staircase they had just come down, intending to fight his way back up the stairs and into the bar, but people were still coming down in droves, blocking his path. Then, as he looked up the stairs, he saw Heather, in the arms of a big bald man coming through the door. Jason pushed closer. "Give her to me, bro," he said.

"Wait," said the man. "Look at her leg."

Jason looked and saw that Heather was in serious trouble, her left foot partially destroyed. "Oh my God, oh my God," she was saying. "What happened? Jason, what's going on?"

The big man—Jason thought he was a bouncer from the bar but learned later he was Matt Chatham, a former linebacker for the New England Patriots—laid Heather gently on the ground. "Please call an ambulance," she told her friends. Her friend Jess got on the ground beside her, resting her head on Heather's shoulder and holding her hand, while Jason punched in 911 on a cell phone. "We're behind the Pelham," he told the operator, mistakenly giving the name of a bar back in Newport. One of his friends quickly corrected him. "Sorry, behind Forum," he said into the phone. No one else nearby in the alley had been hurt, and strangers gathered around them, trying to help.

"Do you think we should move her?" a man asked Jason.

"Don't move her!" a woman ordered sharply.

Another woman hunted around in the alley until she found a sheet of wood five or six feet long, big enough to carry Heather out on if they had to. Heather tried to stay focused on one task: somehow getting herself to a hospital. She knew it had to happen fast, but the wait in the alley seemed to take forever. A nurse and a doctor appeared and asked for a belt. Her friend Tommy pulled his off and gave it to them. Someone fastened it as a tourniquet on her leg. Still no ambulance appeared in the alley.

Her friend Jess was crying now, her face close to Heather's. "Don't leave me," Heather told her softly.

Shana Cottone leaned all the way out the window on the passenger side of the police van as it inched up a side road, away from Boylston, screaming at the people in the street to get out of the way. Her sense of urgency had not abated, but she felt a little safer, now that they were heading away from the scene of the bombing. They turned left onto Huntington Avenue. She took out her phone and dialed her father in New York. "Dad," she said when he answered, "we're being attacked. I'm okay. I'm trying to get people out. I love you." She hung up. The van was passing quickly through the Back Bay now. They turned onto Stuart Street and then onto Charles, between Boston Common and the Public Garden, two of the city's swaths of downtown green, the Common much older than the country.

The back of the police van was another world, hard and windowless and completely dark. The two firefighters knelt on the metal floor as the vehicle careened across the city, each holding one of the severely injured victims. They struggled to protect the wounded from the rough ride, to keep them from sliding off the bare metal benches while still gripping the tourniquets on their legs. Foley was afraid that Marc, the man he cradled, might think that he had died, because of the pitch-blackness in the van. He reached into his bunker coat, found a tiny light and switched it on. Marc was asking for his fiancée and child; he was fading in and out of consciousness. They were so close now, a minute or two away, but it wasn't clear if he had that long.

They turned right on Beacon Street, then cut left to zigzag down historic Beacon Hill, on narrow streets lined with well-kept brownstones, to Massachusetts General Hospital. The van's driver sped toward the emergency room entrance, slamming the vehicle into reverse to back into the ambulance bay. As they rolled in reverse toward their destination, the cell phone Marc was clutching started ringing. Somehow, he managed to answer the call from his fiancée, thrusting the phone at Foley and begging him, "Please, talk to her." Normally, at accident scenes or in ambulances, Foley avoided speaking to family members. At this moment, though, he could not refuse. He took the phone. "This is a Boston firefighter," he said. "We have your husband, we're at Mass General, you need to come here."

Outside the van, in the concrete chamber where ambulances delivered patients, security guards were banging angrily on the sides of the vehicle, bellowing at the driver to move it out of the way. They knew about the explosions at the marathon; they were out there waiting for the victims to show up. "We've got ambulances coming!" they yelled at Jim Davis in the driver's seat. Shana jumped out and ran around to the back of the van, yanking open the doors. Light flooded into the cab, revealing the horrific tableau. Shana helped Pat Foley carry out the injured man as the security guards looked on in shock. "They're bringing them in paddy wagons!" one of them exclaimed. Marc looked gray and lifeless as they laid him on a gurney. Never had Foley so longed to hand over responsibility. But as he prepared to step away, a nurse spoke sharply. "Don't let go of that tourniquet," she warned him. Together, then, they were moving through the door and down the hallway, the firefighter running alongside the gurney, his hand still on the belt, his viselike grip still holding back the flow of blood.

Jason Geremia looked up at the metal staircase behind Forum and saw paramedics with blue gloves coming down it, carrying a back-board used for moving victims. They were coming for Heather; they were going to get her out of this alley and into a hospital. Jason and his friends followed as the paramedics carried her back up the stairs and through the wreckage in the restaurant. They approached the front door; the scene up ahead, the smell like gunpowder, was shocking. *This is what soldiers see all the time*, thought Jason. *But I've never been to war, and I'm not prepared.* Police let two of Heather's friends follow her outside, but they turned away Jason and the others at the door, sending them back through the restaurant to the alley. Out in the street the ambulance was waiting; the EMT put Heather inside it. Her friend Jess tried to climb in the back with her, trying to keep the promise she had made back in the alley. "No, no," the paramedics told her. "You can't come with us." "It's okay," said Heather. "It's okay. Let's go."

A paramedic put a needle in her arm and started an IV. Someone cut off her clothes with a pair of scissors. She could hear the driver screaming at the people in the street: "Make a hole! Make a hole!" The thought of being stuck there filled her with fear. *Please*, she thought, willing the crowd, *please move out of the way.* As they lurched through the streets toward Kenmore Square and Fenway Park, where she had started her day, heading for Brigham and Women's Hospital, Heather asked the EMT to call her parents. She had lost her cell phone, but she knew their home number by heart.

Her mother picked up the phone at home in Rhode Island. The paramedic told her that Heather had been hurt, that they were heading for the hospital, and that she should come to the Brigham. He paused, listening to her questions. "I can't talk anymore," he said before hanging up. "Just come as fast you can." Then the ambulance was jerking to a stop. The doors swung open and Heather was moving fast, into the teeming nerve center of the ER. *I made it*, she thought with relief. *I finally made it.* It was the last thought she would remember having before everything went black.

The two firefighters had run beside the gurneys into Mass General, gripping the two victims' tourniquets as they sped through the maze of corridors. Finally, deep within the emergency department, the nurse in charge cleared them to let go. The two patients, Marc and Roseann, disappeared, headed straight for surgery. Pat Foley and Mike Materia stood in the middle of the hallway looking at each other. Neither one of them knew how to get back out. Then they looked down at the floor and saw the trail of blood, clearly marking the way they had come in. They followed it out, back to the waiting police van. Foley realized that his hand was aching from holding the tourniquet so tight for so long.

Outside, Shana was waiting with Jim Davis, ready to take them back to Boylston Street. The back of the van was slick with blood, but the firefighters climbed in. They were already covered with it anyway. It felt almost impossible, what they had to do next—going back to the street to face it all again. But it was their job, their duty. They steeled themselves to it as best they could. They had no choice.

Only forty minutes had elapsed since the bombs exploded, maybe less. Yet the scene had been transformed when they climbed back out of the van. Everyone was gone; everything was silent. There were no more bleeding people in the street, no more screaming bystanders. There was only a sea of debris, scattered metal barricades and gently drifting paper and bags dropped by spectators in agony or in flight. It was still late afternoon, but the unreal quiet belonged to the darkest hour of night.

CHAPTER 6

"THESE BASTARDS GOT US"

Terror comes into focus

Ed Davis couldn't believe what he saw when he first got to Boylston Street after 3:00 P.M. The Boston police commissioner walked toward the wreckage from the second explosion, outside Forum. Two lifeless bodies lay still. Shrapnel and human limbs littered the bloody ground. The heart of Boston resembled a smoldering battlefield. Everything had gone quiet. The tens of thousands of spectators who had filled the sidewalks a short time earlier were largely gone. Now it was just police officers, presiding over the aftermath, securing the crime scene. Davis paused for a moment. Studying the severity of the damage, he understood in his gut that the two blasts, at Forum and a block away in front of Marathon Sports, had been no accident. Someone had detonated powerful bombs aiming to kill and maim. Davis felt the way he had felt twelve years earlier, upon learning that a second plane had hit the World Trade Center in New York. The conclusion, on this April afternoon in his own city, was just as inescapable: "These bastards got us."

Davis was almost sure, from the start, that this was terrorism. At home just before 3:00 P.M., he had barely hung up from the White

91

House conference call on gun control when his phone rang. It was his superintendent in chief, Daniel Linskey, who was speeding toward Boylston after hearing another cop screaming for help on the radio. Davis heard sirens in the background as he listened to Linskey. There had been two separate explosions, Linskey told him. "I'm not sure what we got, boss, but I think it's bad," he said. "I'm hearing multiple amputations." That was all it took for Davis to believe Boston had been attacked. The amputations gave it away: That kind of trauma was typical of improvised explosive devices, or IEDs, placed on or near the ground. Right after Linskey's call, as the commissioner raced back downtown in his car, he called Rick DesLauriers, the special agent who ran the FBI office in Boston.

"Rick, look, I don't know what I've got," Davis told him, "but I need to roll whatever SWAT teams you have available to Copley Square."

DesLauriers hadn't yet heard of the explosions. "I'll get everything I can to you as quickly as I can," he told Davis, promising to meet him at the scene.

Davis also called Timothy Alben, the head of the Massachusetts State Police, asking for his SWAT teams. Alben had been at the starting line, in Hopkinton, and was heading back to his home in Western Massachusetts when he got the call. He turned around and drove back east. Having studied terror attacks around the world, Davis felt fairly certain there would be a third device, perhaps aimed at first responders. Not only were his officers scattered everywhere on Boylston Street, the targets in other corners of the city were many—from tourist-jammed Faneuil Hall to major transportation hubs. The commissioner was gripped by a powerful sense of foreboding and urgency. One or more terrorists had launched a vicious assault on Boston, and they were still out there somewhere.

Panic rippled across the city as law enforcement descended on Copley Square. Word of the explosions spread rapidly, through social media and frantic bulletins from TV, radio, and print reporters, many of whom had been wrapping up their marathon coverage for the day. Steve Silva, a Boston.com sports producer working at the finish line, was one of the first to broadcast news about the blasts on Twitter: *God help us*, he tweeted minutes afterward, sharing a photo of the chaos on the street. Everyone seemed to know someone who had run the marathon, or someone who was watching it near the finish line. Sitting at their desks, driving in their cars, nervously turning on TVs in their hotel rooms, Bostonians and out-of-town visitors scrambled to decipher what had happened, and to account for loved ones. Communication failures amplified the hysteria. The wireless networks for Verizon, Sprint, and AT&T were quickly overwhelmed, leaving people at the scene unable to call out, and preventing outside callers from reaching people in Boston. Runners and spectators tried to share phones, flocking to those that seemed to work. Two runners of South Asian descent, a man and a woman, approached Terry Wallace, who had been waiting for his wife, Michelle Hall, to finish the race. The woman was nearly in tears. They were desperate to tell their families they were okay, but no one would share a phone with them. Wallace did so willingly and they were deeply grateful.

Twitter and Facebook, meanwhile, lit up with firsthand accounts and pictures, each one more difficult to believe than the last. The images on TV and online were so shocking, so out of custom for Marathon Day, that they were almost impossible to digest. And the threat seemed to be spreading. Word came of a mysterious fire at the John F. Kennedy Library, a few miles away, which had broken out about the same time as the blasts. Alarm swept Boylston Street when a dropped bag under the VIP grandstand triggered fears of a third, unexploded device. Davis moved to lock down the street, pushing people and police off Boylston so bomb squads could go in and pick meticulously through the sea of debris, rooting out suspicious packages. They blew up at least one bag. It turned out to be harmless, but it was a jarring moment for the first responders, who heard the controlled explosion and wondered if a third bomb had gone off.

One of Davis's immediate tasks was to establish a command center where law enforcement leaders could gather and plot a coordinated response. He went looking for space. He tried the Marriott Copley Place first, but the hotel had already set up for a function in its ballroom. He had better luck across the street at the Westin Copley Place. By 4:00 P.M. the top brass had gathered there, a dozen of them around a single table, including Davis, DesLauriers, Alben, US attorney Carmen Ortiz, and Daniel Conley, the district attorney for Boston. Within an hour the crowd in the room had swelled to one hundred. More officers kept coming: city, state, and transit police; FBI; the federal Bureau of Alcohol, Tobacco, Firearms and Explosives. At least thirty agencies would take part in the investigation before it was over, hundreds of police and federal agents working out of the Westin. Davis called on every police officer in Boston to return to duty. They were dispatched across the city, charged with being a visible presence and calming fears at hospitals, train stations, and historic landmarks, where public anxieties were peaking. Others fanned out to hospitals to interview witnesses. Over the course of an hour, Boston's mood had swung from carefree to deeply anxious. Any bag left momentarily unattended could spark dozens of nervous calls to police.

Katherine Patrick had only been a street or two away when she heard two blasts. She saw people running. She called her father, Governor Deval Patrick, who was on his way home for a quiet afternoon.

"What's going on?" said Katherine, a twenty-three-year-old working for a social justice organization in Boston. "I'm scared."

"I don't know what's going on," he said. His first instinct, a paternal one, was to reassure. "I'm sure it's okay," he told her. *Maybe race organizers used some kind of celebratory cannon this year*, the governor thought.

The impulse to explain it away, to grope for a benign explanation, was widely shared. In the confusing minutes after the twin blasts, everyone wanted it to be manhole explosions—Boston had seen several in recent years—or another blown electrical transformer. Hadn't one caught fire just a year before in the same neighborhood? The thought of bombs at the finish line was too unlikely and monstrous to accept. "I was really resistant to the growing evidence that something terrible had happened," said Peter Sagal, the host of NPR's *Wait Wait . . . Don't Tell Me!* and an avid runner, who had led a visually impaired competitor across the finish just minutes before the explosions. Even after someone showed him photos of bloodstains, he told himself it could be Gatorade. "I was completely in denial."

Patrick's hopeful illusions were quickly dashed. After he talked to his daughter, his phone rang again. It was Kurt Schwartz, the state's emergency management chief. He and Patrick had been through a lot together—floods, blizzards, hurricanes, power outages, and a spate of snowy roof collapses. Schwartz was at the finish line. He spoke of explosions. *A lot of people are hurt and down*, he reported. *It's a mess.* Schwartz's voice was thick with emotion; Patrick had never heard him like that. The governor knew, at that moment, that he had to get to Boylston Street. His state police detail resisted, saying it wasn't safe. So he went to the State House instead, though state police weren't wild about that, either, fearing that it could be a potential target. By 4:00, Patrick had joined the other principals gathering at the Westin. President Obama called and spoke to the governor around 4:30, pledging the full resources of the federal government to the investigation. Patrick also conferred with FBI director Robert Mueller III and with Janet Napolitano, the US secretary of homeland security.

The mayor of Boston, Tom Menino, had made it to the Westin, too, after checking himself out of the hospital. His doctors had tried to stop him; it was only two days since his surgery, and he wasn't supposed to put any weight on his leg. Menino wasn't having it. "Give me some clothes and a wheelchair and let's get out of here," he told his staff. Someone grabbed a white hospital sheet from a supply closet to drape over his lap, to hide his catheter from view. The mayor felt he had to be visible right away—not for the sake of his profile, but to reassure the city he had led for twenty years.

. . .

Dave McGillivray had changed into running clothes and arrived in Hopkinton, ready to begin his customary run of the marathon course. He was standing near the town green at the starting line, stretching and mentally preparing for the 26.2 miles. Two state troopers on motorcycles were nearby. As always, they would escort the race director through the course. About five minutes after McGillivray arrived, his friend Ron Kramer, who, according to their tradition, always drove him out to Hopkinton, got a phone call. He hung up and summoned McGillivray over.

"My daughter just called," Kramer told him. "She said a bomb went off at the finish."

The words were chilling. At first, McGillivray thought they couldn't possibly be true. Disbelief shifted to fear. He started to worry not only about the runners and spectators but about his own family, who were on Boylston Street. He called his wife. No answer. He had to get back to Boston. Kramer asked the state troopers, who were just learning of the explosions over their radios, to escort them to the city, and fast. McGillivray hopped back in Kramer's Nissan convertible and they followed the troopers to the Massachusetts Turnpike. They raced back east at one hundred miles per hour. "It was a NASCAR experience," Kramer said. McGillivray was nervous and wanted to slow down, but Kramer didn't want to lose their escort; the troopers had told him to stay close. Going in with police would be their only chance to get into the scene.

When they arrived, Boylston had been largely evacuated. McGillivray went right to the medical tent. The gravity of what had happened was quickly apparent. First responders were treating the injured on cots. The scene was bloody. He would describe it later as organized chaos. He didn't say a word to anyone, not wanting to interrupt the emergency care. "I knew right away—this isn't where I belong," he recalled. McGillivray tried to walk out of the tent and onto Boylston, but police stopped him.

"You can't go up that way, sir," an officer said.

McGillivray explained that he was part of race management. Did that mean the area was off-limits even to marathon officials?

"That's correct," the officer said.

"Okay, sir."

That's when it hit McGillivray that the 2013 Boston Marathon was no longer his. Nor was it even still a race. Athletics, competition— those things didn't matter anymore. Now it was all about security and emergency medicine. An hour earlier, Boylston Street—like the entirety of the course—had been McGillivray's domain. He could go anywhere he wanted. Now he had no more authority than a bystander. The realization was difficult for a man who, for so many years, had been Mr. Marathon, the guy who knew this event more intimately than anyone else.

There was, though, one thing he could still do, and that was to take care of the runners. Almost six thousand had yet to finish. They were cold, scared, and exhausted. Many hadn't connected with family yet. They needed to collect their bags. Out-of-town runners needed help getting to their hotels, or to friends' houses. McGillivray and a few others began grabbing the runners' bags off the school buses where competitors usually retrieve them after the race, wheeling them away from the blast sites in bins. The task was stressful in its own right. McGillivray had managed to connect with his family, so he knew they were okay. But as he and his team worked, they didn't know if other bombs would explode near them. Was there one in that trash can right over there? They had no idea. "We were in a minefield for all we knew," McGillivray said.

After a few hours, as afternoon turned to night, a clearer picture started to emerge of what had happened. Two IEDs had been left on the Boylston Street sidewalk, about 210 yards apart. The devices had been made from six-liter pressure cookers, filled with explosive powder and shrapnel like nails, BBs, and ball bearings. The IEDs, concealed in two black nylon backpacks, had battery-powered triggers and were set off with remote detonators, the shrapnel and metal from the pressure cookers shooting out like bullets in all directions.

Once the sweep of Boylston Street was complete, and authorities were certain there were no more bombs, the investigation launched. It was the largest crime scene in the history of the city: Initially fifteen blocks—later reduced to twelve—in the heart of one of Boston's best-known, best-loved, safest neighborhoods. Hundreds of investigators started working around the clock, collecting fragments of evidence from streets, buildings, and rooftops, labeling each one with the location where it was found. They spray-painted a massive orange grid onto Boylston, dividing the pavement into numbered squares for scrutiny, and they moved with careful urgency: Rain or wind might soon move in, threatening the evidence. The word went out to hospitals from the command center: The embedded shrapnel fragments surgeons were pulling from victims' ravaged flesh were evidence; every nail and shard of metal needed to be saved.

President Obama addressed the nation after 6:00, delivering a briskly paced three-minute statement. "We still do not know who did this or why," he said, "but make no mistake . . . we will find out who did this, and we will hold them accountable." He stopped short of calling what had happened terrorism; he would wait to use that word until the next day. The president reflected on the meaning of Patriot's Day, "a day that celebrates the free and fiercely independent spirit that this great American city of Boston has reflected from the earliest days of our nation . . . a day that draws the world to Boston's streets." He invoked the city's strength—"Boston is a tough and resilient town. So are its people"—and the empathy that had swept the country: "The American people will say a prayer for Boston tonight."

The prospect of a bombing at the marathon finish line, as far-fetched as it might have sounded, was a threat that public safety and race officials had talked about in the past and actively tried to prevent. That was just the nature of things after 9/11—the same held true for any big public event that drew many thousands of people to a confined space. Early in the day on April 15, police had begun sweeping both the starting line and finish line area for bombs. After dawn, the Boston Police Department's bomb squad started scouring the area around Copley Square, looking in trash cans, flower planters, and the windows of cars and shops. Once they had swept everything, seeing nothing, the squad took up positions around the marathon course, ready to respond if the call came. Right after the blasts, the bomb technicians raced to Boylston Street and began furiously cutting open hundreds of abandoned bags with knives, looking for more explosive devices, fearing for their lives the whole time. No one could blame them for not preventing the bombing—the terrorists, after all, had brought in the IEDs right before setting them off—but they still struggled with the feeling that they had somehow come up short.

The question of which law enforcement agency would lead the investigation was resolved with relative ease, thanks in part to the rapport between Davis and DesLauriers. An imposing figure at six-foot-six, Davis, fifty-six, had led the BPD since 2006, after a long career in his hometown of Lowell, the former mill city north of Boston, where he had worked his way up from beat cop to superintendent. DesLauriers, fifty-three, a native of Western Massachusetts, was a counterintelligence expert known for running risky, diplomatically sensitive operations, including one that traded Russian spies for American agents held prisoner in Russia. He had taken over the Boston FBI office in 2010. The two men, along with other law enforcement leaders, agreed that the FBI, with its superior expertise on terrorism, should take charge of the bombing probe. City and state leaders promised the public there would be seamless cooperation. Governor Patrick would later describe those initial conversations about jurisdiction as among the most important things that happened after the bombing. The potential for friction was huge; the collaborative start was a good sign. Besides, there wasn't time for competition. There were terrorists to hunt down.

One of the first people who drew law enforcement attention was an innocent Saudi Arabian student in his twenties named Abdulrahman Alharbi, who had come to Boston on a student visa in 2012 to study English. Alharbi, who described himself as shy and focused on his studies, stopped by the marathon alone on his way to meet friends and was injured by the second bomb. He was thrown into the street, with burns on his head, back, and arms; an uninjured runner helped him to an ambulance. To his surprise, several police officers climbed into the vehicle with him. At the hospital, FBI agents surrounded his bed and interrogated him for hours. The frightened student handed over his address and Facebook password; that night, authorities swarmed his apartment and some in the media identified him as a suspect. In one of his past posts on Facebook, Alharbi had included images of the Saudi and American flags and written in Arabic, "Thank God, I arrived [in] the [US] after [a] long trip." The media, he said, translated that to the ominous-sounding "God is coming to the US." When his friends tried to reach him after the bombing, the FBI would not let them call Alharbi or tell them where he was, he said later. The young man said that he did not blame law enforcement. But he felt he had been injured twice, by the bomb and by the accusatory coverage. "I don't know if I am gonna be safe . . . because I lost my privacy," he said. "It's not [an] easy thing to just forget."

As darkness fell on Monday, Shana Cottone was still working. Hours had passed since her harrowing ride from the finish line to the hospital in a police van. Now the van—so recently pressed into service as a makeshift ambulance for bombing victims—was being used to transport a police bomb squad as it roamed the neighborhood responding to suspicious bag calls. Shana had stayed with the vehicle after it carried her back to the finish line. Its driver, veteran officer Jim Davis, had an unflappable air that had steadied her through the awful afternoon. He had seen that she was shaken, and he hadn't made her feel stupid about it. *After all this is over, kid*, he told her, *you need to take care of yourself.*

Shana had made one quick detour before heading out again with Davis: back to her parked car to get her bulletproof vest. She could not believe she had been caught without it. Once she had it on, she felt a little better. Still, she longed to get away. She was staggered when she got to Kenmore Square and saw people standing around in the street taking pictures. She couldn't imagine why they would choose to be there, when everything felt so unsafe. She stuck to the widest-open spaces she could find. *Leave now*, she told anyone who asked her advice.

When she finally got home to Hyde Park around midnight, her dog was waiting for her by the door. He had been acting strangely all afternoon, her roommate told her, whimpering as if he knew something was wrong. Shana looked down at the beagle and started to cry. The relief she felt at being home was overwhelming. But her tears signaled a deeper realization, too. Everything was different now, Shana understood. She might never leave the darkness of this day behind.

Karen Rand had arrived at Massachusetts General Hospital by ambulance, one of the severely wounded spectators hit by the bomb outside Marathon Sports. She had been standing near her close friend Krystle Campbell and had suffered massive damage to her left leg. Rand was given a patient number and rushed into an operating room. The handbag that came with her was put in a bag and labeled with the same number. The ER staff looked through it, searching for something to confirm the woman's identity. They found a driver's license with a name: Krystle Campbell. Word that Krystle was apparently at Mass General somehow made it to Patty and Billy Campbell, who came to the hospital believing their daughter was being treated there. Around 2:00 A.M. Tuesday, nurses led the Campbells into an intensive care room, where they expected to see Krystle recuperating.

"That's not my daughter!" Billy exclaimed. "That's Karen! Where's my daughter?"

The hospital staff was shocked. The mistake was innocent but the effect was cruel, and it would be a cautionary lesson about correctly identifying patients going forward. Less than an hour later, a detective from Boston arrived with a photo of Krystle. Her family learned that she was already gone. Krystle had been one of three people killed in the bombing. Billy nearly collapsed to the floor. Instead of greeting his daughter at her bedside, he would soon have to formally identify her body.

Back on Boylston Street, the silence deepened with the night. A chill settled in. Two figures still lay on the ground where they had fallen, covered with tablecloths from a nearby restaurant. The bodies of Martin Richard and Lingzi Lu would remain there until 2:00 A.M. as investigators painstakingly collected evidence around them; Krystle's body had been taken from the street already. Several Boston police officers had promised to stay at the scene, as long as they were needed, keeping a last watch over the bodies. Their vigil comforted Martin's father, Bill, who had been distraught at the thought of leaving his son there.

Not far away, a couple blocks east of the blast sites, Dave McGillivray, Rich Havens—the finish area coordinator for the marathon— and other race officials had spent six hours Monday night lining up yellow bags on Berkeley Street. These were the bags runners used to stow their personal items until after the race—clothes, wallets, plane tickets, money, phones, food. Race organizers put out word that anybody who hadn't yet collected theirs should come there to claim them. As McGillivray and his team spread the bags out, they could hear, from time to time, cell phones ringing inside them, each chirp and tinny melody a loved one's vain attempt to reach a runner. They listened to the phones singing in the darkness, a melancholy sound track to their solemn labor.

CHAPTER 7

OPERATING AT CAPACITY

Saving lives, against the odds

Heather Abbott opened her eyes. She was in a hospital bed, her mother beside her. She didn't know how long she had been unconscious, but memories came back to her in fragments: Waiting at the door of the bar on Boylston Street. The sound of the first explosion; turning her head to look and seeing billowing smoke. Then, searing pain and mounting desperation. She remembered choosing not to look at her foot, knowing from the expressions on her friends' faces that she shouldn't. *I wonder what happened to it*, she thought. She let the thought stop there. Part of her wanted to know and part of her wanted to linger in the uncertainty. Her mother seemed calm and collected, relieved to see her awake. Her father, she would quickly discover, was more upset than she had ever seen him. Watching him struggle, realizing the depth of his devastation, Heather was taken aback. He had always been so sturdy. It was not how she would have imagined his reaction.

Her left leg appeared to be in traction, elevated up above the bed, with a white sheet draped over it. From her small room in the Brigham and Women's Hospital intensive care unit, she could see through a glass wall to the busy nurses' station. Patient rooms fanned out around the station in a circle. A nurse told her they were filled with others who had been hurt at the marathon, but for the moment Heather asked few questions. She knew instinctively she couldn't handle the whole story—not right now. For the moment, the pain demanded most of her attention. She had to concentrate on getting through it, the same way she had narrowed her focus the previous day, after the blast, to the necessity of getting to the hospital.

Already, through the pain and the fog of medication, she knew her friends and family were gathering, bracing to support her through whatever lay ahead. Her mother told her that after she left Boylston Street in the ambulance, her friends had walked to Massachusetts General Hospital to find her. When they learned she was instead at Brigham and Women's, another elite teaching hospital about three miles across town, they took a cab there and waited for hours, in their blood-smeared clothes, to learn her condition. Her friend Julie, a former bartender at Forum who had returned for a Marathon Day shift, had found Heather's wallet lying in the middle of Boylston Street and brought it to the hospital, worried that Heather would need her insurance card. Her friend Al's boss had told him to stay in Boston, and then paid for a hotel room. Everyone was sticking close, and wanted to know the same thing: Would her foot be okay? Would she?

Across the city, at Boston's six major trauma centers, similar scenes were playing out. At Boston Medical Center, Celeste Corcoran, forty-seven, a hairdresser who had never been to the marathon until Monday, lost both of her legs below the knee. Her seventeen-year-old daughter, Sydney, whose femoral artery was ruptured by shrapnel from the first blast, had been saved by a bystander who fashioned a tourniquet. When they were finally reunited, neither could stop crying; they would share a room as soon as they were stable, the beds pushed together so they could hold hands. At Beth Israel Deaconess Medical Center, in the city's Longwood medical corridor near Brigham and Women's and Boston Children's Hospital, Paul Norden, thirty-one, a construction worker, struggled to accept the loss of his leg and learned that his older brother JP, thirty-three, admitted to the Brigham, had lost one of his, too.

Altogether sixteen people—eight women, seven men, and one young girl—would lose limbs as a result of the bombing. All of them had been close to the bombs, but so had others who'd escaped with less severe injuries. It was, in many cases, a matter of feet, or even inches, that determined one's degree of injury. Flying shrapnel added to the randomness. Later, Heather would wrestle with the knowledge that people closer to the bomb than she was had walked away unscathed. Her own two friends, standing next to her at the door of Forum, had not suffered a scratch—though one of them later found a blade-shaped shard of metal shrapnel in her handbag. Two people at the first bomb site would lose both legs—Celeste Corcoran and Jeff Bauman, the stoic, ashen-faced twenty-seven-year-old man aided by bystander Carlos Arredondo, the "man in the cowboy hat," at the bombing scene. A photograph of Arredondo racing down Boylston Street, pushing Bauman in a wheelchair while gripping the tourniquet on his leg, had become one of the week's iconic images. Bauman's father, unable to reach his son after the blasts, only learned that Jeff was hurt when he saw the photo. "Unfortunately my son was just in the wrong place at the wrong time," the senior Bauman wrote Tuesday morning on Facebook, breaking the news to his friends and family.

Within twenty minutes of the blasts, thirty of the most critically injured patients had been "red-tagged"—marked as urgent cases for immediate transport—and distributed roughly evenly among the city's largest hospitals, through a central dispatch center at Boston EMS. At the Brigham, the first patient from the finish line had arrived at 3:08 P.M. Monday, eighteen minutes after the first bomb exploded, followed by eighteen more in the next thirty minutes. Mass General took in thirty-one in the first hour, including five patients with amputations, received just minutes apart at 3:04, 3:15, 3:20, 3:22, and 3:27 P.M. At Boston Medical Center, surgeons performed a total of seven amputations on Bauman, Corcoran, and three other patients. It made for a nightmarish scene in the ER. Badly wounded patients lay on gurneys looking at one another as they awaited surgery, blood everywhere and agonizing screams—"Oh my God, my foot!"—ricocheting off the walls. There were three amputations at Beth Israel, two at the Brigham, and one on a seven-year-old girl at Children's Hospital. In some cases, the decision to amputate was uncomplicated, because the patient's foot or leg was gone, completely destroyed, or nearly severed. With others, the decision was less clear. At Boston Medical Center, surgeons consulted with one another to make sure more than one doctor reached the same conclusion. "What we like to do before we take off someone's leg—it's extremely hard to make that decision—is often we get two surgeons to agree," Tracey Dechert, a trauma surgeon at the hospital, said that day. The consultations—"Am I right here? This can't be saved?"—gave doctors reassurance, she said.

The array of other injuries was dizzying. Patient admission logs kept at Tufts Medical Center showed the relentlessness and range of the damage:

3:33 P.M. Female with third-degree burns and shrapnel wounds
3:35 P.M. Male with shrapnel and ruptured eardrums
3:35 P.M. Male with a complex penetrating wound

Soft tissue injuries, nerve injuries, bone fractures, abrasions, and embedded foreign bodies—nails and ball bearings—followed. In the midst of the onslaught, Tufts officials were forced to evacuate their ER because of a bomb scare; bomb-sniffing dogs brought in to check out a suspicious package appeared to confirm that it contained explosives, forcing all emergency patients into the hospital lobby for thirty minutes. Another bomb scare disrupted at Mass General, where the hospital was briefly placed on lockdown because of a suspicious package in a parking garage. Meanwhile, well into Monday night, patients were still showing up at the hospitals—at Tufts, a runner suffering from exposure checked in at 6:14 P.M.; a spectator with hearing loss arrived at 7:01; more burns and abrasions followed at 7:23.

The following day, new patients with hearing loss and head injuries arrived—along with the first wave of those seeking help for invisible wounds, like the "witness with anxiety and depression" noted in the Tufts log at 3:30 P.M. Tuesday. In all, 275 people would be treated at hospitals.

In the midst of so much pressing need, there were inevitable inconsistencies, and patients who experienced gaps in the level of care. Allison Byrne, who had just run the marathon and had a large piece of shrapnel lodged in her left leg, sat in the ER holding her own tourniquet for hours after being brought in a police car to Boston Medical Center. She had just run twenty-six miles, but she wasn't given much water, couldn't get to the bathroom, and had to beg for Tylenol. In the case of some of the doctors and nurses, she found their bedside manner and communication wanting.

As the hours crept by Monday night, and as dawn approached on Tuesday, the tally of the wounded mounted. City officials and shaken, sleepless residents waited for the death toll to creep upward, too. It seemed inevitable, given the power of the explosions and the witness reports from the scene, the videos and photographs and bloodstains on the sidewalks. Yet the number of fatalities remained at three. The first identified was Martin Richard, whose name had begun circulating in the city, and on social media, before 9:00 P.M. Monday; at 1:00 A.M. Tuesday, the *Boston Globe* confirmed it via Twitter. The world learned Krystle Campbell's name later Tuesday. Boston University said Tuesday the third victim was a student, though it took until Wednesday for Lingzi Lu's name to be made public. It was hard to believe there would be no further fatalities, but hopes grew with each passing day. Every injured person who had been transported alive from the scene to a hospital—even a few who had lost all or nearly all of their blood, who may have come within minutes of death, like Marc Fucarile—had survived. It only seemed more stunning the longer it stayed true, a tribute to the frenzied medical response at the bombing scene and the skill and readiness of Boston hospitals.

It was a strange truth that many would acknowledge in the days and weeks that followed: If there had to be a terrorist attack some-where in the US, the finish line on Boylston Street, with the medical tent already in place and six of the top hospitals anywhere within a mile or two, was about the best place it could happen. Such a concen-tration of skilled surgeons, nursing staffs, and operating rooms was extremely rare. The underpinnings of Boston's medical infrastruc-ture had been established early, in the eighteenth century, giving the city a huge head start on its evolution into a health-care mecca. Har-vard Medical School had been founded in 1782. Massachusetts Gen-eral Hospital, one of the first hospitals in the country, opened its doors in 1811. In 1846, the first demonstration of ether anesthesia took place in the so-called ether dome at Mass General. During the famous surgery, the patient on the table suffered no pain—an inter-nationally heralded breakthrough. Its success was further confirmed a month later when MGH doctors amputated an anesthetized pa-tient's leg. The use of ether would transform the practice of surgery and profoundly improve public health, cementing Boston's place as a center of innovation. After Harvard's medical school relocated, in 1906, to five marble-fronted buildings on Longwood Avenue in Bos-ton, a medical building boom followed. The new campus was sur-rounded by marsh and farmland, open space filled by new centers for treatment and research. The growth led to more medical milestones, including the first fertilization of an ovum in a test tube and the first successful human organ transplant.

The hospitals had a rich history, but their preparedness for mass casualties on Marathon Day was largely due to recent training. In the decade since 9/11—since the nation had been forced to accept that terrorist acts could happen in America—hospital leaders and public health agencies had incorporated that reality into their planning for emergencies. They reviewed the latest literature on mass casualty events and hosted conferences on how to respond. They updated their communications systems. When reports of the bombing began to spread via Twitter and text messages, the hospitals had some idea what to expect. They sprang into action, emptying their ERs of less serious patients, preparing operating rooms for vascular and orthope-

dic procedures, and ordering additional blood supplies from outside
the city. When the day nursing shift at the hospitals ended at 3:00 P.M.,
those nurses were asked to stay, doubling the size of the staffs on hand
when victims began showing up. Many off-duty staff members showed
up to help even though they weren't scheduled to work. In part because of the grim legacy of 9/11, it was understood from the first reports that this event would be unprecedented and all-consuming.

Three miles away from the hospital room at Brigham and Women's
where Heather had awoken on Tuesday, David King was facing families' urgent questions at Mass General: *Will my daughter live? Will
she need more surgeries? Will they have to take more of my son's leg?
Will he walk again? When?* They craved certainty, but with so much
still unknown, that was more than King could give. There would
come a time when answers would be clearer, but with some of the
victims facing more surgery or sedated, the time for such projections
was still days or weeks away. The families needed someone to sit
down with them now, to hold their hands and explain what was happening. King didn't have time for that. He was moving too quickly,
consulting with colleagues, evaluating patients, assessing which ones
should head back to surgery and which ones needed to rest. He relied
on the ICU nurses to engage with the distraught family members. As
distracted as he was by the work, he registered how compassionate
they were, the pains they took to make terrified parents and spouses
and friends feel calmer and more comfortable.

It had been a long night for the trauma surgeon. His work had
begun the previous day, just as he was heading home after the marathon. He had run twenty-six miles in three hours and twelve minutes
and he was ready to rest, to sit down and drink some Gatorade. After
finding his family at the finish line, he had lifted his six-year-old
daughter onto his shoulders, while his wife, Anne, pushed the two-
year-old in her stroller. They had planned to take the subway, but the
lines were long, so they piled in a cab and headed home to Cambridge. The ride across the river took less than ten minutes, but by

the time they got there, King had received a swarm of text messages. He always got supportive notes from friends when he had a big race—he liked to save them to read when he got home, after he had showered and swallowed some ibuprofen—but this looked like an unprecedented influx. While his wife went around the corner to pick up a pizza, King brought the kids upstairs and scrolled through his messages. *Are you okay?* one of the texts asked. Another mentioned an explosion. King tapped the screen to call up some breaking news from Fox or CNN. The websites wouldn't open—another bad sign. Something had happened. He had to get to the hospital. Anne had seen the news on the TV at the pizza place; she arrived home ready to drive him to work.

He arrived at Mass General around 3:15 P.M., a few minutes behind the first patients from the bombing, carrying a banana and wearing surgical scrubs he had hastily pulled on at home. He dove right in, running upstairs to grab the cap and protective glasses he would need in the operating room. Speeding back downstairs and into the ER, he came around the corner and had a clear view of four or five patients lined up in the trauma bays, a series of small exam rooms all in a row. Normally the curtains around the bays were pulled closed, but today, in the chaos and confusion, they were open, giving him an unobstructed panorama of the injuries. That was all it took for him to be sure: A man-made explosive device had blown up at the marathon. He had seen these injuries countless times before, thousands of miles away, as a combat surgeon treating wartime casualties. Most of his work in the army reserve with his forward surgical team was on bombing victims: 75 percent of injuries suffered by American soldiers in Iraq and Afghanistan were caused by explosive devices. Only 20 percent of the wounds came from guns.

King moved toward the most severely injured patient he could see: a blonde woman covered in black soot whose leg had been brutally burned and broken by the bomb. It was Roseann, the woman Shana Cottone had found lying in the street. Shana had helped deliver her to the ER just minutes earlier, in the back of a police transport van. "This lady looks like she's dying," King said to another surgeon.

"Does she have a chest X-ray?" He reached out a hand to check the tourniquet on her leg, making sure that it was tightened to his satisfaction. He glanced at the unit of blood hanging up over her head and checked that it was flowing at the correct rate. Then he pointed at a young surgical resident standing nearby. "Let's go," he said. They moved out of the ER at a brisk clip, pushing Roseann's gurney down a hallway with white tile walls. Ten seconds later they were in an elevator, ascending from the first floor to the fourth; two more turns of the hallway and they were in the OR, past the big white doors marked RESTRICTED AREA. A full team was already there prepping the room: a dozen people, maybe more, dressed in blue scrubs and masks, scrambling now to save Roseann's life. Saucer-shaped lights glowed bright over the table; cameras at the center of each one would capture the surgeon's every movement and project it onto big flat-screens mounted high on the wall for his team. "We'll start with the abdomen," King told them. "Then the leg." As he waited for the anesthesiologist to put Roseann under, King pulled out the banana he had been carrying and ate it. No more than five minutes had elapsed since he had walked into the hospital.

Had the blonde woman been the only bombing victim at Mass General that day, her journey to the OR probably would have taken longer, with more stops along the way. A chest X-ray was the bare minimum of information needed for surgery; ideally, she might have had several other X-rays or a CAT scan. But the circumstances of the bombing— with dozens of patients flooding the hospital, and an unknown number yet to come—changed everything. There was no way to calculate the right amount of resources to expend on each, because they did not know when the demand would cease. It was, in a strange way, like the starting line at the marathon: The hospital had to move each wave of patients out of the emergency room and into operating rooms swiftly, to make sure they could keep up with the next wave gathering behind. Trauma teams and specialists worked side by side in a blur, exchanging patients seamlessly, any preexisting disagreements swept aside by the rising sea of need. Normal electronic record-keeping had gone out the window. King was taking notes on index cards stashed in his pockets;

when he ran out of cards, he jotted reminders to himself on the leg of his blue scrubs with a black Sharpie marker, lines of scrawled ink creeping up his pant leg from his knee. The overload had driven staffs at other hospitals to similar measures, and would lead, in the case of Krystle Campbell, to that rare and wrenching misidentification.

King's fundamental approach to surgery on victims of a bombing was the same whether he was in rural Afghanistan or in a top-notch Boston hospital. In either situation, he followed his "medical rules of engagement," a list of reminders he had posted on the wall in the ER. Chief among them was this: Do not be distracted by the obvious. The most "visually stimulating" injury—that is, the one that looks the most gruesome and dramatic—"is almost never the one that kills them," he explained. "The leg might be ugly and obvious, but it's probably not the one that's fatal." Problems that were invisible on the outside—perforated organs; uncontrolled internal bleeding; system-wide vascular breakdown—could create an irreversible downward spiral. He had to look further, probe deeper, and consider carefully where to go first when he got into surgery. It could mean the difference between death and survival.

They all knew Monday night's work was just the beginning. The first operations aimed just to stop the bleeding, remove the shrapnel, and limit the risk of infection. They would let the patients rest before heading back to the OR to continue their work on wounds that had been left open for that purpose. The goal was to minimize the stress on the sickest patients, breaking up the complicated repairs they needed into a series of smaller, discrete tasks. There would be days of follow-up surgeries ahead, patients who might require three, four, a dozen or more operations. King and a handful of his colleagues sat down together in a conference room late Monday night and reviewed a list of all the patients and their injuries. It was the first chance he had had to consider how he felt, and the first thing he realized was that he was wild with thirst. He had finished the marathon nine or ten hours earlier, and all he had eaten since was a banana. A medical student, dispatched to the ICU pantry to find him something to drink, came back with packages of Saltines and graham crackers, a can of

Coke, and a carton of milk. Chewing on the crackers, King felt awful. He would finally go home and to sleep at around 2:00 A.M.; before the sun rose Tuesday, he was headed back to work. There wasn't any time to watch the news or read the paper. He knew, at once, less than most people about what had happened and far more than most would ever want to know.

With the eyes of the world still fixed on Boston Tuesday morning, the names of the wounded were beginning to leak out. Already, friends and family members of the most severely injured were setting up fund-raising pages on the Internet, drafting paragraphs describing their loved ones, and their injuries, and uploading photographs taken in happier times. It was a big step to go public, to give up a victim's cloak of anonymity even before the prognosis was clear, but a sense of urgency crept in as the national media descended. With millions watching, the public's shock had quickly turned to sympathy. It had become clear that many of the victims would be facing long and costly rehabilitations. There was tremendous potential to tap the mass impulse to help, but the impulse wouldn't last forever.

An online campaign for Jeff Bauman, the man who lost both legs, raised $745,000 in nineteen days, attracting gifts from more than sixteen thousand people. By Wednesday, the world would know the names and faces of Patrick Downes and Jessica Kensky, attractive young newlyweds who'd each lost a leg in the bombing. By Thursday night, as they lay in two different hospitals just three days after the bombing, donations to their fund-raising site would reach $300,000. Over the next four months, the total would nearly triple, to $875,000. Donors who clicked on the site for Patrick and Jessica lingered over a photo of the pair taken on a carefree stroll before the tragedy; in it, they walk together holding hands through Harvard Square in Cambridge, Jessica smiling as she looks back at Patrick, the skirt of her red dress flaring as she strides ahead. The poignant image seemed to capture all the innocence and freedom they had lost.

No photograph would more perfectly distill Boston's lost innocence than one of Martin Richard that ricocheted around the globe the day after the bombing. On Monday night, the news that an eight-year-old was among those killed had made the unimaginable day feel unbearable. Martin and his family—his parents, Bill and Denise, and his brother and sister, Henry and Jane—were well known and much loved in their corner of Boston. Bill had spent years volunteering his time to improve their neighborhood and was one of the people most often credited with its renaissance in recent years, its new businesses and brightly refurbished subway station and swelling civic pride. His efforts had deeply endeared him in Dorchester, a working-class haven with a long Irish heritage, and now the most diverse corner of the city, with Vietnamese phở shops scattered between the traditional Irish bars like The Blarney Stone and The Banshee. In the midst of change, violence had persisted on some streets, gangs and guns that changed how people looked at Dorchester. Some who had the means had left for good, fleeing to the safer suburbs south of Boston. Others, like the Richards, chose to stay, digging in and deepening their commitment.

As the awful news spread through the neighborhood, many residents were mute with grief, shaking their heads and waving away the reporters who had descended. They had just begun to absorb the overwhelming facts: Bill and Denise and their three young children had been standing next to the second bomb when it exploded. Both parents had been injured, Denise suffering a serious eye injury, and Bill enduring shrapnel wounds, burns, and hearing loss. Their oldest child, Henry, had escaped serious injury. But their youngest, seven-year-old Jane, who loved Irish step dancing, had lost her left leg below the knee. And Martin—the baseball-loving boy with the big brown eyes—was gone forever. It seemed more than any family could bear. At the beautifully restored Victorian home where the family lived, Martin's classmates filed up the steps one by one to leave flowers and notes and balloons by the door. Meanwhile, on the Internet, a photograph of the freckled child holding up a handmade sign had gone viral. NO MORE HURTING PEOPLE. PEACE, the boy had written with colored markers.

The Richards were among the families who met with Governor

Deval Patrick as he visited six of the city's hospitals Tuesday and Wednesday. Patrick spent time with Bill, Denise, and Henry. The governor didn't see Jane; she was in surgery. Bill told Patrick of a photograph he had of Martin, as a toddler, holding one of the governor's campaign signs. They talked about how the family could go about rebuilding their lives without the whole world watching. They wanted to maintain their privacy. Denise had the impossible task of simultaneously mourning her son and staying strong, to aid her own recovery and that of her family. Patrick wasn't sure, in these visits, what to say. All he knew was that he didn't want to say much. He figured the bombing victims and their families probably didn't want to hear it. What he could offer, he felt, was a dose of emotional support, a warm hug, a quiet reminder that he cared.

That held true for the caregivers, too. Just before 8:30 A.M. on Wednesday morning, Patrick arrived at the emergency department of Brigham and Women's Hospital. The plan was for him to slip into the hospital quietly, without the media knowing, greet employees in a small staff lounge, and maybe make some remarks. Patrick began walking around the emergency room, chatting quietly with secretaries, nurses, housekeepers, anyone he came upon. He shook hands, he gave hugs, he asked how they were doing. They were simple, unremarkable gestures, but something about his solicitousness gave license to people to open up and confront their own emotions. Many broke down in his presence. "People who had been saying, 'No, no, I'm fine' up until that moment with him seemed to say, 'It was really hard. It was really awful,'" said Erin McDonough, the hospital's senior vice president of communication and public affairs, who was there. "It started to feel okay to say you're not okay." Patrick approached one nurse who had been working on Monday. She'd seen the carnage wrought by the bombs. Her husband, a paramedic with Boston EMS, had been one of the responders who tried to help Martin Richard on Boylston Street. Patrick walked over and embraced her. He thanked her and her family, but didn't say much more. He didn't need to. They stood, arms locked, for several moments.

Patrick figured that the adrenaline that had been propelling the medical teams since Monday afternoon would soon begin to ebb, that the enormity of it all would soon sink in. His message, when he finally made it to the ER lounge, was simple. "I told them I wanted them to know that they were appreciated, that I was proud of them, but that they also needed to look after themselves," he said. The Brigham, like the city's other top hospitals, boasted some of the most accomplished doctors and nurses and technicians in the world, wizards of medicine whose skill and experience would save lives that week they had no business saving. Underneath, though, they were still people. Their own emotional wounds, which they'd tried, out of necessity, to ignore since the bombs had gone off, would also need tending.

As dusk fell on Tuesday outside her hospital room, Heather Abbott was feeling reassured: The terrible thing that had happened to her could have been worse. She had learned the answer to her question— the question she had hardly dared to ask—and to her surprise, she still had her foot. It was there, underneath the sheet that covered her leg. She was one of the lucky ones. She could hardly believe it. But she wasn't out of the woods yet—the doctors had made that clear. In the hours after the bombing, surgeons had removed blood vessels from her undamaged right leg and grafted them into the left in the hope they would take over the work of circulating blood through the devastated foot. But it was too soon to tell if the transplant would take. If it failed, much more painful options might await her.

Heather's close friend Jason Geremia had been with her at the bar by the finish line. Now he was beside her in the hospital. A home builder from Newport who was nearly ten years her senior, he had always been protective, like an older brother. Late into Monday night, after the bombing, he had waited downstairs with their other friends, in a room filled with the families of other victims. Every group of loved ones he saw was different—five people here, a couple there, a girl by herself in the corner—but almost every one of them was crying. There was food and water in the room, and at some point as the hours crawled by, a priest appeared. Jason found himself talking to the man, asking him why God would let something like this happen.

"God didn't do this," said the priest. "Evil did it."

"But God created everything," said Jason. "Didn't He?"

Yes, the priest acknowledged. He was ready to say more. But just then a doctor walked into the room, looking for Heather's friends and relatives.

It was hard to know how to react to the news he brought. Jason had wanted more than anything to believe that Heather's foot could be saved. For the moment it had, and that was a huge relief. But the doctors warned them that things could change quickly. If blood couldn't get to the foot through the transplanted veins—if the foot turned gray—they would have to consider amputation.

To Heather's mother, Rosemary Abbott, the wait for information Monday night seemed endless. She and her husband had rushed to Boston from Rhode Island after the call from the ambulance. They knew nothing about the bombing at first; they thought Heather had been in an accident. They had found their daughter's friends at the hospital—and had seen the bloodstains on their clothes—but Jason and the others shared few details about what had happened, believing it was better to leave that to the doctors. For six or seven hours she waited to learn more, with no idea how dire the situation was. When at last, around 11:00 P.M., a doctor called to tell her the surgery was over, Rosemary still thought maybe Heather's leg was only broken. Instead, he said her daughter's foot had been severely damaged but that it had not been amputated. Shock washed over Rosemary as the words sank in. She had been waiting and worrying for hours, yet she had not imagined anything this bad. It was gut-wrenching, but there was no time to dwell on it. Heather was out of surgery, headed to the ICU, and her mother needed to get there and reassure her.

"You're alive," she told her daughter. "We will deal with this."

In the midst of all the worry and the waiting, an unexpected visitor had shown up at the Brigham. Heather's ex-boyfriend had rushed to the hospital as soon as he'd heard she was hurt. Their on-again, off-again relationship had ended badly a few months earlier. Now, in the wake of the bombing, he wanted to start over. He was emotional when he finally saw Heather, late that night in her room in the ICU. "I'll never let you down again," he promised. She was groggy, vulnerable; still, she had her doubts. She had been hurt before. The stakes were a lot higher now. She wanted to believe him, though. So she said okay.

Her mother stayed beside her through that first long night, leaning forward in a chair beside the bed, resting her head gently on the mattress. "Talk to me," Heather said, and so Rosemary did, speaking softly to her until Heather fell asleep. The busy ICU beeped and hummed around them. Nurses moved in and out, monitoring her condition as the night outside went from black to gray. The watching and waiting continued all the next day. Heather drifted in and out, in pain and medicated, but she understood that a gamble had been waged. The surgeons had done their best to give her foot a chance. The passing hours would reveal their failure or success. There were no guarantees, but there was reason to hope for the best: a full recovery and return to normal life. Lying in her bed, she tried to focus on the hope. It was hard to do in the midst of so much pain.

Even with his legs gone and his life hanging in the balance, Jeff Bauman knew he had something vitally important to share. After he was rushed to an ambulance after the bombing, Bauman began talking about the suspicious man he'd seen standing near him—the one with the hat, sunglasses, and backpack—with whom he'd exchanged a stare just before the blast. Bauman told someone at the hospital the same thing. When he woke up after surgery, FBI agents were waiting for him. As Bauman described the man he felt certain was responsible, a sketch artist began to draw. The furious work of finding the bombers was on.

CHAPTER 8

THE HEAVIEST TOLL

Three voices, silenced

The mission was one no mother should ever perform, nor even contemplate. But late on Tuesday afternoon, barely twenty-four hours after her daughter had lost her life on Boylston Street, Patty Campbell summoned all her strength, stepped out onto the weathered wooden porch of her two-family home in Medford, and prepared to deliver the most painful words she would likely ever say. She surveyed the pack of reporters, photographers, and camera operators staring up at her from the sidewalk along Park Street, in a quiet residential neighborhood bordered by the highway and the Mystic River. The cameras clicked away, capturing every frame of her stunned movements, every angle of her shock. Wearing a black jacket over a blue shirt, Patty put on her glasses and approached the bank of microphones. She looked down at the notepad cradled in her shaky hands.

"We are heartbroken at the death of our daughter, Krystle Marie," she said. "She was a wonderful person."

Every word was a struggle. Her voice broke, her breathing heavy. She took her glasses off. Her son, Billy, stood to her left in a white

119

Boston Red Sox cap, his right arm hung tight over her shoulder. Her brother John Reilly walked up on the other side and put a hand on her back. She fought on.

"Everybody that knew her loved her," Patty said. "She had a heart of gold. She was always smiling, friendly. You couldn't ask for a better daughter."

Her face was a portrait of agony; still she pressed forward.

"We can't believe this has happened," she said. "She was such a hard worker at everything she did. This doesn't make any sense."

She looked out pleadingly at the dozens of gathered reporters, who were quietly taking in her statement, and threw her hands up, as if looking for an answer. As if one of them might explain how it was that she could be standing in front of them here today, on a porch her daughter had been up and down countless times. How it was that Krystle, such an outsized presence in their lives, could suddenly be silenced.

"What kind of daughter was she, ma'am?" a reporter asked as she turned to walk away.

"She was the best," Patty said.

Her family led her back inside the house.

Two blocks east of the finish line, smack in the middle of Berkeley Street, a few thousand unclaimed runners' bags lay in rows. It was Tuesday morning. The night before, marathon officials had hastily arranged them in numerical order. Now runners were arriving to fetch them, flashing their bib numbers at a checkpoint to prove ownership. It was not supposed to be this way. They had expected to cross the finish line triumphantly, receive a coveted race medal from a volunteer, and collect their stuff from school buses parked nearby. Instead the whole place had become a crime scene, their marathon experience forever scarred. It was nothing compared with what the Campbells were facing, but the running community had lost something, too.

So on Tuesday, race officials did their best to restore some of the ceremony the bombing had taken away. They parked a cherry-red GMC van stocked with medals in the middle of the baggage area and began bestowing them on runners who hadn't been able to finish. The transactions were brief, as marathon representatives carefully draped blue-and-yellow ribbons around people's necks. But they meant something. Some of the runners were distraught. Race officials became tearful, too. "Quite a few people were crying, on both sides of the fence," said Matt Carpenter, a member of the Boston Athletic Association's organizing committee. The moment Carpenter will never forget came when a middle-aged woman from Hong Kong approached him with her bib number. He awarded her a medal, and she broke down. He held her for five minutes. "I will be back next year," she told him.

In the afternoon, marathon officials took the medals and bags over to a former armory a few blocks away, a building known as "the Castle." Here, they laid down a nearly three-foot piece of the blue-and-yellow adhesive finish line brought over from Boylston Street. Runners who hadn't finished the marathon were invited to step across the tape and receive their medals. Volunteers snapped photos and offered applause. For some of the runners, it was a complicated moment, their emotions a mix of heartache, pride, and anger. One woman remained composed as she received her medal and her bag. But then she dug out her cell phone, which she had stowed before the race. The voice mails from loved ones in the twenty-four hours since the bombing plunged her back into Monday's terror.

The hours after the attack were like that, Carpenter said, a blur of dread and sadness. Many of the staff, board members, and volunteers of the BAA felt the same way. Their organization had put on the Boston Marathon for 117 years—before World War I even—and here they were in 2013, badly shaken, unsure how they would get past this year. Tuesday morning, after Governor Deval Patrick briefed the public on the start of the investigation, he slipped over to BAA headquarters behind Copley Square for a brief visit. The task was similar to the one he would perform at the hospitals: offering support, words of comfort, and an acknowledgment of their grief. Everyone gathered in a conference room, and the governor walked around and shook hand after hand. For Dave McGillivray, Patrick's visit was a source of consolation, but the race director couldn't dwell much on his feelings. The practical challenges and immediate demands were all-consuming. Calls and e-mails streamed into the BAA, from runners, from media, from people across the world offering support and assistance. More urgently, the BAA had thousands of marathoners for whom it had to account and care. "We didn't have time to reflect and pause and think about what happened," McGillivray said. "We had to give answers and directions." Then he walked back into his house north of Boston for the first time after the bombing and saw, in the eyes of his seven-year-old son, Luke, just how much had changed. "Dad," Luke said the minute he came in the door, "I don't want you to ever direct that race again."

As nightfall arrived on Tuesday, a thousand people gathered in Garvey Park in Dorchester. In the deep blue April twilight, they lit candles in memory of Martin Richard, the yellow flames flickering inside small cups. They sang "God Bless America." They wept for a loss that would never make sense. None of what had happened made sense—every death, every grievous injury was its own injustice. But to lose Martin, an eight-year-old boy out enjoying a spring day in the city with his family—this one cut especially deep. "My grandson plays sports with little Martin," said Maria Deltufo, a lifelong resident of Dorchester. "When it's somebody in your neighborhood, and your hometown—and such a little boy that is so full of life and so happy . . . The whole family is now destroyed senselessly."

Many children at the vigil had known him; they had gone to school or played together in the neighborhood. They had played together at the very park where they gathered to remember his life. Martin told the best knock-knock jokes, his friends said. He always won at math games. He reached out to classmates who were isolated. "He sticks up for kids," recalled Colin Baker, nine. "If somebody was left out, he would come say, 'Want to join my group?' " The more the world learned about Martin, the larger his absence loomed: Who would stick up for the kids who needed it now? "It should not have happened to him," Colin added. "It should not have happened to nobody."

Her friends, in the hours after the bombing, had taken to Facebook, Twitter, and the Chinese social media site Sina Weibo, frantically looking for information. Lingzi Lu was missing. They urged police and the news media to help find her, posting pictures of the Boston University graduate student, with her seafoam-green nail polish, her warm smile and dark, piercing eyes. "Lingzi, where are you now?" her roommate asked in a Weibo message. "I know you get lost so easily. Don't worry. We will find you." Her roommate also contacted BU's Chinese Students and Scholars Association, an organization of Chinese students and employees at the university, and the group's members began trawling the streets. When Lingzi didn't call after the bombing, her parents and extended family in China grew worried, too.

One friend, Yijing Lu, drove from hospital to hospital, eventually landing at Boston Medical Center. There, Yijing found what she thought was a glimmer of hope. She was told the hospital was treating an unidentified woman of Asian descent, and that the woman wasn't stable enough yet to handle visitors. So Lingzi's roommate and friends gathered and waited. Hours later, they learned the patient was not Lingzi. And it was there at the hospital that the terrible news came: Their friend had been killed. First, they sat in stunned silence. Then her roommate began quietly telling stories about Lingzi, about what she had been like. What they had just learned was too much to comprehend. Better to focus on what had come before.

On Wednesday morning, tributes to the promising young statistician began appearing at the foot of a statue in front of Marsh Chapel on campus—flowers, a pair of running shoes, messages of remembrance. Joy Liu, a twenty-three-year-old journalism graduate student, left a green scally cap with a shamrock on it and a note that said, "From Boston and Beijing with love, RIP." Freshman Jiani Jiang, nineteen, another native of China, visited the makeshift memorial to pay her respects to Lingzi, whom she did not know but whose death made her feel sad and homesick. "There are a lot of foreign students who want to go home now," she said.

A few miles north, word of Krystle Campbell's death spread like a crushing wave across Medford, from the high school where her strong personality stood out, to the streets around her parents' home, to city hall, where the flag was lowered to half-staff. It was hard enough trying to absorb the blow the bombing had delivered to Boston. Now they had lost one of their own. "To deal with those emotions of shock, of anger in the early stages, and then finding out that one of the three victims was actually a young lady from our city, just compounds the sadness and the anguish," said Medford's longtime mayor, Michael McGlynn, who reached out to the Campbells on Tuesday and would help them navigate the rocky weeks to follow. The Medford High School Lady Mustang softball team dropped their heads for a moment of silence at its Wednesday game and dedicated the balance of the season to Krystle. Later that evening, the city came together at Grace Episcopal Church for a prayer service. Many other tributes, benefits, and rituals of mourning followed.

The shattering news rippled, too, through the cousins, the aunts, the uncles, and other relatives, through her extended family at Summer Shack, through her new colleagues at Jimmy's, and through the many other lives Krystle had touched. The general sense of shock was now painfully, impossibly specific. "Of all the people that were there, and three were killed, and one is Krystle—it's unbelievable," said Bryan Conway, a boat captain who worked alongside her on the harbor islands. "I would like to say that she was in a better place now but she's not," another friend wrote on Facebook. "Because THIS is her place—right here, right now, with her family and friends smiling, laughing, and making everybody's day better."

Maybe it was her outspokenness, or maybe it was the red hair, or the distinctive blue eye shadow. But college professors who had had her in class a decade or more before—professors who had known hundreds of students since—remembered her instantly when Krystle's name hit the news. Robin Gomolin had taught her in sociology classes at the University of Massachusetts Boston and spent time with her in a study group that used to meet Saturday mornings. Krystle, to her, was a striver, someone who hadn't always had it easy but so badly wanted to do well in school. Tuesday morning, Gomolin was driving over the Charles River in her car when she heard the name on the radio. *It couldn't be*, she thought. She asked her daughter to check it out. Her daughter texted her a picture and Gomolin's heart sank. Robert Tarutis, whose Western civilization class Krystle had taken at community college in the fall of 2002, had much the same experience. The minute he saw her picture on the Web, he knew it was the same charming, talkative Krystle he'd known when she was a nineteen-year-old. "Even after all those years, I remembered the name and the face," he said. "That was a very sad day."

For most of Greater Boston, the rest of Marathon Week would be a fearful experience, with threats of further attacks and deep apprehension that the bombers were still out there. For the Campbell family and for Krystle's friends, it would be a week of unrelenting sorrow. Instead of organizing the next get-together, the next family gathering, the next night out, they were now planning her final rite of passage. They arranged for a wake at a local funeral home on Sunday evening, and a funeral service at St. Joseph Church, right in Medford center, on the following Monday morning. It was, for some who knew her, a classic case of not knowing what you have until it's gone. "She was stolen," Bryan Conway said. "She was *stolen*."

CHAPTER 9

HIDING IN PLAIN SIGHT

From billions of pixels, a break

Ain't no love in the heart of the city, his message began.

It was just hours after the bombing, and Dzhokhar Tsarnaev was already on Twitter, commenting on the tragedy as if watching it all unfold from a distance. As if he were just another pot-smoking, soccer-playing, social media–savvy nineteen-year-old college kid in a hoodie.

Stay safe people, he wrote.

At 2:50 P.M. on Monday, the bombers had walked away from Boylston Street and disappeared into the city's thrum, havoc burning in their wake. With surgeons racing to save lives, with police standing vigil over bodies, with investigators combing the wreckage for evidence, and with the public panicked at the prospect of more bomb blasts, one, and perhaps both, of the Tsarnaev brothers went grocery shopping. According to a receipt later recovered by police, at least one of the brothers made a purchase at a Whole Foods store across the Charles River in Cambridge, about a half mile from their family home.

Tamerlan seemed to lay low after slipping away from the marathon; authorities later declined to share what, if anything, they knew of his movements after he dropped his backpack outside Marathon Sports. Dzhokhar was a different story. At 12:34 A.M. Tuesday, he returned to Twitter, posting a message more opaque, more serious than his first after the attack: *There are people that know the truth but stay silent & there are people that speak the truth but we don't hear them cuz they're the minority.* Twelve hours later, around lunchtime on Tuesday, he showed up at Junior Auto Body in Somerville, a short walk from the family's home on the Cambridge-Somerville line. He wanted to pick up a white Mercedes that he had left two weeks earlier, a car he had said belonged to a girlfriend. The rear bumper wasn't fixed yet. Dzhokhar told the mechanic, Gilberto Junior, he would take it anyway.

"I need it now," Dzhokhar said.

Normally he was relaxed and pleasant, chatting about soccer, weed, and girls. That Tuesday, Dzhokhar appeared anxious. He was biting his nails. His knees shook so much that Junior thought the kid had been popping pills.

The proximity of the bombing to world-class hospitals had been one blessing. The abundance of commercial and retail buildings near Copley Square would prove to be another. Shops and banks lined Boylston Street on both sides of the finish line area, from the Lord & Taylor department store on one side to the Sugar Heaven candy store on the other. Businesses occupied the upper floors. The Boston Public Library was right there, too. The array of retail outlets and attractions made Boylston a huge draw for consumers and visitors; it also meant security video cameras were just about everywhere. For law enforcement, this held huge promise. At least one of the cameras had almost certainly picked up the bombers walking through the vast crowd at the finish line. The trick was figuring out which one. "We were very confident that there were enough cameras down there that we were going to capture something," said state police colonel Tim Alben. "The sheer volume of stuff made it difficult to sort through."

Within minutes of arriving at the scene Monday afternoon, Boston Police commissioner Ed Davis sought out Sergeant Detective Earl Perkins, a video specialist with the police department's intelligence-gathering unit, the Boston Regional Intelligence Center. Davis directed Perkins to hit up every potential source of video up and down Boylston. Perkins and his team, working alongside state police and FBI agents, quickly began tracking down store owners and managers, collecting footage from them, and converting what they received to formats that allowed for efficient review. In addition to the stores, marathon spectators were another potential source of video, as many had used their smartphones to capture the triumphant finishes of loved ones. The bombers must have walked right by at least one of them. In the hours that followed, the FBI set up a special website where the public could easily upload video clips.

Investigators gathered raw footage from anyone they could find. Kiva Kuan Liu, a twenty-three-year-old Boston University graduate student, had been filming for a documentary near where the first bomb exploded. She was summoned to Tufts Medical Center around 10:00 P.M. to be interviewed. In a drab hospital meeting room, four investigators grilled her. When her memory failed her, they persisted. "They were very picky about details," said Liu, who was not injured in the blast. Liu volunteered her Panasonic video camera, which she had borrowed from BU. Every clip, every camera, every snippet that authorities collected could be the one that unlocked the case. There were thousands of images to look through, but time was short. With every hour that passed, the risk of the bombers' escape, or of another attack, seemed to grow.

Law enforcement had set up their primary command and control post at the Westin. But they also commandeered the Lenox, a hundred-year-old luxury hotel right on Boylston Street between the two bombing sites, turning the whole place into a technical operations center. The 214 well-appointed guest rooms housed federal agents and other law enforcement officials who had come in from around the country to help. Evidence-gathering teams took over the hotel's function rooms. Over seven days, Davis said, the place came to resemble a military reservation, with local, state, and federal authorities in every nook working the investigation. "You'd go into the bar and there'd be twenty people having lunch talking about the case," Davis said. "And then you'd go upstairs and there'd be fifty people in the main ballroom, and everybody was handing out assignments. A very, very dynamic place." It was also a haven of sorts, with its lamplit lobby, carved lion heads, and low-slung leather armchairs. Outside the windows, beyond the front door that had been broken by the crowds desperate to escape the bombs, teams in Tyvek hazardous waste suits picked up evidence.

The Lenox had been fully booked, as always, for the marathon, with guests including elite runners from around the world. After the bombing shut down the neighborhood, guests couldn't get back to the hotel. The staff spent days packing up every guest room and shipping belongings back to those who had fled. The influx of FBI agents was disconcerting, but it gave the hotel staff a purpose. Most volunteered to keep working, determined to show the police the same hospitality as guests who paid $400 a night. It was not a perfect fit—some of the hard-nosed cops roaming the place hardly knew what to do with all the solicitous inquiries about their needs, and they kept their rooms so neat housekeepers couldn't tell which rooms were occupied—but as the week went on and their exhaustion peaked, the agents' appreciation of their plush accommodations deepened. "Some of them pulled me aside and said, 'You know, we're usually in a tent, barely eating, using Porta-Potties, and to be able to take a hot shower . . .' That helped us get through it, too," hotel sales director Scott Grigelevich said.

Hotel workers also took comfort in the generosity of other businesses that rallied to help them feed 1,500 investigators a day at a time when trucks could not get through with their regular deliveries. When food supplies at the Lenox ran dangerously low, the general manager of the nearby Fairmont Copley Plaza Hotel walked over with an enormous slab of bacon on his shoulder. Smith & Wollensky, a Back Bay steak house, sent lunch for seven hundred people. Still, the work could not distract the hotel staff completely. Tending to business that week in his office on the second floor of the hotel,

Grigelevich said, "There were times I couldn't stand to look out the window at the baby carriages" still sitting abandoned in the street. He longed for the disarray below to be swept clean. But no clean sweep would come for days, until agents had recorded every detail.

Investigators used two locations to sift through all the security footage that was coming in. The first was a room at the Lenox, where Perkins had set up his temporary headquarters. Authorities also took over a cavernous, century-old former army warehouse in the Black Falcon Cruise Terminal in South Boston. Half of that space was converted into a video center, the operation growing to include a number of computers, where shifts of investigators sat and carefully combed through frame after frame. The heavily secured space, right on Boston Harbor, wasn't heated, so they brought in mobile heating units and piped warm air in through wide yellow ventilation tubes. The other half of the warehouse was used for evidence collection. Investigators gathered bloody clothing and other debris brought over from Boylston and arranged it, starting around 11:00 P.M. Monday night, in a manner that mimicked the scene of the bombing. It looked, to Davis, like one of those big hangars where crash investigators try to reassemble downed airplanes.

Between the Lenox and Black Falcon, investigators spent hour after hour reviewing video, looking for something that didn't belong. Different cameras offered different angles, different levels of quality, and thus varying degrees of use to those working the case. The repetition could be numbing. One agent reviewed the same video clip four hundred times. Everyone yearned for a breakthrough, some suspicious movement or odd-looking bystander to emerge from the billions of pixels filling their vision.

By Tuesday afternoon, Dzhokhar was back on campus at the University of Massachusetts Dartmouth, acting like he had no care in the world, walking nonchalantly around his dorm, Pine Dale Hall, and chatting with acquaintances. "He was not startled. He was not scared. He was not anything," student Andrew Glasby said. "He was just the same old Dzhokhar." Dzhokhar even offered Glasby a ride back up toward Boston later in the week.

At 9:05 P.M. Tuesday, Dzhokhar used his swipe card to enter the campus fitness center. Fellow student Zach Bettencourt saw him there and mentioned his shock at the bombing. Bettencourt made a comment about this kind of thing usually happening in other parts of the world, and Dzhokhar agreed. "He was like, 'Yeah, tragedies happen like this all the time. And it's sad,'" Bettencourt told a reporter. Dzhokhar also posted more Twitter messages Tuesday, including one about a photo of a bombing victim. Internet rumors had swirled about the injured woman in the picture, claiming her boyfriend had planned to propose but found her dead.

Fake story, Dzhokhar tweeted.

The next night, Wednesday, he stopped by a get-together at an Italian restaurant where some of his fellow intramural soccer players had gathered, students recalled. He slept in his room, number 7341. "He was just relaxed," one student said. Indeed, Dzhokhar appeared to be trying to resume his normal life, evidently unconcerned that he might be caught. Not only was he not in hiding—he was all over campus.

I'm a stress free kind of guy, he had tweeted early Wednesday morning.

With investigators working behind the scenes, the public and the media began sleuthing on their own. On sites like Facebook, Twitter, and reddit, social media users, relying on snippets of police scanner traffic and photos of the finish line, turned to crowd-sourcing to isolate and identify potential suspects. These online vigilantes may have been driven by good intentions, but they would, over the course of Marathon Week, finger the wrong young men, in some cases to damaging effect. In an apology posted a week after the bombing, Erik Martin, the general manager of reddit, a massively popular messageboard site, wrote, "Some of the activity on reddit fueled online witch hunts and dangerous speculation which spiraled into very negative consequences for innocent parties. The reddit staff and the millions of people on reddit around the world deeply regret that this happened."

In particular, reddit apologized publicly and privately to the family of Sunil Tripathi, a twenty-two-year-old Brown University student who had gone missing on March 16, a month before the marathon attack. For a time, much of the speculation on reddit and elsewhere online about the bombing culprits swirled around Tripathi, because of his perceived physical resemblance to Dzhokhar. Compounding the problem, a number of prominent figures in the press spread his name to their own followers and friends on social media. The episode became a source of deep pain for the Tripathi family, already devastated by the young man's disappearance. The very next week, Tripathi's body would be pulled from the Providence River in Providence, Rhode Island. His tragedy had nothing to do with Boston's.

It wasn't just "new media" that got caught up in the speculation. On Thursday, April 18, the *New York Post* featured, on its cover, a giant photo of two young men from Massachusetts, later identified as Salaheddin Barhoum and Yassine Zaimi, at the finish line of the marathon, one wearing a backpack, the other carrying a duffel. Under the banner headline "BAG MEN," the story said that authorities were looking for the two in connection with the bombing. Barhoum, a sixteen-year-old high school student, and Zaimi, twenty-four, a part-time college student who worked at a financial services firm, both lived in cities just north of Boston. Both had come from Morocco and were legal residents of the United States. Both loved running, which is why they were at the marathon. Being erroneously connected to the bombing probe, their lawyers said, damaged both of them emotionally. Weeks later they would file a defamation lawsuit against the *Post,* which would stand by its sensational presentation.

In the rush to figure out the real story, other mainstream media outlets got it wrong at times, too. On Wednesday, relying on a source familiar with the investigation, the *Boston Globe* posted a breaking-news report online that a suspect had been arrested and was on his way to federal court. Other media outlets, including the Associated Press and CNN, put out similar bulletins. Hundreds of reporters and photographers descended on the Moakley Courthouse in South Boston. The Coast Guard and Boston Police Department Harbor Patrol kept watch over nearby waters. Inside, courthouse staff flocked to the emergency magistrate's courtroom, anticipating a hearing. They began discussing whether they should move the hearing to a larger courtroom with more seating, and whether to provide a live, closed-circuit feed to yet another courtroom, in anticipation of an overflow crowd.

Watching the drama unfold on live television, the US attorney's office denied the reports of an arrest and called court officials to tell them there would be no hearing. By then, word of the arrest turned into an avalanche of chaos, complicated by the "code red" that was broadcast over the intercom at 3:01 P.M. The building's management company had received a bomb threat, and the US Marshals Service ordered an evacuation. Outside, judges mixed with members of the public who had come to catch a glimpse of the commotion. It was a code none of the lawyers had heard before, and none of them knew what it meant. But they could tell from the seriousness in the announcer's voice that something was up. "This was different; this was louder," Boston-based lawyer Jonathan Shapiro remembered thinking as he descended seven flights of stairs to exit the building. Outside, seeing the patrol boats with machine guns and the crowd in the streets, he was struck by the oddness of the moment. "I've never seen anything like it," he said. After a sweep by federal agents, the area was cleared at 4:41 P.M., and courthouse employees were allowed back in.

It was early Wednesday morning. The day was still dark. Investigators, working around the clock since Monday afternoon, continued to sift carefully through surveillance video, hoping for a lead. In the predawn hours, there at the FBI's Boston office in the middle of downtown, a break finally came. And when it did, it was clear as day. Investigators, including Boston police officers who sat on the city's Joint Terrorism Task Force, saw Dzhokhar first, though they didn't know his name yet. There he was, walking easily along Boylston Street, his white hat turned backward, slipping a backpack off his shoulder in front of Forum restaurant, and then walking away. Moments later, when the bomb went off behind him, he didn't react, didn't even turn around. It was a sure giveaway: Everyone else around him fled in panic; his face remained stoic. Investigators played the tape over and over. With each viewing, their confidence grew. This seemed like the *Eureka!* moment everyone had been waiting for. "It was right there for you to see," said Tim Alben, who would later be shown the video, the source or sources of which authorities declined to disclose. "It was quite clear to me we had a breakthrough in the case."

Later Wednesday morning, Ed Davis was at FBI headquarters in Boston for a top secret briefing with Washington. Afterward, he walked upstairs to a big, open command center where dozens of federal agents were at work. In a smaller side room where some technical equipment was kept, Kevin Swindon, an FBI supervisory special agent who oversaw the collection, review, and analysis of all computer and video evidence, showed Davis the footage. As FBI officials kept playing back the images of Dzhokhar, Davis noticed something else—another suspicious man who was perhaps twenty or thirty feet away from Dzhokhar but seemed to share his gait. "It was almost like they were walking in concert," Davis said. The Boston police commissioner took note of the second man's sunglasses and the black hat pulled tight over his head. "I didn't like him from the beginning." They reeled back the video some more, Davis and federal agents crouching over one another's shoulders to see the images on a computer screen. They had hit upon Tamerlan, too.

Figuring out who the bombers were would be the next urgent task. But investigators now knew what their suspects looked like, and that was a huge step forward. "The day before we had no idea who did this," Alben said. "We were all hopeful. When you were finally able to see it, it was exhilarating to know you made this kind of progress." Alben would later say that he had been struck, in watching the videos, by how little attention marathon spectators paid to the young men in their midst. He said he wasn't looking to place blame, but that people had to be more vigilant. "I mean, I don't go into a movie theater without looking around to see who's sitting next to me or who's a couple of rows away," he said in an interview with a Boston sports radio show. "Every time you go into a major event like this you've got to be on your game. You've got to be at least looking around and seeing what your surroundings are."

After Alben saw the crucial footage on Wednesday, he briefed the governor, Deval Patrick. He showed Patrick photographs of Dzhokhar taken from one of the videos, describing seeing on the tape how the nineteen-year-old had dropped his bag on Boylston Street. It was a chilling sight, but at this point, a welcome one. Alben gave his boss the good news: "We think we have a break."

CHAPTER 10

PICTURE OF MALICE

Somber morning, violent night

T he doctors and medical teams showed up in scrubs. The runners and race volunteers wore their marathon jackets. The politicians donned crisp suits, four former governors among them. Soldiers arrived in camouflage fatigues. Emergency medical technicians kept on their khaki uniforms. Police came in blue. The wounded hobbled in on crutches. Together, about two thousand people crammed into the Cathedral of the Holy Cross in Boston's South End for an interfaith service, hoping to hear President Obama deliver words of comfort for their rattled city. It was Thursday, three days after the attack on the marathon, the shock still fresh. The diversity of attire in the pews said something about how many people the bombing had touched, how many had been working around the clock to heal and protect. "I wish I brought a suit," said X-ray technologist Mervyn Williams as he glanced down at his blue fleece embossed with the words BOSTON MEDICAL CENTER DEPARTMENT OF RADIOLOGY. He had been working when the bombs went off and casualties streamed into his hospital. "But I'm so proud to wear this jacket."

The presidential visit came as Boston remained on edge, still desperate for answers, still deeply anxious that the terrorists were at large and more violence might follow. In this state of high alert, jittery citizens did their best to open themselves to Obama's calming message and his call for resilience. It was part of the job, this solemn presidential ritual of showing up where disaster strikes—to the hamlet on the plains flattened by a tornado, to the small town swallowed by biblical flooding, to the suburb rocked by a mass shooting. It was now Boston's turn, sadly, and the city needed it. Obama's objective, he explained, was simple: to tell Boston that the nation had its back. "Every one of us," he said, "stands with you." He recounted fondly his formative experiences in the city, first as a law student at Harvard and later, in 2004, as a young state senator from Illinois. It was here, at that year's Democratic National Convention, that Obama had delivered his stirring address about renewing a common purpose in American politics, a speech that had put him on the political map and on the road to the White House. Nine years later, here he stood, speaking tenderly about each bombing victim who had died, visibly shaken as he spoke of young Martin Richard, recalling the blue poster the boy had made, with two red hearts, a blue peace sign, and those haunting words: "No more hurting people. Peace."

The president praised the spirit shown by the first responders, the spectators, and the runners who had dashed toward danger on Monday. "You've shown us, Boston, that in the face of evil, Americans will lift up what's good," he said. "In the face of cruelty, we will choose compassion. In the face of those who would visit death upon innocents, we will choose to save and to comfort and to heal. We'll choose friendship. We'll choose love." He quoted Dick Hoyt, the man who for decades had pushed his disabled son in a wheelchair through the marathon course, who said, "We can't let something like this stop us." Obama continued, "That's what you've taught us, Boston. That's what you've reminded us—to push on. To persevere. To not grow weary. To not get faint. Even when it hurts. Even when our heart aches. We summon the strength that maybe we didn't even know we had, and we carry on. We finish the race. We finish the race." When he was done, the president wiped a tear and took a seat.

From the moment the sanctuary fell silent, and the first notes of "Amazing Grace" rose from the choir, it had felt as though the whole town were there under the majestic stone arches of the cathedral, in person or in spirit. The ailing mayor, Tom Menino, had been discharged that morning from Brigham and Women's Hospital, where he had been recovering from surgery. Three days earlier, against his doctors' wishes, he had checked himself out of the hospital after the bombing. He had returned there late Monday night. Now he was out for good, but still under strict orders from his doctors not to put any weight on his right leg, which he had fractured in a fall a week earlier. The mayor arrived at the cathedral in a wheelchair, and as far as his aides knew, he intended to stay in it, even when he went to the podium to speak. But at this moment, when his city needed him, Menino knew he had to stand. He told no one of his plan, except for his son Tommy, who guided his wheelchair to the front of the church. They paused there as his aides exchanged worried glances. Then with a terrible grimace, Menino pushed himself to his feet to speak. His love for Boston and its people had never been stronger, he said. "Nothing will take us down, because we take care of one another," he vowed, his voice ragged. "Even with the smell of smoke in the air, blood on the streets, tears in our eyes, we triumphed over that hateful act on Monday afternoon."

Many had waited in line outside since 4:00 or 5:00 A.M. to get a ticket to the service, huddling together for warmth, a few wrapped in the thermal blankets given to marathon runners. Others held signs, American flags, and worn leather Bibles. Those who didn't get into the sanctuary or an overflow auditorium hung around anyway, listening as the service was broadcast into the April morning. Some had been close to Monday's explosions, some removed by blocks, others by just steps. They had heard the boom, had felt the ground rumble. They had smelled the acrid air. Now they wanted to be here, needed to be here.

Any presidential visit demands high security; this one more than most. No one knew the bombers' intentions, or what exactly their quarrel was. No one knew if they would consider Obama a target and attempt some further act of terror. And no one, at that moment, had any idea who they were or where they were. "The urgency and the national implications of this event were [like] nothing anyone had experienced before," recalled Boston Police superintendent William Evans, the department's point man on the streets. "We knew we had a terrorist incident here and national security was riding on this. The whole nation was watching." The roads surrounding the cathedral were cordoned off. Bomb-sniffing dogs patrolled the area. The threat may have been vague, but it was real. The air crackled with it.

To the family of Krystle Campbell, that threat had already visited, leaving them with a grief that felt like too much to bear. Thursday morning, before the interfaith service, the FBI had swung by their house in Medford, picked up Billy Jr., Patty, and Krystle's brother, Billy III, and ushered them to the church. They were led into the sacristy off the sanctuary. The president and first lady came in and offered quiet hugs and words of condolence. Their sincerity was evident. Billy Jr. could see that Obama was having a difficult time. "He was totally dumbfounded," Billy said. As comforting as it was, the moment was hard for the Campbells, too—venturing out in public to receive the president of the United States, so soon after losing Krystle. "We did a lot of this to honor our daughter," Billy said. "That's what my wife kept telling me and my son—we're not doing this for us, guys; we're doing this because Krystle would want it."

Shana Cottone filed out of the cathedral with the crowd. It had been three days since the twenty-seven-year-old police officer had been on her knees on Boylston Street, surrounded by the victims of the terrorist attack. In the time that had passed, she had scarcely stopped thinking about the blonde woman with the badly damaged leg, the woman whose hand she had gripped tightly as they waited for an ambulance. Today she was finally going to see her again.

The minutes they had spent together at the finish line were engraved on Shana's memory. She had known right away that she would never be the same, but she wasn't sure how she would ever get over it if the woman from Boylston Street didn't make it. *Please don't let her die*, Shana had silently pleaded on Monday night, after she finally made it home to Hyde Park. *Please don't let it be her*, she thought over and over when she heard that two people were dead, and then three. She felt connected to the woman in a way she had never felt about anyone at a crime scene. The badly injured people she had previously encountered generally ended up that way because they were up to some kind of trouble, or because they chose to stick close to trouble-makers. This was different. These victims had done nothing but go to a race. Shana couldn't bear how innocent they were, how vulnerable and unsuspecting.

She knew the woman's first name was Roseann. On Tuesday, she went online and typed it into Google. Right away she found what she was looking for: a fund-raising website set up by Roseann's friends, with a smiling photo of the woman whose face she couldn't forget. The website said that Roseann had been badly hurt, that she had lost her leg, and that her recovery would be long and difficult. But she was alive, and she was going to survive. Shana copied the link to the fund-raising website and quickly sent it to all her e-mail contacts, with a note demanding that they forward it on to their friends. Then she clicked on another link that allowed her to contact the website's creator, a woman who had known Roseann since high school. Shana typed a message, explaining who she was. She was on her way to the cathedral for the service Thursday morning when she got a call from Roseann's sister, asking her to come to the hospital when it was over.

Shana was a little worried about the visit. She badly wanted to see Roseann, but she was feeling the emotional strain of the week, and she didn't want to fall apart at the hospital. *Nobody wants to see a crying cop*, she thought. She had gone to see a primary care doctor on Tuesday, to check out muscle pain from her work at the scene, and returned to work on Wednesday, but she knew she needed more help, in the form of counseling. "I could lie about it," she said, "or I could do something about it. I don't want to be the person who doesn't address it." Police from different districts around the city were now taking turns directing traffic around the crime scene; Shana knew she couldn't go back there yet, so she asked for a different assignment. She knew some of her colleagues wouldn't understand. For many cops, there is a stigma attached to any sign of weakness. Better, they thought, to suffer in silence.

Searching for Roseann's room at Mass General, Shana put on her game face. She could play the tough cop; that would get her through. Her eyes scanned the room, past the worried faces of family members, until she found Roseann. She approached the bed. It was hard to get close, with all the machines and people, and impossible to really talk. But it was enough, for now. Roseann's family hugged her and thanked her for what she had done. Shana absorbed the care Roseann was getting, the loved ones all around her, and recorded those pictures in her brain. They wouldn't replace the others—the ones from that day in the street—but maybe they would somehow blur together, softening the jagged edges of her memory. "We will get the people who did this," Shana told the woman in the bed and her family. "I promise you, we will get them." It sounded like a cop cliché, but it was what she could give them, and God knows she meant it. The nightmare was still there when Shana closed her eyes; she wanted it to end more than she could say.

David King had been awake most of Wednesday night, preparing for the president's visit to Mass General. When he had first received the call from the White House, asking him to send information on the victims at the hospital, he had assumed they wanted a medical briefing, a description of each person's injuries and progress. He wasn't surprised at that, and he could provide it. The staff member on the phone had corrected him, explaining that they needed something deeper. The president wanted to know who these people *were*: where they came from; what had brought them to the marathon. Listening, King realized he didn't have the answers. He was going to have to find out, and quickly. To complicate matters, he couldn't let the patients know exactly why he was quizzing them all of a sudden. For security reasons, he could only tell them that a mysterious "someone" might visit them—and that he needed their permission to share their personal medical profile with the mystery visitor. Some of the patients were weary of visitors. A few were suspicious. One demanded to know if King was really a doctor. Still he kept at it, room after room, hour after hour, visiting eleven of the most seriously injured and emerging with a newly detailed picture of each one. Drained by his efforts, but confident now he could complete his assignment, King wrote up the profiles and sent them to the White House. The next call came at 7:00 A.M. Thursday: He had done his job well. The president had what he needed. And now they wanted King to be Obama's guide, introducing him to every patient.

Obama had lunch when he got to Mass General after the interfaith service, in a private room with some of his aides, a few hospital staff, and Menino. The mayor was amazed to see the president actually eating a sandwich. Every other time they had dined together, Obama never seemed to eat a thing. After lunch, King brought him to see the patients. The bombing victims were split between two ICUs, on two different floors. The surgeon guided Obama from room to room in the first intensive care unit, giving him a few minutes alone with each patient. They stepped into an elevator when he was finished there, headed for the second ICU.

"How do you think it went?" Obama asked King after the doors closed.

"I think it was perfect, Mr. President," King said. "I think you inspired them."

"No, no—that's not it at all," Obama corrected him. "They inspired *me*."

King considered what the president was saying. He thought about how little he had known about the bombing patients until he had embarked upon his mission for the White House. He had been in surgeon mode, focused for days on the work of "fixing holes," but now he caught a glimmer of the larger picture. The surgeries were important, of course, but he had needed this reminder of the real lives inside the bodies he was mending.

After Obama had toured both ICUs, King brought him to a

nearby conference room. Rather than trying to secure the rest of the hospital, where other, less badly hurt marathon patients were scattered, officials had brought the patients here, many of them in wheelchairs, to hear from the president and shake his hand. Having toured city hospitals earlier in the week, and now at Mass General alongside the president, the governor, Deval Patrick, was struck by how positive the survivors' outlook was. "They were grateful for the care; they were grateful for the responsiveness," he said. "They were grateful to be alive."

Obama had spent ninety minutes with patients at Mass General, staying beyond the time allotted on his schedule. When the meeting in the conference room wound down—after he had spoken individually with every patient there—the president was whisked away by his team. He was gone in an instant, it seemed to David King, as if he had vanished in a puff of smoke. The doctor was beginning to turn his attention back to his regular workday—wondering what backlog of tasks now awaited him—when he felt a mild twinge of irritation: *I just spent an hour and a half introducing that guy to people, and he never even said thanks.* A minute or two later, as if on cue, a lone Secret Service agent reappeared and approached him. "Are you Dr. King?" the man asked. "I have a message from the president. . . . He's sorry he didn't get a chance to thank you. And he really appreciates your help."

At Thursday's service, when the president had delivered a public warning to the bombers, his words were generic, almost boilerplate. "We will find you," he said. "We will hold you accountable." Wasn't that what political and law enforcement leaders always said at moments like this? Boston wanted to believe him, wanted it to be true. But it was such an easy thing to say. As far as the public knew, no progress had been made in finding the perpetrators. Were they still in the area? In the country? Would they ever be found? It had been nearly seventy-two hours since the explosions. The hunger for progress was palpable.

As Obama spoke those words, though, he surely knew more than he was letting on. It had been more than twenty-four hours since investigators had zeroed in on the two suspects, the men they were calling White Hat and Black Hat. As the president traveled to the cathedral in Boston, US Homeland Security secretary Janet Napolitano acknowledged publicly the existence—and promise—of the surveillance video. Speaking elliptically, Napolitano told a hearing of the House Homeland Security Committee that the FBI had come upon some footage that had "raised the question" about some suspicious characters. She said she would not characterize them as suspects, however.

For investigators in Boston, the men's menacing presence on Boylston Street had left little doubt about their involvement—that these were the guys they wanted. The only question was how to go after them. Investigators initially tried using facial recognition technology to identify Tamerlan and Dzhokhar Tsarnaev, but the angle at which the cameras had caught them—looking down at their faces, and from the side—made that difficult. That meant the images could not be readily cross-checked against photos stored in government databases. This left authorities with two primary options: release the photos right away and seek the public's help in identifying the suspects, or keep the pictures private and see if law enforcement could somehow covertly track them down. Behind the scenes, state, local, and federal law enforcement leaders debated vigorously which path to take. Either way, the stakes and the risk were grave.

Later in the day on Wednesday, around a table at FBI headquarters, Boston Police commissioner Ed Davis made his case to Rick DesLauriers, the local FBI chief. Davis, worried principally about public safety, wanted to put the photos out there, believing it would hasten the arrest of the suspects and minimize the potential for further mayhem. FBI officials, focused on building the strongest criminal case they could, were initially cool on the idea. They came from a different culture. They specialized in working discreetly, methodically building cases over time, acting only when everything was in hand. One concern, for example, was that showing the suspects' photos would prompt the men to destroy evidence, making it more difficult to prosecute the case. "If your main goal is prosecution, then you look at things one way. If your main goal is a larger goal of public safety, you might make different decisions," Davis said. "They don't necessarily line up." Tim Alben, the head of the Massachusetts State Police, also worried that putting the pictures out would cause the suspects to flee, or go underground. "You always want to apprehend someone when you have control of the situation," he said. "Not when someone has been tipped you're coming through the door."

Around 6:00 Thursday morning, DesLauriers called Davis. He told the police commissioner he had been thinking about it all night, and that he had come around: He now agreed that they should put the photos out. "Everybody wanted to do the right thing," Davis said. "Ultimately, we came together on it." Local FBI leaders, though, were getting push-back from Washington. It took much of Thursday to get all parties on board. Finally, in midafternoon, the FBI put out word: It would update the public on the bombing investigation at 5:00 P.M.

Sixty miles away, on the campus of UMass–Dartmouth, Dzhokhar Tsarnaev's life as a carefree college sophomore was about to end. He had one hour of anonymity left. At 4:02 P.M., with the FBI preparing to release photos of the men they wanted, Dzhokhar used his swipe card to enter his dorm room. It would be the last time he used the card on campus. Dzhokhar had already made what would be his last posting on Twitter the previous day. He had retweeted a message from a Zimbabwean scholar, Mufti Ismail Menk, that was almost absurdly off point, given his current situation: *Attitude can take away your beauty no matter how good looking you are or it could enhance your beauty, making you adorable.* After that, silence. He and his brother had enjoyed three days of relative freedom since the bombing. But they had failed to prepare for what was coming, as if they had imagined they'd never be found. They had little money. They seemed to have no plan. And they had run out of time.

At 5:20 P.M., DesLauriers strode to a podium set up in a third-floor ballroom at the Sheraton Boston, flanked by the state's top law enforcement figures. Since the bombing, he said, the FBI, Boston Police, and other agencies had chased down thousands of leads and tips. Now it was time to ask for assistance. "Today, we are enlisting the public's help in identifying the two suspects," he said. As DesLauriers spoke, the world got its first glimpse of two of the most wanted men in the city's history. There, unveiled on two display boards set up to his left, were eight photographs culled from surveillance video, four of suspect number one—dark coat, black hat, sunglasses, with a bulky backpack—and four of suspect number two—white hat turned backward, tufts of dark curly hair peeking out, a bag slung over his right shoulder. Underneath each image were the words ARMED AND DANGEROUS. News photographers' cameras began clicking furiously. TV cameras zeroed in. In a week full of dramatic moments, this was one of the biggest. Here, for the first time, were the faces of Boston's terror.

In an instant, the images traveled the globe, showing up on TV screens, smartphones, and computers far and wide. Their faces quickly lodged in the public's consciousness, unforgettable after a single study. Mindful of the errant speculation by online vigilantes, DesLauriers pointedly urged the public and the media to rely on these images alone in trying to help. He laid out the case for why authorities deemed them suspects—how video cameras had captured the men walking together along Boylston Street, how White Hat could be seen dropping a bag in front of Forum restaurant minutes before the bomb there exploded. "We know the public will play a critical role in identifying and locating these individuals," DesLauriers said. "Somebody out there knows these individuals as friends, neighbors, coworkers, or family members." The nation, he said, was counting on their help and also their discretion. God forbid anyone should try to detain the suspects themselves. "We consider them to be armed and extremely dangerous," he said. "No one should approach them."

Back at UMass–Dartmouth that night, Pamala Rolon, a senior

and a resident assistant in the dorms, returned from class and turned on the TV news. Pictures of the bombing suspects flashed across the screen. One of them looked faintly like a guy she knew on campus. "We made a joke, like, 'That could be Dzhokhar,'" she said. "But then we thought it just couldn't be him. Dzhokhar? Never." It made no sense; the slacker college kid she knew would never be capable of something like this. One of Dzhokhar's Twitter followers sent him a copy of his image from the FBI pictures, writing, *Is this you? I didn't know you went to the marathon!!!!* By the time Dzhokhar arrived back in Cambridge sometime that night, his face was known to millions. Tips about his identity, and that of his older brother, had begun pouring in to federal agents. The brothers' sudden notoriety may have inspired their desperate plan to escape to New York, where authorities came to believe they saw their next target: Times Square, the fabled "crossroads of the world." But the Tsarnaevs hadn't set aside money or even a getaway car for the journey—they had to figure the green Honda Civic Dzhokhar drove would soon be known to police. They were also short on weapons; police would later recover only one handgun and a BB gun that they could trace to the pair. In Thursday's waning hours, Dzhokhar and Tamerlan set out to expand their arsenal, and they had an idea where to look.

Sean A. Collier was born to be a cop. There was little doubt he would be one day. As the second-youngest of six siblings in the Collier household, raised in the Boston suburb of Wilmington, north of the city, he used to make siren noises as he chased his brother Andrew around. "You're breaking the law!" he'd yell. "You're breaking the law!" In the car, if they passed someone who had been pulled over, young Sean would sing the theme song to the show *COPS*. As his sister Nicole Lynch explained to CNN, Sean was born with an instinctual sense of right and wrong. "There was no in between," she said. "Either you did the right thing or you did the wrong thing. And if you did the wrong thing, you needed to be punished." He also possessed a deep sense of compassion, as if he felt an obligation to look out for others. Once, as a six-year-old, he was sitting in the booth of a Papa Gino's Pizzeria with his mother, Kelley, and his little brother, when he noticed a woman sitting alone nearby, crying.

"Mum," he whispered. "You've got to go talk to that lady."

Kelley glanced at the woman and told her son it was best to leave the woman be.

"Sean," she said, "I'm sure she just wants to be alone."

"Maybe she has no one," Sean replied. "You're a nurse, Mum. Please go talk to her."

Her son's appeal to her conscience too strong to resist, Kelley walked over to the woman and asked if she was okay. The woman said she was fine, but that she appreciated the gesture.

Sean was known, too, for his love of American flags, drawing them constantly with crayons, pencils, and markers and then handing them out to family, friends, and strangers. He was also known for a charitable side that showed early. In high school, moved by stories he'd heard on the radio of kids overcoming cancer, he went home one night and made a donation to the Jimmy Fund, which supports cancer research at Boston's Dana-Farber Cancer Institute. He set up an automatic withdrawal from his bank account, commencing a stream of gifts that would continue for the rest of his life.

After high school, Collier studied criminal justice at Salem State University, traveling to England to learn about rehabilitating offenders and researching the plight of Mexican women used as drug mules. He graduated from the university with honors in 2009. Tamerlan Tsarnaev partied with friends at Salem State around the same time, the first of two periods in which the men may have encountered each other—a potential link law enforcement officials would later decline to discuss. After college, Collier worked in information technology for the police department in Somerville, a dense, diverse city just north of Boston, but he longed to join the police ranks himself. He graduated from the MBTA Transit Police Academy in 2010, and then in January 2012 he got his first real police assignment, joining the security force of the Massachusetts Institute of Technology. He became one of nearly sixty officers charged with protecting the Cambridge campus and its roughly eleven thousand students. It didn't take long for Collier to build relationships within the MIT community. In a place that draws students, faculty, and visitors from every corner of the world, Collier had a knack for making foreigners feel welcomed and comfortable. "Sean was one of these guys who really looked at police work as a calling," said MIT police chief John DiFava.

Collier joined the MIT Outing Club and enjoyed climbing New Hampshire's Mount Washington, even in winter. For one "retro" hike, he donned plaid flannel and yodeled from the heights at the top of his lungs. He played on a local kickball team that called itself Kickhopopotamus, participating in a national tournament in Las Vegas. And he was active in Somerville boxing circles—the second instance in which he may have crossed paths with Tamerlan, who trained at one of the city's gyms for a time. Collier's dream was to become a police officer in Somerville, where he lived. And it looked promising. He had scored well on a civil service exam. Around Easter, in late March of 2013, he told his family he was going in for a final interview. Afterward he announced proudly that he had gotten the job and would be sworn in in June. The news was bittersweet for John DiFava. The MIT chief knew Collier's departure would be a big loss for his department, but he also knew Collier had been pining for a job like this. "I said, 'Sean, you owe me nothing. You've done a fine job for me,'" DiFava said. "I would never stand in the way of someone trying to do better for themselves. I was thrilled for him."

On the night of Thursday, April 18, Collier was nearing the end of his 3:00-to-11:15 P.M. shift. In the days after the marathon bombing, DiFava had ordered additional security for the MIT campus. Collier was stationed at the corner of Vassar and Main Streets, near Cambridge's Kendall Square, a typically placid neighborhood that served as Boston's unofficial headquarters for innovation and technology. Collier was positioned at a spot where drivers would sometimes take a chance, making an illegal shortcut through campus to avoid a red light. Putting an officer there both discouraged cutthroughs and provided a high-profile police presence for the MIT community, at a time when no gesture of reassurance was too much. Around 9:30 P.M., DiFava pulled his car next to Collier's cruiser.

The chief asked his young officer what he was up to.

"Just making sure everybody behaves," Collier told him.

The two men chatted easily for several minutes. And then DiFava pulled away.

Shortly before 10:30 P.M., Tamerlan and Dzhokhar Tsarnaev, their photos now plastered everywhere, drove undetected toward the MIT campus in the green Honda Civic. They had packed the car with five explosive devices, a Ruger P95 9mm semiautomatic handgun, additional ammunition, a machete, and a hunting knife. They approached Collier's cruiser from behind. As Collier sat behind the wheel, they ambushed him, shooting him five times at close range, twice in the head. An assassination. "He didn't stand a chance," said DiFava, who was home barely a half hour before getting the devastating news from his deputy. The two bombing suspects then sought to steal Collier's weapon but couldn't figure out how to remove it from its locking holster. Within minutes, the Tsarnaev brothers were gone, their attempts to add a gun to their stash having ended in failure.

As news of the shooting spread around campus, to the media, and to Boston-area police, the awful truth emerged. The beloved twenty-seven-year-old with big promise and a bigger heart, the man who loved his new black Ford F-150 truck, who loved country music, who paused at noon when Boston's country music station, WKLB-FM, played the national anthem, was gone. The grief, though, was accompanied by an even greater sense of urgency. After three quietly tense days of investigative work, the sirens were blaring again. The Tsarnaev brothers, five hours after their photos had been broadcast worldwide, had resumed their reign of terror—police officials knew it in their gut. The murder of a campus police officer was highly unusual. Surely it was connected, even if much of the public—assuming they were even still awake—wouldn't know of the link until morning.

Collier's death would be a violent prelude to a violent night, making the president's visit to Boston Thursday morning feel like a distant memory. State police colonel Tim Alben was in Springfield, in Western Massachusetts, when he got the call from one of his deputies. State troopers, he was told, were on the scene at MIT. Ed Davis had already gone to sleep. He awoke to a similar phone call. The commissioner got up, got dressed, grabbed his gun and his badge, and hustled out. He ordered police out in force on Boston streets. He wanted bars and hospitals on high alert. From the moment they heard the news, neither man had much doubt: The terrorists had struck again.

CHAPTER 11

"DEATH IS SO CLOSE TO ME"

Hell in a Mercedes

The man jumped out of his car. He approached Danny's passenger window, talking loud and fast, and rapped on the glass. Danny lowered the window. The man reached inside and opened the car door from the inside. He climbed in, shut the door, pointed a silver handgun at Danny, and demanded money. Danny, who had grown up in China, assumed that he was the victim of a classically American violent crime, a stickup. He told the man that he didn't carry much cash, but to take anything. He handed over $45 from inside the armrest. He gave the man his wallet. The man then asked Danny an unexpected question: Had he heard about the bombing at the Boston Marathon? Danny said he had. "I did that," the man replied, his voice full of pride. "And I just killed a policeman in Cambridge."

Danny's heart dropped. He had been following the news closely enough, had studied the surveillance images of the suspects. But he had not recognized Tamerlan Tsarnaev sitting inches away in the passenger seat, not thinking he was this skinny, this white. He couldn't believe what was happening. *How could this be possible?*

Danny thought. Tamerlan's instructions to him were simple: "Don't be stupid."

It had all begun with a text message. At work earlier that night, Danny—who asked to be identified only by his American nickname—had gotten a message from a friend. Nothing special, just a quick note, a simple hello. He was busy, so he didn't answer right away. He worked late, not getting out until 10:00 P.M. Afterward, he needed to unwind. So he took his black 2013 Mercedes-Benz ML350 out for a spin in the darkened city. Just him, his music, and the hum of a car he had come to love. It was his little ritual, his way to relax, his right arm usually on the wheel, his left resting on the door. His life, at that moment, had seemed ascendant: from a province in Central China, to graduate school at Northeastern University, to a start-up in Cambridge's Kendall Square, the hub of the Boston-area technology industry.

On this night, the Thursday after the marathon bombing, he tried to drive down to Boylston Street, but it was still closed. So he took a route that roughly tracked the Charles River, no destination in mind, eventually ending up on Brighton Avenue, in a dense neighborhood west of downtown, home to thousands of college students. Suddenly, he remembered: He'd never written his friend back. He pulled to the curb to text a reply. Just as he was starting to type, he saw, in his mirrors, an old sedan slam to a stop behind his Mercedes. It struck him as strange—the speed and suddenness seemed out of place. *People don't park like that*, the twenty-six-year-old thought to himself. *Maybe our cars had scratched and I didn't notice*, Danny thought. *Maybe the other driver wants to swap information.* It was nearly 11:00 P.M.

After Tamerlan got in, he ordered Danny to start driving—right on Fordham Road, right again on Commonwealth Avenue—the start of an achingly slow ninety-minute odyssey through the peaceful, sleepy streets of Greater Boston, the outside world oblivious to the unfolding terror inside the dark Mercedes. As the night deepened, Danny thought these were very likely his final minutes alive. He silently analyzed everything Tamerlan said and how he said it, mining for clues about where and when he might be killed. *I don't want to die*, he thought at one point. *I have a lot of dreams that haven't come true yet*. He privately gamed out the scenarios: Should he plot a white-knuckled escape from the car? Should he beg for mercy? Should he just wait it out, hoping he would eventually be let go?

"It's not so easy," Danny replied when Tamerlan first told him to start driving. He was nervous, his hands shaking. He could barely control the wheel, the car veering out of lane. Tamerlan, not wanting to draw attention, told him to relax. Drive like nothing happened, he told him in a calming voice. Play it cool. Danny's heart was pounding. *Just don't kill me*, he thought. *Don't hurt me*.

They continued west. Tamerlan asked Danny where he was from. "I'm Chinese," he said, thinking it might help to emphasize that he was not American.

"Okay, you're Chinese," Tamerlan said. "I'm a Muslim-American."

"Chinese are very friendly to Muslims!" Danny assured him. "We are so friendly to Muslims!"

As they talked, Danny cast himself as a recent immigrant with no friends and limited command of English. He apologized for his halting speech. In truth, he was hiding behind that self-portrait, trying to buy time to strategize. Trained as an engineer, he made scrupulous mental notes of street signs and passing details, even as he abided Tamerlan's command not to study his face.

"Don't look at me!" Tamerlan shouted at one point. "Do you remember my face?"

"No, no, I don't remember anything," he said.

Tamerlan laughed. "It's like white guys—they look at black guys and think all black guys look the same," he said. "And maybe you think all white guys look the same."

"Exactly," Danny said, though he thought nothing of the sort.

It was one of many moments in their strange conversational chess match, Danny playing up his outsider status and playing down his wealth—he claimed the car was older than it was, and he understated his lease payments—and Tamerlan trying to make Danny feel sufficiently at ease, so he wouldn't do anything to draw attention to the car. When Tamerlan asked him what he was doing in the United States, Danny didn't tell him he had a job, in part because he didn't want Tamerlan to think he had any close relationships with people—people who might grow worried about Danny's whereabouts and call the police, which he feared might drive Tamerlan to do something rash. Better to figure out his own way out of this, Danny thought. So he told Tamerlan he had just finished a graduate degree at Northeastern and been in the United States only eighteen months. "Oh," Tamerlan said. "That's why your English is not very good." It seemed to help that Tamerlan even had trouble with Danny's pronunciation of the word "China." In truth, Danny had come to the United States in 2009 for a master's degree, graduated in January 2012, and returned to China to await a work visa. He came back in early 2013, leasing the Mercedes, moving into a high-rise with two Chinese friends, and diving into his work at a start-up.

Eventually Tamerlan put the gun on the armrest, satisfied that Danny was behaving as directed. He asked for the PIN for Danny's ATM card. Danny contemplated giving him a fake one, but thought better of it. When he told Tamerlan his PIN, Tamerlan asked him if the number was his birthday. It was really the birthday of Danny's close friend, but Danny didn't want him to think that he had any friends, lest Tamerlan think someone was waiting for him. So he told Tamerlan it was his girlfriend's birthday, and that his girlfriend lived in China.

"Does anyone care about you?" Tamerlan asked him.

"There is no one who cares about me," Danny replied.

Tamerlan wanted to know about Danny's roommate: Were they friends? "No," Danny assured him, even though he was quite close to his roommate, a woman from China he'd met on his first trip to the United States. They had sat next to each other on the plane. She had gone to Northeastern University, too. Danny was driving fast. Tamerlan asked him to slow down, not wanting a police car to notice them. Directed to a quiet neighborhood in East Watertown, Danny pulled up as instructed on an unfamiliar side street, steering to the curb behind a parked Subaru. Tamerlan got out of the car, taking the key from the ignition, to prevent Danny from speeding away. He ordered Danny into the passenger seat, making it clear he would shoot him if Danny attempted an escape. Danny hopped out of his car, walked around the back, and got in on the passenger side.

A sedan had stopped behind them. It wasn't until now that Danny realized that the car, a green Honda Civic, had been following them the whole time. A man got out and approached the Mercedes. The passenger door was still open, and the man was standing right next to him. This time, Danny had no trouble recognizing the face: It was the skinnier, floppy-haired suspect in the photos and videos released by investigators earlier that evening. He didn't know either of their names yet, but he was face-to-face with Tamerlan's younger brother, Dzhokhar. For several minutes, with Danny in the passenger seat, the brothers transferred heavy objects from the smaller car into Danny's SUV. *Luggage*, Danny thought, hearing four or five pieces being loaded inside. *Maybe they're trying to run away.* That's how the script would play out if this were a movie, he figured. Tamerlan got behind the wheel. Dzhokhar climbed in the backseat. Danny's hopes for release were dashed. He was a hostage; he'd better get used to it.

Tamerlan asked Danny how to operate the transmission, and Danny showed him. They pulled away, cruising over side roads in silence. They turned onto a dead-end street. A dread came over Danny. *Is he going to kill me there?* he thought as he looked ahead at the darkness where the road stopped. But Tamerlan made a U-turn and kept going through the quiet neighborhood, no other cars around, no people, no lights. Tamerlan had told Danny that both brothers had guns.

"Are you going to hurt me?" Danny finally asked him.

"No, relax, man," Tamerlan said. "I'm not going to hurt you."

Tamerlan explained that they planned to drop him off somewhere remote, and that he would probably have to walk several miles to find anybody. If he was lucky, Tamerlan said, someone would come pick him up. Danny was hardly relieved, though. He didn't quite buy it. If it were him, he thought, he wouldn't do that. Surely the brothers knew

Danny would call the police as soon as he could. Why put themselves at risk of capture? *They have already killed a lot of people*, Danny thought. *It wouldn't matter if they killed one more.* Running through his mind were scenes from the life he might not live to see: his hopes for the burgeoning start-up, and the girl he secretly liked in New York. *Oh my God*, he thought, *I have no chance to meet her again.*

Death, Danny thought at one point, *is so close to me.*

No, Danny concluded. He couldn't count on being released. He needed to escape. But how? They continued on to Watertown center so Dzhokhar could withdraw money from a Bank of America ATM using Danny's card. Dzhokhar got out of the car. Danny, shivering from fear but claiming to be cold, asked for his jacket, which was in the backseat. "Can I have my coat?" he asked Tamerlan, thinking it might offer a chance to secretly unfasten his seat belt. His only shot at freedom, he thought, would come while one of the brothers was out of the car. Tamerlan said no. A few moments later, Danny asked again, almost begging. "I'm really cold—can I have my jacket, please?" This time Tamerlan agreed, turning into the backseat to grab it. He checked the pockets and handed it to Danny. Danny unfastened his seat belt to put the jacket on. *I should run*, he thought, though all he could see were locked storefronts. Danny knew Tamerlan expected him to quickly put his belt back on. Danny tried to do it behind his back. The buckle clicked.

"Don't be stupid," Tamerlan said, sensing even without looking what Danny was up to. "Do it right. Do what you should do."

"Sorry," Danny said meekly, obeying his captor's orders.

It was one of Danny's lowest moments. Not only had a chance to run evaporated, now Tamerlan knew what he was thinking. Surely he would be on high alert now. Escaping would be more difficult. Dzhokhar returned to the car a few moments later. They continued west on Route 20, in the direction of Waltham and Interstate 95, passing a police station. Danny tried to send telepathic messages to the officers inside. He imagined dropping and rolling from the moving car. He felt hopeless.

.   .   .

Back in Cambridge, cops from Boston and surrounding communities descended on the area around MIT, heartbroken to learn of Sean Collier's murder and now doubly motivated to hunt down the killers. Some went directly to the scene of the shooting, but many others fanned out to nearby streets, hoping to catch sight of something suspicious. Ed Davis met the MIT police chief at Massachusetts General Hospital, where Collier had been taken, and called in a Boston Police "critical incident" team to help Collier's family. Davis sent ballistics and K9 specialists to MIT to assist state police in combing the scene for evidence. Police also chased a potential tip, which turned out to be a false alarm, to a hotel in Dorchester. A few miles west, the Mercedes cruised through the night, no one wise to who was inside.

Danny studied the brothers as they drove, developing his own sense of them. Tamerlan seemed the bad guy, threatening and menacing. Dzhokhar came off as friendlier, chattier—asking questions, talking about music and iPhones, typical college-kid stuff. In the car, the discussion turned to how much money Danny had in his bank account, what his credit limit was, what year his Mercedes was, and whether he could take the SIM card out of his iPhone. *He doesn't look like a terrorist*, Danny thought. He overheard them speak in a foreign language—"Manhattan" the only intelligible word to him—and then ask in English if Danny's car could be driven out of state. "What do you mean?" Danny said, confused. "Like New York," one brother said. But if the two fugitives were planning a dash out of town, they were remarkably slow to move, almost aimless in their actions. They didn't seem headed for anywhere in particular. Three days out from the crime of the century in Boston, they displayed remarkably little urgency.

The tank nearly empty, they stopped at a gas station. The pumps were closed. After pulling away, Tamerlan asked Danny to turn on the radio and show them how to use it. The older brother then quickly flipped through stations, seemingly avoiding the news. He asked if Danny had any CDs. No, he replied. Doubling back, they returned to the Watertown neighborhood where Dzhokhar had joined them. Dzhokhar hopped out and seemed to fetch a CD from the other car. FAIRFIELD STREET, Danny read on the sign, thinking, *Maybe I'll be alive and I can tell the policemen that.* The brothers popped in an instrumental CD that Danny thought sounded Middle Eastern, believing it to be religious music.

Just before midnight, Danny's iPhone buzzed. A text from his roommate. Tamerlan got nervous; he demanded to know who it was and what the text said. Danny said it was his roommate, asking in Chinese where he was and telling him that there had been gunshots at MIT. Tamerlan laughed. "Oh, something happened in Cambridge?" he said. Barking at Danny for instructions, Tamerlan used an English-to-Chinese app to text a clunky reply. "I am sick. I am sleeping at a friend's place tonight." But it came out garbled, not the way one would ordinarily respond. The roommate texted back and asked if he was sure he was okay. *If you're not,* she wrote, *let me know. If you are,* she said, *you don't have to write back.*

About ten minutes after the first text, Danny's phone rang. It was his other roommate, suspicious about Danny's cryptic replies. Tamerlan was furious. "Who is this?" he demanded. "Who is calling you?" He picked up the gun, pointed it at Danny, and told him to answer. "If you say a single word in Chinese," Tamerlan said, "I will kill you right now." He ordered Danny to tell his roommate, in English, that he was sleeping at a friend's place. Danny didn't answer the call in time, but the roommate quickly called back. Danny was nervous. He was praying. He knew a small mistake could cost him his life. The roommate asked where he was. Danny didn't even say hello. He said he would be sleeping out tonight. "Why are you speaking in English?" his roommate asked. "Are you okay?"

"I have to go," he said. "I'm sorry, I have to go."

"Okay," his roommate said.

Click.

"Good boy," Tamerlan told him. "Good job."

Now more than an hour into their meandering journey, the brothers drove along the Charles River, back toward Boston, in search of gas. Crossing the Charles into Cambridge, the SUV came upon two gas stations, a Shell station on the left and a Mobil on the right. Tamerlan steered into the Shell station, pulling the right side of the car up to the gas pumps. Dzhokhar got out to fill up using Danny's credit card. Danny, back in familiar territory, began thinking again about an escape, especially with Dzhokhar out of the car.

Dzhokhar quickly knocked on the window. "Cash only," he said. Danny knew this was good news. He knew Dzhokhar would have to walk into the store, away from the car. Dzhokhar asked Danny how much money it took to fill the tank. Danny said he didn't know. Tamerlan told his brother to buy $50 worth and peeled off the money.

Danny watched Dzhokhar head inside, trying to decide if this was his moment. Not only was he now alone with Tamerlan, but the doors were unlocked. Tamerlan had unlocked them to let Dzhokhar out and had never bothered with the relocking. But Danny, employing the cool calculus of an engineer, knew he had to still do several things almost instantaneously: unfasten his seat belt, open the door, and jump out. He rehearsed the sequence in his head. He knew that if he wasn't quick enough, Tamerlan would kill him on the spot. *This is your best chance*, Danny thought to himself. *It's your moment.* His fear, the image he played on a loop in his head, was that they would drop him off at some distant spot, tell him to run, and then shoot him in the back as he fled. Unless he could get away, he convinced himself, this would be his fate.

Even without looking at him directly, Danny could see that Tamerlan was preoccupied. He had stashed the gun in the driver's door and was fidgeting with a GPS device. Danny collected his thoughts and counted quickly to four in his head, allowing himself one more integer than the typical three count, given the gravity of what he was about to do.

One. Two. Three. Four. Go.

In a flurry, Danny released the seat belt with his left hand and opened the car door with his right. He scrambled out, slamming the door behind him. He felt Tamerlan try to grab him, Tamerlan's hand brushing against his. But Danny had tucked his left arm into his body. Tamerlan couldn't get a grip. Tamerlan reacted fast, but Danny had him beat.

"Fuck!" he heard Tamerlan shout. "Fuck!"

Danny sprinted between the passenger side of the Mercedes and the gas pumps and darted toward River Street, not looking back, drawn to the lights of the Mobil station on the other side. He didn't know if it was open or not. He prayed it was. The angle he was running at, he figured, would make it difficult for Tamerlan to shoot him. He glanced quickly to see if any cars were coming but barely gave it any thought.

He dashed into the Mobil station, talking rapidly at the clerk behind the counter. Danny implored him to call the police. "They are terrorists!" he said. "They have guns! They're trying to kill me!"

Danny begged him to lock the door, but he wouldn't. The clerk was skeptical.

"Please call 911!" Danny pleaded, crouching behind the counter. "Please call 911!"

The clerk then heeded his cry and picked up the phone. Danny ran into the storage room as the man dialed, shut the door behind him, and sat down. The clerk brought the phone to him, passing it to him through a crack in the door. Danny was terrified. If the brothers stormed in, he was cornered. He feared they would come and shoot him dead at any second. The police dispatcher on the line told Danny to relax, to take a deep breath. "Come quickly," he said. "Please." A few minutes later, there was a knock at the door.

It was the attendant. "Sir," he said, "the police are here." Danny walked outside the room, elated to see the swirling blue lights. He told the officers everything—that they were the bombing suspects, that Tamerlan had even boasted about what they had done, and that they had guns. The police asked if Danny knew where they were headed. Maybe back to Watertown, Danny said. He knew there was an easy way to find out. Danny told the police that not only was his iPhone still in the Mercedes, but that his car had a GPS and roadside assistance system they could track. Danny told them what it was called—mbrace—and gave them his full name and address, so they could identify the car. Police called Mercedes from the store.

In the hours ahead, police would laud Danny's quick thinking, saying his escape had helped avert further mayhem. Indeed, for the first time since Monday's bombing, investigators, even if they weren't certain of the brothers' names, now had a way to track the suspects' location in real time. Tamerlan and Dzhokhar were still on the loose—armed, dangerous, their intentions unclear—but the trail was finally hot. All of Boston—much of the world, really—wanted them caught, wanted the week's terror to end. But the brothers weren't finished yet. Not even close.

CHAPTER 12

SHOWDOWN

Bullets in the dark

he report crackled across the radio in Joe Reynolds's squad car. "Wanted for carjacking that occurred in Cambridge, possibly related to the Cambridge incident." It was the voice of a Massachusetts State Police dispatcher. The Tsarnaev brothers had murdered Sean Collier. They had kidnapped Danny at gunpoint, then recklessly let him escape. No one knew where their plans would lead them next. But police were desperate to stop them, to put an end to a terrifying week. The dispatcher relayed Danny's frantic account: that the marathon bombers had taken him hostage, threatened to kill him, stolen his car, and were on their way to attack New York next. In fact, the stolen black Mercedes was nowhere near New York. Pings from the vehicle's global positioning system showed that the Tsarnaevs were less than five miles from their own apartment in Cambridge—and very near Reynolds.

Reynolds had spent seven years as a police officer in Watertown, an unpretentious community northwest of Boston known as a melting pot of immigrants, young professionals, and working-class families. He typically worked nights, and his midnight-to-8:00 A.M. shift on Friday, April 19, had barely begun. At 12:42 A.M., the voice on the radio issued a warning: The stolen car was on Dexter Avenue, a slumbering neighborhood of tidy houses and modest duplexes, where many residents decorated their homes with flower boxes. Reynolds turned onto Dexter, heading northbound. He drove a couple of blocks and then came upon the brothers, whose two vehicles, the stolen Mercedes and the green Honda Civic, were parked on the side of the road, facing south. He locked eyes with Tamerlan as he passed.

"I have the car," Reynolds said into the radio. "Do you want me to stop it?"

"Don't stop the car until I get there," the patrol supervisor, Sergeant John MacLellan, replied. "Wait for help to come."

MacLellan raced to the scene. Reynolds swung a U-turn. The brothers, driving both cars, pulled away from the curb and turned left from Dexter onto Laurel Street. Reynolds followed cautiously. Tamerlan and Dzhokhar then came to an abrupt stop after about one hundred feet, one behind the other, and hopped out. Tamerlan walked toward Reynolds's police car, raised his arm, and began shooting from a distance of several houses away. Bullets cut through the darkness, dinging off the cruiser. Reynolds ducked below his dashboard and jammed the car into reverse, trying to gain distance from his attackers. As he peeled back about thirty yards, he radioed to dispatch: "Shots fired! Shots fired!"

For more than three days, a coalition of local, state, and federal law enforcement agencies had been hunting day and night for the marathon bombers, eager to finally put Greater Boston at ease. Now the showdown had arrived, in a town where police rarely had cause to fire their guns outside the practice range. Police officers, including those guarding the crime scene at MIT, sped toward the fight. They knew nothing of the brothers' arsenal, which included a handgun and at least two kinds of homemade bombs. Dozens of cruisers lit up the night with their flashing blue and white lights. They converged on the bridges over the Charles River, all booking toward the action. With little time for police to coordinate, the scene would quickly turn chaotic. Officers flooded in, many from outside Watertown, and bullets began flying in many directions. The crossfire would prove nearly fatal to one of their own.

As MacLellan rounded the corner in his brand-new black-and-white Ford Expedition, a bullet pierced the windshield, buzzing so close to his face that it lodged in his headrest. He took cover behind the engine as he tried to wrestle his semiautomatic AR-15 out of its locked case. When he couldn't get it, he put the Expedition back into drive, jumped out, and let it roll toward the brothers as a diversion, which he thought might buy him time to take cover or get a better shot at the assailants. There was little refuge on that stretch of Laurel Street; the lone tree nearby was barely a foot in diameter. MacLellan dashed behind it. A third Watertown officer, Miguel Colon, had pulled up to the scene. He turned on the spotlight of his police car. A bullet blew it out almost immediately.

By now, Laurel Street slumbered no more. Neighbors awoke to a battle so improbable they assumed the commotion had to be something far more benign. Peter Kehayias, a sixty-five-year-old restaurant chef, figured it was kids playing with firecrackers. He opened a window in the TV room of his two-family house.

"Get the hell out of here and go to your own neighborhood!" he shouted.

"Get inside and shut your window!" an officer yelled back. The Tsarnaevs were right there in the street.

"Give up—there's no way out," Kehayias heard an officer yell at the brothers. "Give up."

Tamerlan offered a taunt in return. "You want more?" he said. "I give you more."

Kehayias's wife, Loretta, a special-education teacher in Cambridge, picked up the phone and called 911: "Do you people realize there is a cop out here and there are two guys? They're shooting at him!"

The reply was immediate: "Yes, we know, lady." *Click.*

Dzhokhar helped Tamerlan load a fresh clip into a gun. Next he reached inside the car for a duffel bag. The battle had just begun, and now it took an ominous turn. The brothers began hurling homemade explosives at police, including pipe bombs and then something more alarming. Dzhokhar pulled out a larger pressure cooker bomb—the kind of device he had used to murderous effect on Marathon Day—and tossed it toward police. The explosion shook the neighborhood and set off a bright yellow flash, momentarily turning midnight darkness to day. Lizzy Floyd was crouching with her husband beneath a bedroom window on the second floor of their home. The force of the explosion knocked a framed photograph of a New Hampshire harborside scene off her shelf.

Jeff Pugliese, a thirty-three-year veteran of the Watertown police force and a firearms instructor, had recently gone off duty when he learned about the firefight over his radio. He sped to the scene in his family's minivan, jumped out of the car, and ran to the back of the houses on Laurel Street. He hopped a fence or two and then circled back, creeping down a narrow patch of grass mere feet from where Tamerlan was firing away. The two took shots at each other, nothing but two old Mercedes in a driveway between them. Peter Kehayias feared for Pugliese's life. "Jesus, he is going to get killed," he said to his wife. But Pugliese proved to be a much better shot than Tamerlan. Pugliese believed he hit Tamerlan a number of times. Tamerlan didn't hit a thing, spraying bullets into the side of a house before seeming to run out of ammunition. He threw his gun at Pugliese, hitting him in the left arm. Tamerlan tried to run. Pugliese, with the aid of other officers, chased him down and tackled him in the street. Tamerlan, in a rage, continued to struggle, but Pugliese and MacLellan pinned him on the ground. As they reached for handcuffs, Reynolds looked up to see the lights of the Mercedes moving toward him. Dzhokhar had jumped in the SUV. Tires screeching, he had spun around and was barreling straight at the spot where the officers wrestled with his brother.

"Sarge, Sarge!" Reynolds yelled. "Look out—he's coming!"

MacLellan jumped off. Pugliese grabbed Tamerlan's belt and tried to pull him out of the way.

"Jeff! Jeff!" MacLellan shouted at Pugliese. "Get off!"

The car blew by. Everyone was sure Pugliese had been hit. But he had rolled clear at the last moment. The car missed him by inches.

Tamerlan was not so lucky. Dzhokhar ran straight over his older brother, dragging him some thirty feet down the street as he fled west in Danny's Mercedes. The headlight beams bounced up and down as the car rolled across the body with a sickening thump. Tamerlan was left lying on his stomach, clinging to the final moments of his life. He tried to lift up his head. Blood pooled around his body, streak marks visible on the street where the SUV had dragged him. Pugliese ran over, put cuffs on him, and pressed a foot into his back. Then he called for an ambulance. At long last, Tamerlan was theirs. Other officers chased Dzhokhar into the night. But with the gunfire in the street finally gone quiet, police now faced another critical concern.

"Gunshots. Officer down."

The alert pierced the silence of the firehouse just before 1:00 A.M. Watertown firefighters Patrick Menton and Jimmy Caruso—both trained as emergency medical technicians—jumped into an ambulance and roared toward Laurel Street, Caruso at the wheel, Menton in the passenger seat. They said little as they drove. "Officer down" were about the most urgent two words imaginable. Even more so for Menton. His younger brother Tim was a Watertown police officer. Menton wondered: *Is my brother in trouble?*

"Get some rubber gloves out," Caruso told his partner as they raced toward the area. "Get ready."

EMTs are instructed never to enter an unsecured crime scene. This lesson is drilled into them: If you're hurt, you're useless. But as their rig rolled down Laurel Street, Caruso and Menton tore up that rulebook. In the chaos of the crossfire, Richard "Dic" Donohue, a thirty-three-year-old police officer with the Massachusetts Bay Transportation Authority, had been shot in the thigh. "I'm hit!" Donohue yelled when the bullet struck him. His partner tackled him, to get him out of the line of fire, and then tried to find the wound and apply pressure. Two Harvard University police officers, Ryan Stanton and Michael Rea, rushed over with tourniquets to stanch the flow of blood. A Boston cop, Ricky Moriarty, began doing chest compressions.

Donohue's condition deteriorated quickly. He was at grave risk of bleeding to death. "We're losing him! We're losing him!" one neighbor heard desperate voices screaming. "Get an ambulance here now!" A dazed Jeffrey Ryan stumbled out on his porch on Dexter Avenue to witness the frantic efforts to save Donohue in his driveway. Police asked for towels, and he and his wife rushed some out. "We need to get him out of here!" officers shouted in the darkness. "He's bleeding bad! We need to go!"

An awful coincidence had unfolded: Over the course of a few hours, Sean Collier and Dic Donohue, friends, former neighbors, and classmates from the MBTA Transit Police Academy, had both been shot—one fatally, the other barely hanging on. Like Collier, Donohue had grown up north of Boston, in the well-kept suburb of Winchester. He was an avid runner, competing in cross-country and track in high school. He graduated from Virginia Military Institute in 2002, majoring in history. He served as a US Navy officer before joining the MBTA police force in October 2010. Earlier in 2013, he had received a commendation for helping to save someone else's life, having rushed into the Chinatown T station to stem the profuse bleeding of a stabbing victim. He and his wife, Kim, had a six-month-old son, Richie. As it happened, Donohue's grandfather several generations removed, Lawrence Brignolia, had won the 1899 Boston Marathon, the first Massachusetts man to do so.

Late Thursday night, Donohue had been one of the officers responding to the scene of Collier's murder, hitting the lights in his cruiser as soon as he heard that an officer was down. Once he found out what happened, he sent a few solemn text messages to friends, breaking the tragic news: It was Sean. Like other officers, he then raced to Watertown once reports of the firefight started streaming in. He got to the scene, jumped out of his car, and began firing alongside other police. Then he was hit.

With Donohue down, Caruso went to the rear of the ambulance to retrieve the stretcher, but officers had already carried Donohue from the driveway and put him in the back. The stretcher never left the truck. Donohue had a three-quarter-inch wound at the top of his right thigh, a single bullet having severed his femoral artery. He was in cardiac arrest. He had no pulse. His eyes were open. His color was gray. "He was deceased" is how Caruso would describe it later. No one by his side, though, was going to let him die. Caruso ripped Donohue's blood-soaked pants apart, desperate to find the source of the bleeding. He grabbed two multitrauma dressings, big gauze pads, and pushed them into the wound. Menton provided breathing for the breathless patient, using a "BVM," a bag valve mask, which sent puffs of air into Donohue's lungs. Alongside them, State Trooper Christopher Dumont, who had jumped aboard, began performing CPR. "We need a driver! We need a driver!" someone shouted. Moments later the ambulance lurched forward.

Caruso and Menton were so consumed with their tasks that both assumed the other was driving. Behind the wheel in the front of the cab was Menton's brother Tim, the Watertown police officer who moments before had been involved in the shoot-out, a bullet having pierced his windshield. Tim Menton didn't really know how to drive the ambulance, but he figured it out, speeding toward Mount Auburn Hospital in Cambridge, the closest emergency room available, arriving within minutes. His actions proved to be critical. "If we didn't have three people in the back of the truck, I don't know how it would have worked," Pat Menton said. "Because we were each doing a vital thing to save his life. We had to go." Caruso kept pressure on Donohue's wound at the hospital, letting go only when Donohue was wheeled into surgery. By the time doctors got to him, he barely had any blood left in his body. It took them forty-five minutes to get his heart beating again. The Menton brothers reunited in the hospital parking lot—Pat hadn't realized that it was his brother driving the rig. It turned out that Tim, before climbing into the ambulance, had been one of Donohue's first caregivers, using a towel to apply pressure on his wound. It was there in the parking lot that they smelled it—the awful, metallic odor. Tim hadn't known how to release the ambulance's emergency brake. They'd driven nearly two miles to the hospital with it on.

Donohue's wife, Kim, was asleep in their home around 1:30 A.M.

when she was awoken by her son's cries. "The baby just went nuts—just was hysterical," she would later tell *CBS News*. As she tended to him, the doorbell rang. She opened the door to see Steven O'Hara, a sergeant with the MBTA police. She knew instantly what his presence meant. "You are my worst nightmare," she told him, her mind racing. "Tell me if Dic is dead, right now," she said. "Don't walk in this house; don't come past that door. Tell me if Dic is dead." He was still alive, O'Hara told her. But only just. When she got to Mount Auburn Hospital, they had a priest waiting. They handed her Dic's phone, his badge, his wedding ring. After his eight hours of surgery, she was finally allowed to see him. He looked, to his wife, like he was dead. She pulled the doctors aside. "He has to come through," she implored. "It's not a question. You can't come back in this room and tell me anything else."

The rapidly unfolding Watertown battle, with the unique threat of homemade bombs and the crush of police, gave officers little chance to orient themselves at the scene in a coherent, strategic manner. Police converged on the Tsarnaevs from multiple points, many or all of them firing away; one account put the total number of rounds discharged at roughly 250. Just whose bullet it was that nearly killed Dic Donohue was not immediately clear—that would be up to authorities to determine over the ensuing months. Witness accounts in the days after the firefight, though, suggested that he was likely hit by friendly fire. Jane Dyson, who lived 140 feet away, reported seeing Donohue hit as police trained their guns on the black Mercedes, in the final volley of shots as Dzhokhar fled. Police at that point were the only ones doing the shooting—Tamerlan had already thrown his gun at Officer Jeff Pugliese. At least two other witnesses backed up Dyson's account.

As bad as Donohue's wound was, the night nearly got much worse for police. Amid the chaos, there was a report that one of the suspects was attempting an escape in a black pickup truck. A short while later, a state trooper saw a black pickup near the scene. Evidently thinking it fit the profile, and without waiting to be sure, he raked the vehicle with bullets, emptying the clip of his M4 gun. But the black pickup carried two police officers, one from Boston and the other a state trooper, who were responding to the call like everyone else. The bullets, which left an S-shaped trail on the truck, somehow went between them, missing both men, but not by much. "It was very, very bad," said Boston Police commissioner Ed Davis. In a separate incident nearby, a bullet grazed another transit police officer in the buttocks. "The control of fire in a situation like that is something we really have to work on," Davis said. In a military encounter, he said, you typically know where the good guys are, and where the bad guys are. "In this particular case, cops converged on that scene from three hundred sixty degrees. They hear the gunshots, that's how they locate where the action is. But when they get there, they're in a circle. And a circle ambush is deadly to everybody."

The fog of confusion extended beyond the immediate scene of the firefight. Several blocks away, officers at one point stopped a car they thought was suspicious. The police activity around the car only attracted more police, including Dan Linskey, the Boston Police superintendent in chief, who assumed this was where the fight was. Believing the man in the car to be hostile, officers had him on the ground and were stripping his clothes off to check for explosives. He was cuffed. "It's him. It's him," someone said. "He's not cooperating." Police at this point were lined up on both sides of the man's car, dozens of guns pointed at him. Linskey issued orders to get the man's ID and run his license plate. It took several minutes for police to determine that the man lived nearby and was not one of the suspects. Linskey and other officers then had to run several blocks to reach the actual scene. There were a "significant amount of resources that were shunted" to the wrong spot, Davis said.

As Watertown Police chief Edward Deveau said afterward, nearly all of the police officers in Watertown early Friday morning were from out of town. Most didn't know the streets, didn't know the neighborhoods. All they knew was that two bad guys were nearby trying to kill officers with bullets and homemade bombs. "Everybody's doing the best they can," Deveau said. "But it's chaotic because of what's going on." No one doubted that assessment. No one faulted police for putting their lives on the line to go after the guys everyone so badly wanted—even more so following the cold-blooded execution of one of their own. It became clear, though, that the response early Friday held some lessons to be learned for next time—that as brave and savvy as some of the police actions were, there were also, in retrospect, some grave mistakes. Thanks to the work of his fellow officers, firefighters, and emergency room doctors and nurses, Dic Donohue had made it. But it had been way too close.

Max Kerman, twenty-five, was getting ready for bed as Dzhokhar careened down Spruce Street in the Mercedes. A former high school football and basketball standout, Kerman heard the distant gunfire and stepped out on the second-floor porch to investigate. Just then the car came into sight, flying up a hill, its front end damaged, one headlight out, and the passenger-side windows blown out, Dzhokhar not bothering to slow at a tight curve. About forty-five seconds later, Kerman estimated, an unmarked police cruiser came up the hill with lights blazing, then slowed in front of his house. Kerman pointed down the street and screamed at the cop: "Keep going! Keep going!" Having left his older brother in a heap, Dzhokhar had smashed into Joe Reynolds's squad car and then made it only about a half mile away before he dumped the Mercedes and took off on foot. It would prove to be enough of a head start. As police chased after him, they were slowed by three things: the rush to save Donohue's life, parked police cars clogging the road, and fears of unexploded bombs in the abandoned SUV. Within minutes, the uncommon brilliance of the early morning firefight had given way to a pursuit through the darkness.

When officers came upon the battered Mercedes, they approached it warily. They didn't know if Dzhokhar was still hiding inside, or whether he had booby-trapped it with explosive devices. Eventually, they determined that no one was in the car and that it posed no risk. "He probably didn't even realize how effective he was being," Davis said. "They were all focused on the car, and he got into backyards and managed to hide out." Scores of police swarmed the neighborhood and began checking houses. They did a room-by-room search of Austin Lin's house on Spruce Street before evacuating Lin and his grandmother to the police station. Residents of six other nearby houses were hustled out in bathrobes and sweatpants—most of them clutching cell phones—for the night. "They had SWAT teams, dogs, and the National Guard going through backyards and checking basements and garages," said Mary Karaguesian, who watched from her home. "But they didn't find him." Police thoroughly swept Kerman's backyard several times.

Dzhokhar enjoyed an added advantage: He was able to exploit out-of-town officers' unfamiliarity with Watertown. "It wasn't like everybody just watched him go down the street," Deveau said. "One of the disadvantages that we have is the rest of the officers aren't familiar [with the area]. We know Watertown. My guys know Watertown. So when they're yelling he's on whatever street, ninety-five percent of the people that are here—if not more—have no idea what that street means." As the minutes ticked by, there was a dreadful sense that Dzhokhar was going to elude them, that he was slipping away. "You're in the middle of perhaps the most stressful set of crimes you will ever deal with as a police officer," said Tim Alben, the state police colonel. "One person on the scene is dead or dying; a police officer sustained life-threatening injuries. And in the middle of this, this kid has fled into the neighborhood."

Police would later recover only a handgun and a BB gun from the shooting scene. In the heat of the pursuit, though, officers assumed Dzhokhar was armed, possibly with a suicide vest. "They didn't want to see an officer blown up," Deveau said. Search teams with dogs were called in—Boston police had dogs, as did the state police, local departments, and federal agencies. But with so many people around, it was difficult for them to pick up the scent. Officers found blood and urine at a nearby house, but still, the trail dried up. One bloodhound sent officers in the entirely wrong direction. Dzhokhar had smashed his cell phones so he couldn't be tracked. Police decided to pull back, regroup, and devise a fresh plan. After all the drama, and getting so close to capturing Dzhokhar, the manhunt was back on.

Within a half hour of Dzhokhar's escape, Boston Police superintendent William Evans was in Watertown. It had already been a long day for the thirty-two-year veteran of the Boston Police Department, who earlier in the week had completed the Boston Marathon himself. Evans was assigned to secure the area where the firefight had just ended. "It was an ugly scene," he said. Indeed, this quiet corner of Watertown became one of the most complex crime scenes in the history of the Massachusetts State Police. More than 250 shell casings and several IEDs—exploded and not—would be recovered throughout the neighborhood. Investigators collected the remains of a pressure cooker bomb that had detonated into the side of a parked car. A stop sign riddled with bullet holes was removed from one corner. Houses were pockmarked. Laurel Street had to be evacuated. An entire community had been traumatized. And relief was still nowhere in sight.

Dr. David Schoenfeld was reading on his couch early Friday morning when the gunfire and explosions erupted near his Watertown home. Anticipating massive casualties, he told his wife good-bye and bolted out the door to the hospital where he worked—Beth Israel Deaconess Medical Center, in the heart of Boston's medical district. Less than ten minutes after he arrived in the emergency department, his instincts were proven right. The wounded man who came in, however, would test the sacred credo by which doctors and nurses operated— that your first task is always to save the patient's life, regardless of who the patient is.

At about 1:20 A.M., EMTs wheeled in Tamerlan Tsarnaev, handcuffed, unconscious, and near death. His tattered clothes had already been cut away. More than a dozen police officers surrounded him. Emergency crews were performing cardiopulmonary resuscitation on him. His injuries were severe—burns on his right shoulder, multiple gunshot wounds, and a gaping slash on his torso. Trauma teams had been alerted that one or more people injured in the gun battle, possibly a suspect, or a police officer, or both, were on the way, and they wore protective gowns and gloves. They checked Tamerlan for radioactivity with a Geiger counter—a rarely used protocol, but one that felt appropriate here—but they found none. "I don't think people were worried for their safety," Schoenfeld said. But "we knew this was not a normal night for trauma."

Doctors placed a breathing tube in Tamerlan's throat and tubes in his chest to release pressure from his lungs. Schoenfeld helped coordinate the efforts to save Tamerlan's life, grabbing a tray with instruments for the team to use to cut open his chest and check for heart damage. But Tamerlan had lost massive amounts of blood from his wounds and was suffering cardiac and respiratory arrest. Doctors could not revive him. They declared him dead at 1:35 A.M., about fifteen minutes after he was brought in.

His death meant that somewhere, hiding in the cold darkness of Watertown, Dzhokhar was left with a new reality. He had helped kill his older brother. Whatever he would do now, whatever remained of his violent mission, it was now his to carry out alone.

CHAPTER 13

DISQUIET

In a silent city, the hunt begins anew

awn broke Friday on a still-life city. Streets empty. Sidewalks lonely. Stoops vacant. Businesses dark. Houses closed up. A transit system shut down. The clamorous night, with the frenzy over the terrorists' photos, the killing of Sean Collier, and then the clash in Watertown, had given way to a silent morning, eerie and frightening in its tranquility. It was the last day of school vacation week. The weather looked promising. A perfect day to hit the playground, to ready a backyard garden for spring. Vacationing families were on their way home, their fridges empty, planning to pick up takeout for dinner. But this was not that kind of Friday. At daybreak, Dzhokhar Tsarnaev, his name now becoming known to the public, was still unaccounted for. With the strain of the week's drama weighing heavily, and conviction mounting that the crisis needed to end, authorities turned to a radical plan: locking the whole city down until the second suspect was in custody. They knew the idea would be controversial—a major American city going dark to smoke out a wayward nineteen-year-old. Who had ever considered such a thing?

Could it even be done? And yet no one would accept Dzhokhar slipping away again. No one could abide more violence.

From the first moments after the shoot-out, as Dzhokhar's trail
went cold, Governor Deval Patrick conferred hourly with aides about
the status of the hunt. By about 4:00 A.M., with no arrest at hand and
the MBTA bus and train system about to start up for the day, Patrick
and top law enforcement officials had a decision to make. Having
ditched the Mercedes SUV, Dzhokhar was believed to be on foot.
Watertown was now overrun with cops, so it was all but impossible
for him to escape by car. That left public transportation: What if he
managed to sneak onto a bus, or a train? Then he could get anywhere
he wanted. Police had established a security perimeter in Watertown,
around the area where Dzhokhar had slipped away. Patrick and law
enforcement leaders devised what seemed like a prudent plan. They
would ask residents within the perimeter to "shelter in place" while
SWAT teams conducted house-by-house searches. They would sus-
pend T service through Watertown. And they would ask people in
surrounding communities to remain vigilant.

But as the governor was on his way to make that announcement,
he began receiving reports of suspicious activity elsewhere: a taxi
suspected of carrying explosive devices that had reportedly come
from Watertown and been stopped in Boston's Fenway neighborhood; a police pursuit at South Station, a major transportation hub,
and another at the federal courthouse nearby. Even though the FBI
had zeroed in on two suspects—and one of them was now dead—the
full complexion of the terror plot was still unknown. Were other ac-
complices out there lurking, waiting to strike again? "There was a
high level of anxiety about, frankly, how much we didn't know, and
how big this might be," Patrick said.

Suddenly a more expansive lockdown seemed necessary. So Patrick turned to the playbook he and his emergency management team
had employed with success before, though never for something like
this. Just two months earlier, with a massive blizzard enveloping Massachusetts, Patrick had ordered everyone but essential workers off
the roads and shut down public transportation. The sweeping deci-

sion had its critics—"tyrannical," some complained—but it had the desired effect: keeping accidents to a minimum and allowing a more rapid and effective cleanup. The gravity of the terror threat now seemed to justify something even more sweeping. Still, this was a huge imposition—not only shuttering public transit but asking all of Boston and several neighboring communities not to go outdoors. Not to work, not to shop, not to play, not even to take the dog for a walk. The behind-the-scenes debate was a robust but collaborative one, with Boston mayor Tom Menino and other leaders weighing in. Everyone knew it was a major decision, one sure to spark dissent. And they were happy to let Patrick be the one who made it. "Everybody got that this was a big call," Patrick said. "And that the governor gets the big calls."

Patrick went before the TV cameras in Watertown that morning and delivered the heavy, unsettling message to residents of Boston, Watertown, and the surrounding communities of Cambridge, Newton, Belmont, and Waltham, nearly 950,000 people in all: Stay inside, lock the door, and don't open it for anyone but properly credentialed law enforcement officers. "There is a massive manhunt underway," he said. "We've got every asset that we can possibly muster on the ground right now." Nervous parents drew the blinds, trying to explain to their children why they couldn't run out into the beckoning sunshine. Watertown prayed for its safety, watching columns of police in full SWAT gear canvass its streets. The same nagging thought crept into the minds of many: *What if the bomber is hiding near my house?*

Police drew up a map that included roughly twenty blocks around the spot where Dzhokhar had dumped the Mercedes. Using Google Maps, they divided the area into five quadrants. Tactical teams, each composed of as many as three dozen officers, then went to work scouring Watertown block by block. Tim Alben, the state police colonel, promised the governor they would not stop until they had Dzhokhar. "We are going to start going house to house on every single street," Alben recalled. "We're going to knock on every person's door." More dogs were brought in. Watertown issued reverse 911 calls to its residents about what was happening outside their windows. People began tweeting about the battalions of police trawling their sidewalks and backyards.

Over the coming hours, the police tactical units knocked on hundreds of doors, from single-family homes to individual units of big apartment buildings. Watertown, in parts, was dense. There were lots of places to hide, which meant lots of places to check. They rooted through yards, sheds, barns, pickup trucks whose beds were loaded with debris. They looked under porches and in basements. They asked people if anything seemed amiss on their properties. Often, residents asked for the scrutiny, wanting police to search every room in the house, or to survey the upstairs, because they thought they had heard footsteps. "They were kind of begging us—'check the attic, check the basement, check the car,'" said Mike Powell, a police officer and SWAT team member from the nearby city of Malden. It was a balancing act—police didn't want to brush aside anyone's nervous request, but they knew they had a job to finish. "We were trying to answer every call we possibly could while clearing the area and fulfilling the mission to search our quadrant," said Boston Police superintendent William Evans.

For police, the assignment was already stressful enough, but no one wanted to let anything slip by. They all understood what was at stake. "He could be anywhere, and you would hate to be the team that goes in there and misses something that could eventually be disastrous," Powell said. "That was the most intense part—making sure we look everywhere and do it right." Police knew the risks and urgency of their work, but they also knew they had to approach each house with calm and sensitivity, a task complicated by their conspicuous weaponry and armored vehicles. "One poor house we had to ask occupants to leave, and they had little kids," Evans said. "I said, 'Those poor kids, walking out and seeing a lot of police officers out there.' My heart sort of broke we had to do this." Residents praised the officers for their politeness, and for helping to bring a sense of security to a panicked neighborhood. Homeowners and renters offered them water and oranges. They offered their bathrooms. Throughout, residents tried to carry on as normally as possible, planning bar mitzvahs, taking naps, keeping young children away from televisions and the wall-to-wall coverage of the manhunt. The TVs proved useful to the search teams, though. They would catch glimpses of the news in every house, allowing them to remain up-to-date on what was happening elsewhere.

Throughout the day Friday, police raced around Watertown chasing suspicious reports that filtered in. There was the 911 call about a woman reportedly being held hostage inside her home by a man with a gun. The person seen running into a home on Oak Street. The man speaking Russian who had crossed a secure line. The kid in a sweatshirt walking through a backyard. The young man sitting on a porch with a laptop, which seemed possibly connected to another report that Dzhokhar was online threatening retaliation for his brother's death. Then there was the guy with circuit boards in his car who ran away when a Boston Police team confronted him. Making matters worse, the man's family shut themselves inside a house. "Now everyone's in a panic," said Rich Correale, the Malden SWAT team leader. They didn't know if the man had some connection to Dzhokhar. They feared he may have a bomb in the car. After forty-five minutes of negotiation, police finally got the family out of the house and did a thorough search, even calling in a bomb squad. It turned out to be one of many false alarms. "At least a dozen [times] just inside the perimeter, and then at the same time in the command post, we're hearing different stuff that didn't turn out to be accurate," said Watertown Police chief Ed Deveau. "But you have to run it down." Watertown would receive 566 calls to 911 on Friday. The day before, there had been twenty-eight.

Authorities ran the manhunt operation out of a makeshift command post set up near Watertown's Arsenal Mall. There was a certain historical resonance in that. It is a shopping mecca these days, but in the early nineteenth century the US military established one of its first arsenals there. Metalworkers built cannons for the Civil War and guns for both world wars. On this Friday, it resembled an army outpost once again, with thousands of uniformed officers using it as a staging area for this strange new twenty-first-century battle. The assemblage of police assets was like something out of childhood dreams: every manner of squad car, emergency response truck, and special operations vehicle imaginable gassed up and ready to go. It was here, too, where political leaders had their own brush with anxiety. Around midday, as Patrick and Menino were preparing to brief the media again, there was a man in the street, not far from where the media had assembled, who said he had an explosive device and was going to blow himself up. Police had to move Patrick and Menino to the other side of some buildings while they checked it out; just another false alarm, in the end. "That," Patrick said, "was the nature of the day."

As the hours ticked by, nervous faces peered warily out the windows of Watertown's homes and apartments, wrestling with whether to watch or retreat behind the curtains. They were frightened, but they were interested, too. Nothing like this ever happened here, and it probably never would again. It was unnerving, yes, but also a spectacle, a Friday they'd never forget, all of it captured by national TV, which they kept on all day; there was little else to do, after all. They may have been bit players in the drama, but it was their town and their drama. Perah Kessman, a twenty-nine-year-old mental health clinician and university lecturer, had been up all night, unable to sleep after seeing dozens of police cruisers race by her Arsenal Street apartment toward the firefight. She kept watch out her window, reassuring her nervous mother on the phone. "It's pretty jarring," she allowed. As the day wore on, Kessman and many others in Watertown couldn't resist wandering gingerly out of their homes, curious, dazed, and increasingly stir-crazy, just to take stock of it all. They watched in disbelief as convoys of armored trucks, state police cruisers, ambulances, and fire engines from across New England roared up and down their streets, trying to read news in their speed and direction. They stiffened at the growl of low-flying helicopters overhead. They leaned on one another for news and comfort. They gripped their smartphones like lifelines. Some turned to alcohol to calm their nerves. It didn't take much to get edgy: *Why is there an unmarked white box truck rolling toward the police cordon? Why does that police dog look like he's found something?* The whole day was like one big pregnant moment, and no one knew how it would end.

Aided by the darkness, Dzhokhar had slipped away from the Mercedes and into the early-morning quiet of the Watertown neighborhood, past the pine trees, along the chain-link and wooden fences, among the well-kept single- and multifamily homes, their sleeping residents oblivious to his silent flight. Walnut Street, near where he'd left the car, was relatively busy, but not at this hour. Even with an army of officers on his trail, it wasn't hard to evade detection, to creep quietly through backyards and behind parked cars, to slide by the flag poles, painted garages, and stone walls. Behind a home on Franklin Street, a short L-shaped road connecting Walnut and a major artery, Mount Auburn Street, Dzhokhar came upon a boat, wrapped and stored for the cold months. It lay fewer than twenty houses away from where he had fled from the car. This, he decided, would be his hiding place. He wriggled inside.

With the whole world looking for him, Dzhokhar hunkered down inside the boat and used a pen to scrawl a note on its inside wall and beams. It was a confession of sorts. He seemed to take responsibility for the marathon bombing, praised Allah, and cast himself and his brother as martyrs, paradise as their reward. "The U.S. Government is killing our innocent civilians," he wrote. "I can't stand to see such evil go unpunished. We Muslims are one body, you hurt one you hurt us all." In the message, there was a brief hint of regret for what he had done. "Now I don't like killing innocent people it is forbidden in Islam," he wrote. But it was justified in this case, he asserted. "Stop killing our innocent people," he wrote, "and we will stop."

Heather Abbott was not following the search. The shelter-in-place request, disruptive to so many hundreds of thousands of people in Boston, meant little to her and the dozens of others who had been badly hurt by the bombs at the marathon, who were stuck in their hospital beds, looking down on the city from above. They weren't going anywhere, not for a while, and many of them, like Heather, had chosen to block out the hunt for the bombers. They had more important things to focus on. Heather had spent the last two days grappling with a decision only she could make, one that she could never in a million years have imagined facing. No matter how she turned her options over in her head, the one she wanted remained out of reach: the life she had enjoyed before, and taken for granted.

Doctors had saved Heather's left foot on Monday night. The surgeons had rapidly assessed and responded to the damage, opening up the inside of her undamaged right thigh, removing blood vessels, and grafting them into place where the veins inside her foot had been destroyed. They had said from the start that the transplant might not work, and that if it failed she might face a dire choice. Amputation was not off the table. After the transplant, when the doctors touched her foot to see if the nerves were functioning, she had feeling in some places and none at all in others. But blood was circulating again. Doctors who gathered at her bedside were heartened by the sounds they heard through their Doppler probe, a handheld device used to detect blood flow. Heather dared to hope that she would keep her foot.

She had since returned to the OR for two more surgeries. In the last one, doctors had surveyed the damage and repairs, and they had assessed how well the foot might one day function. Then they had come to present her with their findings. Their tone was solemn; the news they brought was not good. The blood was flowing, but her foot was ravaged; if and when it fully healed it would be hell to live with. The decision was hers and hers alone, but it was clear: The doctors thought she should amputate. If she kept the foot she had been born with, she would never run again, they told her. She might be able to walk on it someday. Her left leg would be shorter than her right; she would suffer chronic pain and need more operations. And still her foot would always look deformed. The hospital arranged for her to talk to people who had faced the same decision. One man who came to see her had kept his leg after a motorcycle accident. He suffered chronic pain and addiction to painkillers, and ten years later, he chose amputation. "I wasted ten years of my life," he told her. She wondered, as she listened, if she really had a choice. She was in tremendous pain; every time the nurses changed the dressing on her foot, it became excruciating. She tried to imagine steeling herself to the suffering, maybe for years. The thought—the dread she felt—gave her a moment of clarity.

Meanwhile, the people close to her were struggling, too. Her mother, Rosemary, found the thought of Heather losing part of her leg almost unbearable. Then, after listening intently to the surgeons, she discovered the alternative scared her even more. She reached her own conclusion but said nothing to her daughter. The choice had to be Heather's. Her mother did not want to sway her.

To Heather's close friend Jason, who had stayed by her bedside all week, the talk of amputation seemed to arise out of nowhere. On Wednesday, he had seen her foot for the first time since she'd left Boylston Street in an ambulance. He had braced himself for the worst as the nurse pulled off the sheet. But the foot had looked more normal than he expected—at least the top of it did; he couldn't see the bottom—and the sensors placed on it to check for circulation had broadcast the much-desired thump of flowing blood. Listening, Jason felt a rush of joy. It was working; it was going to be okay. He stepped out into the hallway with two other friends who were there, who had also been at the marathon. They wrapped their arms around one another's shoulders. All three were crying tears of happiness.

It seemed like the next thing Jason knew, everyone was talking about amputation. He didn't understand—how could the outlook be so dire when everything had seemed to be going so well? The problem, he gathered, was the underside of the foot; there was no good way to reconstruct it. He heard the doctors' dark prognosis, the predictions of more pain and suffering. Still he resisted, clinging to a hope that had quickly faded. After one doctor talked to Heather in her room, Jason followed him out into the hall.

"She's my best friend in the whole world," he implored. "Is there any chance?"

"The decision is hers," the doctor said. "But what I said in there is true."

That night Jason and Heather sat alone in her room. No one had rushed her to decide, but Heather knew the time was coming. "What do you think?" she asked.

"I think you've got to try and save it," Jason said.

"I don't want to lose it," Heather agreed. But she could not ignore the warnings, either, from those who had already made the painful passage she was facing. She was, at her core, a practical-minded person. She had always made decisions based on information, not just emotion. There was no way to know for sure which path would bring more pain. She could only make her choice and commit herself completely.

David King was up early Friday morning. The surgeon had to be in Dover, New Hampshire, north of Portsmouth, before 8:00 A.M., to give a lecture at a hospital there. It was a commitment made long before the marathon. He got coffee and went to the gym, and then he started reading the news on his phone. When he realized what was unfolding in Watertown, he wanted to skip the trip and stay in Boston. What if more violence erupted and he was needed at the hospital? He called in to work and asked to stick around, but his boss told him to head north.

The lecture, at Wentworth-Douglass Hospital, was supposed to be about the latest strategies for replacing fluids after blood loss in trauma patients. *No one is going to want to hear about that*, King thought as he drove up I-93 to I-95 and over the border. On a day like this, with the drama still unfolding, he was sure the doctors in New Hampshire would prefer he talk about the bombing and his hospital's response. The week had been a whirlwind—he hadn't had time yet to reflect on what had happened, let alone assemble any notes or photographs—but he usually did just fine speaking off the cuff. The lecture room was packed when he arrived, the crowd much bigger than its normal size. As he had expected, everyone wanted to know about the bombing. His talk, King told them as he began, "was advertised as something else, but that's not what you want to hear about. I'll tell you the story through my eyes, and if you're bored, you can leave." He started talking. Two hours later—long after the lecture had been scheduled to end—the room was still full of people.

The drive to and from New Hampshire was the first time King had had to himself since Monday, the first real chance he'd had to think about the week. The high-octane surgeon—who always had music playing, often at top volume, whether he was exercising or writing e-mails—chose to drive in silence that Friday morning. He found himself reflecting on his time in Iraq and Afghanistan, and thinking about the many soldiers he had treated who had lost their legs. If every one of those cases became big news, like the plight of the marathon victims, he wondered, would it change public attitudes about the wars? He understood why this event was different—these things weren't supposed to happen *here*, in the US, and these victims hadn't made a choice to head into harm's way—but it still bothered him that wounded soldiers so rarely inspired a similar flood of public outrage and concern.

In between his musings at the wheel, King got on his phone with a *Time* magazine reporter. The hospital had been flooded with interview requests from around the world, and King had volunteered to respond to some of them, squeezing calls into his few breaks between patients. He felt a responsibility to make sure the facts were reported correctly and calmly, and he saw an opportunity, too, to help the public understand the work he and his colleagues were doing. He talked to the *Time* reporter as he drove, the answers to the questions coming to him easily. He felt like he had the right words, like his brief sojourn north had helped him process the chaotic events. By 11:00 A.M., the doctor was back in the city. He drove his car home to Cambridge, then walked across the river to the hospital, ignoring the order to shelter, intent on getting to work. The streets were empty, the morning unnaturally silent. The bomber was still at large, and Boston was a ghost town.

. . .

They were starving when they arrived in Harvard Square around 2:00 P.M. Deval Patrick was with about a half-dozen state troopers in full-body gear. Nobody had eaten in hours. They pulled up to Charlie's Kitchen, a longtime Cambridge fixture. They were happy to find the place open. Patrick had to laugh at the irony of it: *We know we've asked everyone to remain indoors and businesses to close, but, hey, can you make us some cheeseburgers?* Everyone in the restaurant applauded the troopers when they walked in. Patrick had just come from visiting Mount Auburn Hospital, where Dic Donohue was recovering from surgery. Patrick couldn't see Donohue but spent time with his wife and his brother. The governor was gratified to see all the support Donohue seemed to have, including from colleagues at the transit authority and in law enforcement. After the meal at Charlie's, Patrick returned to the State House. Exhausted, he lay down on a couch in his office, not bothering to even take off his shoes. He didn't have the energy for that.

Less than an hour later, his cell phone rang. It was the White House. The president was on the line. Obama, with whom Patrick had been close for years, asked him how he was doing, whether he had everything he needed. The president had been following the investigation closely. "He was very current," Patrick said. They talked about the possible threats that were still out there, what they knew of the intelligence. They discussed the latest development, which involved promising police searches in New Bedford, a former whaling city on the state's south coast; authorities had picked up a ping down there from one of Dzhokhar's electronic devices. Then Patrick and Obama discussed the shelter-in-place request. Obama told Patrick what Patrick already knew: that they'd have to lift the request soon, regardless of whether they had found the suspect. They couldn't ask people to stay in lockdown forever. Patrick told the president they planned to wrap up the house-to-house searches by the evening, and then they'd tell the public to resume their lives, carefully.

By 5:00 P.M., with Dzhokhar still at large, William Evans, his police officers, and the rest of the tactical teams back in Watertown were feeling the weight of their work. They were living off bottled water and granola bars. Bathrooms were hard to come by. They were beat from lugging their heavy gear around all day under the sun. The exhaustion, coupled with the frustration of not having found their man, left police spent. "Some of my officers were calling for release," Evans said. "I said, 'Let's hang in there. Let's hang in there.'" As evening approached, Ed Deveau, the Watertown chief, began to worry what all this meant for his community. Where was this guy? Had there been a carjacking police never heard about, giving Dzhokhar a vehicle to escape in? "My other concern was that it was going to be dark in an hour and a half or two, and it was going to give him a chance to move again if he was still here," Deveau said.

Patrick knew, by day's end, that it was time to go back before the cameras. What he had wanted to say—what everyone hoped he would say—was that after hours of searching police finally had their suspect in custody. But that was not in the script. Instead he had to deliver the truth: that authorities did not know where Dzhokhar Tsarnaev was. That after a long, difficult day of methodical searches, there was little to show for it. The Boston Red Sox and Boston Bruins had called off their games. The Big Apple Circus was in town, but there were no clowns or elephants or trapeze acrobats. The city had more or less ground to a halt. And yet the dragnet had come up empty. On the way out to Watertown, where he planned to announce the end of the shelter request, Patrick picked up Menino at the Parkman House, the city-owned mansion where the ailing mayor had been recuperating.

Around 6:00 P.M., the governor stepped up to a bouquet of microphones at the Watertown command post, a blend of determination and disappointment evident on his and other leaders' faces. Menino was by his side in a wheelchair, frustrated by how little they had to report but convinced Dzhokhar was contained in Watertown, and that the shelter order should not drag on any longer. "We can return to living our lives," Patrick said, urging residents to use extra vigilance. Mass transit would reopen immediately. It made for an odd and unsatisfying juxtaposition—residents were being told to resume their lives, but that a terrorist who had helped kill and maim scores of people could still be right there in their midst. "There were the inevitable questions: Are you saying we're safe? Did he get away?" Patrick recalled. "We answered what we could." Patrick himself was still on edge, too, but he understood that they couldn't keep the shelter request in place indefinitely. "Any one of the decisions around the response you knew had consequences, good or bad," he said. "The worst thing would have been not to make decisions. You have to keep moving." Patrick said he had come to understand that you could trust the public with information—that you could be up-front about what you did and did not know, and that people would respect that. "I'm not saying there was unanimity in support for what we had to do," he said. "I think people basically got that we were trying to do what was in their best interest."

In the car on the way home, Patrick felt drained. And he felt uneasy. *Is this going to be a long, painful period of uncertainty?* he thought. *Where could this guy be? Is he up under some house, dead?* The governor called home, where his wife, Diane, and his daughter Katherine had been looking after each other. They decided that, on his way back, he would pick up Thai food from a place in Quincy that they liked, called Pad Thai. They had found it on Yelp a while back. Diane and Katherine placed the order; Patrick didn't have enough brainpower left to do it himself. Comfort food for an uncomfortable night.

CHAPTER 14

TRAPPED IN A BOAT

"He's in custody! He's in custody!"

A ll day long, David Henneberry had been looking out his window at the two fuzzy paint rollers lying on his lawn. They weren't supposed to be there—they had fallen out from under the shrink-wrap cover on his boat. He was itching to go put them back where they belonged, but he didn't want to disobey police. Already, officers driving up and down his street had spotted him on his back steps smoking a cigarette. They had waved, with a look that said, *Okay, but that's far enough.* There were helicopters hovering overhead. Henneberry figured if he got up on a ladder and started messing around with the boat, they would see him and angrily order him back inside. He understood that the situation in Watertown was serious; he was trying to respect authority, he really was. But as he stood there smoking just outside his back door, gazing down at the rollers on the grass not twenty feet away, he felt a nagging irritation. For a guy as meticulous as Henneberry—especially when it came to his twenty-four-foot Seabird powerboat—even that trace of disarray was hard to take.

The boat was Henneberry's greatest pleasure. Now that he was retired from his job as a phone company installer, the sixty-six-year-old Watertown native had more time to enjoy it. In another month, he would have the vessel in the water, and he and his wife, Beth, would settle into their favorite routine. Beth would pack a lunch on Sunday mornings, he'd pick up the paper, and they'd head for the nearby Watertown Yacht Club. There they would hop aboard the *Slipaway II* and meander eastward on the Charles River, around the bend at the Eliot Bridge in Cambridge, past Boston University to the Esplanade. They would often drop anchor there, in the basin between MIT and Kendall Square on the Cambridge side of the river, and, across the water in Boston, Beacon Hill and the golden dome of the State House. They would take their time with the paper and their lunch, and then, when it felt right, make their way back. They loved how easy it was and how free it felt to get away from everything.

It felt like the opposite of all that on this particular Friday in April. They were stuck inside, like all their neighbors on Franklin Street, where Henneberry had lived for forty years. And the situation was unnerving. Somewhere in the area, the authorities said, Dzhokhar Tsarnaev could be hiding. Henneberry had been up late the night before—he was a night owl, a habit ingrained from his many years playing drums in bands at Boston nightclubs—and he had heard the gunfight erupt on Laurel Street. It was little more than half a mile away as the crow flies, across the backyards and quiet, tree-lined streets. He stayed up until 2:30 A.M. watching the news coverage on TV. It almost seemed unreal that the violence that had erupted in Boston on Monday had come to his town, his neighborhood. Early Friday morning, one of Beth's children called to make sure they knew of the lockdown. Beth peered sleepily through the blinds and saw a military vehicle stop on the corner outside. Police dressed in heavy tactical gear assembled on the streets.

The boat in Henneberry's backyard was thirty-two years old, but it was nearly impossible to tell. He had owned it for eleven years, and he had been working on it the whole time. He had restored the cabin, crafted custom covers for the storage bins, laid in a new teak floor. The wood got seven, eight, nine coats of varnish—whatever it took for the shine to meet his standards. It was so glossy you could see your reflection. When winter threatened and it was time to store the boat for the season, Henneberry took pains to protect it from the weather. That was where the fuzzy white paint rollers came in. When the boat was sealed in protective white plastic, Henneberry liked to tuck ten or so rollers up under the bottom edge of the wrap, so it wouldn't chafe against the boat and leave scratches. It was an extra, almost obsessive bit of care. Now two of the rollers were just lying there on the grass. Maybe, Henneberry thought, the wind had blown them out. Or maybe the wooden frame under the shrink-wrap had loosened up. As soon as he was allowed to venture that far, he would go outside and check it out.

He and Beth watched the 6:00 P.M. press conference on the TV in their living room. They watched Governor Deval Patrick announce that "the stay-indoors request is lifted" and then ask the public to remain vigilant. "Remember there is still a very, very dangerous individual at large," he cautioned. Then, as if realizing the ominous tone of his warning, Patrick added a note of reassurance. "We feel confident . . . we can return to living our lives," he said.

It was all Henneberry needed to hear. *Well, they didn't get him,* he thought. *He got away somehow, and now he's in Boston, Worcester, wherever.* Beth was not convinced. *I wonder what they're not saying,* she thought. *I think they think he's still here.*

"I'm going to check the boat," said her husband, heading to the back door.

Henneberry crossed the small backyard to his garage, a low-slung, tidy structure, white with green trim, built along with the house in 1890. He grabbed his stepladder, carried it outside, leaned it up against the side of the boat, and stepped up onto the second or third step. He rolled up a section of shrink-wrap that covered the side door to the boat, put a clamp on it to hold it up, and peered in through the sheet of clear plastic underneath. Sunset was an hour away—there was still plenty of light—and he could clearly see blood on the floor of his boat. There was no mistaking that deep crimson color. He looked forward, toward the cabin, and saw more blood there, under the seats. His eyes traveled back and forth between the two sets of bloodstains, his mind working to make sense of what he saw. His gaze shifted, to the deeper interior—that's when he spotted the body on the other side of the engine box. The person on the floor had his back toward Henneberry, the hood of a sweatshirt pulled up over his head. The body remained perfectly still as Henneberry, stunned, backed away silently down the ladder. Later, he would not remember stepping off onto the ground.

He ran into the house. When Beth saw his face, she knew something bad was happening. Henneberry was shocked and confused, but he knew exactly who was in his backyard.

"I . . . there . . . He's in the boat," he managed to stammer. Beth grabbed the phone, dialed 911, and thrust it at him.

"This call is recorded," the operator told him.

Henneberry recited his name and address. "There's a body in my boat in the backyard," he recalled saying.

"Sir, did you say there's a body in your boat?"

"Yes, there's someone in my boat," Henneberry repeated. "And a lot of blood." He stood at the kitchen sink, watching the boat out the window.

The operator told him that police were on the way. Then he asked if the man was still in the boat.

"I think so," Henneberry said. "But I can only see one side."

Then, without asking the dispatcher if he should, Henneberry decided to go back out and check. Cordless phone to his ear, he walked down the porch steps and back onto the grass. He moved closer to his six-foot wooden fence, peering down the side of it to check behind the boat.

"He's still in the boat," he assured the operator.

"How do you know that?" the operator asked.

"I'm looking at the other side," Henneberry said.

As the operator ordered him to get back in the house, Henneberry turned away from the boat. He was facing his pebble-covered driveway when police came running up it, weapons drawn, yelling, "Get back! Get down! Where is he?" He felt a wave of overwhelming fear—what if they thought he was the terrorist? Frozen there, the phone still in his hand, he saw one officer emerge from the pack, and he realized she was calling his name: "David! David!" He recognized Watertown Police Detective Jennifer Connors, whom he knew from the Watertown Yacht Club. The familiar face jolted him from his paralysis. She grabbed his arm and pulled him down the sidewalk, away from the house. "Jen, Jen," he told her, "get Beth! She's all by herself!"

Around 6:45 P.M., right after Henneberry's 911 call, William Evans jumped in his Boston police car with two lieutenants, racing toward Franklin Street behind a Watertown cop. State troopers and other police officers quickly descended on the property, too. Evans positioned himself in front of Henneberry's house, looking straight up the driveway at the boat. He saw Dzhokhar poking at the tarp. Everyone at the scene began yelling. Police thought he might be trying to get a gun through. "We didn't know what he had," Evans said. "But given what he did at the scene of the marathon, given what he did during the shoot-out, and given what he did to the MIT officer, we knew we were dealing with a serious terrorist here who had weapons to the max." Dzhokhar's movements prompted someone to begin firing at the boat. Other officers immediately joined in, the shots ringing out through the quiet neighborhood. "Hold your fire!" Evans yelled. He believed they had the guy in their clutches, that things were under control. And he wanted to take Dzhokhar alive. The bullets stopped. Evans didn't need guns. What he needed were SWAT officers who could get the suspect out.

Rich Correale, Mike Powell, and Nick Cox had spent all day searching homes and properties in Watertown. The SWAT team officers from the nearby city of Malden had just finished scouring an apartment complex. They were sitting out front of the building, talking to a supervisor from a Boston Police SWAT team working alongside them. Everyone was tired, ready to go home. Suddenly the supervisor got a call over the radio: A resident had seen some blood on his boat. "And we're like, 'Bullshit,'" Correale said. "'This isn't it.'" They had been chasing false alarms all day. This just seemed like another. Police on the radio called for SWAT units. The Boston squad was heading to the house and asked the Malden team to join. They agreed, reluctantly. "We were kind of dragging our feet," Correale said. But as they walked to the van, the radio traffic intensified. Police had seen movement on the boat. The Malden guys heard "shots fired!" and raced to the scene.

With the shelter request now lifted, the streets leading to Franklin were lined with people—"like a parade," Nick Cox said. The Malden team dumped their van and ran the last quarter mile or so, in full SWAT gear, toward Henneberry's house. Uniformed officers directed them to it. Correale, Powell, and Cox didn't know what to expect. Was this it? Was this really him? They reached the bottom of Henneberry's driveway. The boat sat just on the other side of two cars. As more officers arrived, snipers took positions in armored vehicles and in the windows of surrounding houses, their weapons trained on the boat. Correale, seeing guns pointed in several directions, got on the radio at one point and warned about the potential for deadly crossfire. Commanders removed some police from behind the boat.

Everyone's attention turned to getting Dzhokhar out of the *Slipaway II*. Police were on edge, not knowing what his intentions were, what weapons he had, or how hurt he was. They kept their distance at first. They tried tear gas, to flush him out, but he didn't budge. Instead the gas drifted down the driveway, where the Malden team was set up. "We got smoked," Correale said. "The whole place cleared out." Around this time, an FBI tactical unit arrived and took command of the scene, behind a leader from the bureau's Virginia-based Hostage Rescue Team; the FBI would later request that he not be identified by name. The FBI unit was composed of fourteen operatives, including three specialists in crisis negotiation. There were also two "breachers," who had responsibility for preparing the scene for the operation; a K9 specialist, who coordinated all the responding K9 teams; three "assaulters," who helped run the show on the ground; two communications specialists, one right near the boat and another in a vehicle a few blocks away; and two snipers, who got up on a building and provided cover for everyone else. The team leader quickly won the trust and respect of local police, taking their guidance into account, keeping them informed on next steps, and leading with firmness and unexpected humility.

A number of warnings had trickled in over the radio, and it was impossible, in the moment, to weigh their legitimacy. Hovering above in a helicopter, state police outfitted with thermal imaging equipment reported that Dzhokhar looked like he may be trying to start a fire in the boat; dozens of gallons of fuel might be on board. The FBI team leader calmly told everyone to back away. If the boat exploded, he said, the flash would come right down the driveway. "I know this is your party," the leader told Correale. "But we're going to want you to back up." They knew that snipers would likely take Dzhokhar out if he tried anything, but the Malden SWAT officers were prepared for the worst. They'd been told that Dzhokhar had a weapon and had exchanged gunfire with police. Indeed, throughout the two-hour standoff, all kinds of reports were coming over the transom about Dzhokhar's purported arsenal—that he had a rifle, that he was armed with an AK-47, that he wore a suicide vest. "I was under the impression these people had no regard for human life," Powell said. "So I'm thinking this guy's going to go out with the last hurrah, and he's probably going to try to take as many out with him [as he can]."

At one point, around nightfall, Correale's cell phone rang. It was his wife.

"Hey," she said, "you know they have him in a boat?"

"Yep, I know," he said.

"Where are you?"

"I'm in the driveway."

"You gotta be shittin' me! You said you were just watching sidewalks!"

The FBI breachers launched at least four or five diversionary devices into the boat, which produced loud, bright explosions meant to stun and disorient Dzhokhar. The idea was to buy police and federal agents time to safely move in. State troopers had also positioned a BearCat—an armored, military-style vehicle with chunky tires—in Henneberry's backyard. They tried to tip the boat over using the BearCat, but the trailer made that difficult. They punctured the tarp instead. Authorities at one point discussed sending a dog into the boat but concluded it wouldn't do much good; a dog wasn't going to cuff the suspect and bring him out. As the standstill continued, the FBI team leader came over to where Correale's team had assembled, alongside a group of SWAT officers from the transit police and officers from a regional unit called North Metro SWAT. If Dzhokhar wouldn't leave the boat on his own accord, that left one option for taking him alive: They'd have to go get him. The team leader put his hand on Correale's shoulder. "We need to move fast," he said. "Get your team. Get a plan together."

The call came while Deval Patrick was waiting to pay for his takeout order at the Thai restaurant. On the line was Tim Alben, the state police colonel. Alben told the governor the news: "We think we have the suspect." Patrick now had a bundle of Thai food for himself, his wife, and his daughter, but he had to get back out to Watertown, and fast. He called his wife, Diane, and told her he couldn't come home. They arranged a quick transfer of the food on his way back up north. Diane pulled up outside St. Agatha Parish, in their hometown of Milton, and the governor's car did, too. Patrick hopped out, handed over the takeout, and gave his wife a kiss. "Be careful," she said, and he was gone. They raced back downtown, picked up Patrick's chief of staff, Brendan Ryan, and booked it to Watertown, blue lights flashing.

The principals gathered in a trailer at the Watertown command post—Patrick, Alben, Rick DesLauriers of the FBI, and other top law enforcement officials, including an FBI tactical supervisor who, with chewing tobacco in his mouth and a Gatorade bottle as a spit cup, kept in constant communication with the leader of the Hostage Rescue Team at the boat; the FBI would later decline to name the supervisor. The HRT team leader called the supervisor about every five minutes on the phone; the radio frequencies were too jammed with voices. The supervisor in turn provided regular updates to state and local leaders. At times he just put the team leader on speakerphone so those in the trailer could hear directly what was going on. Inside the trailer, a flat-screen on the wall showed the live video feed from a thermal imaging camera on the Eurocopter TwinStar helicopter that Mark Spencer, a state trooper, was piloting above Henneberry's property. For a time, Dzhokhar appeared to be totally still. They didn't know if he was alive or dead. The color of the image on the screen seemed to be fading. Then he moved, and everyone stirred. *He's moving! He's moving!* Menino couldn't get into the trailer because of his injuries, so he sat in the front seat of his SUV listening to the drama on the police radio, fervently hoping that this was really it. The operation seemed to be taking an eternity. *Let's get this over with*, he thought.

As the drama unfolded, the second-guessing began: How had the house-by-house teams not found Dzhokhar's hiding place? Was Henneberry's house within the perimeter that police had spent the entire day searching? A clear answer would prove elusive in the days ahead, as different police officials provided different accounts. What was clear was that no one had come to search Henneberry's house that day—nor his garage, his boat, or his backyard—even though he lived just two-tenths of a mile from where Dzhokhar had ditched the Mercedes. Other residents of Franklin Street who lived farther from where Dzhokhar had escaped on foot did have their properties searched, but the work at times seemed haphazard or incomplete. One neighbor had his barn searched, but not his house. Another had her barn searched, but had to ask the officers to check the structure's cellar. Yet another neighbor, Robert Vercollone, saw a tactical officer conduct only a cursory check under his porch, whose latticework had a gaping hole because of ongoing plumbing work. "It's the perfect size for somebody to crawl through," Vercollone said. "But he didn't poke around any further."

Answers to such questions would have to come later. By this point, with Dzhokhar surrounded by police and federal agents all armed to the teeth, there was no remaining doubt—they had him. The searches may have covered hundreds of homes and saturated whole blocks with SWAT officers, but the manhunt had hardly proved to be airtight. They had not, despite the promises, knocked on every door. And so it had been left to David Henneberry to discover Dzhokhar on his own. The chance encounter in a Watertown backyard could easily have ended with another victim.

Grabbing a Kevlar ballistic shield from a federal agent, Rich Correale began to assemble a team to approach the boat. He, Powell, and Cox would lead, followed by the transit police officers and members of North Metro SWAT. Two FBI assaulters would provide cover. The SWAT unit lined up in a stack in Henneberry's driveway, Correale in front with the shield, the others in a column behind him. The FBI leader returned and briefed them on what he knew. Negotiators were having some luck getting Dzhokhar to cooperate, to follow their instructions, in part by citing a public plea by his high school wrestling coach, Peter Payack, to give himself up. Dzhokhar had lifted up his shirt at one point to show that he wasn't wearing a vest. Correale ran through their plan, how they would go at the boat, try to get Dzhokhar to surrender, and grab him if he didn't. The FBI leader went down the line to each member of the SWAT team. Flashing a thumbs-up, he asked them all: "You good with that?" The leader told them that if they didn't like what they saw, they should pull back.

At that, Correale's team began walking methodically up the driveway. As they reached the edge of Henneberry's house, they heard a voice over a PA system: "Back up!" They stopped, not knowing who was giving the command, or what it meant. It turned out later that there had been some confusion over which SWAT team would advance. The FBI leader told them to keep going, so they did. But again they heard it: "Back up!" Correale thought this meant danger. *They see a gun? A bomb? What are they seeing?* he thought. Again, the FBI leader instructed them to continue. "Fellas," he said, "they're not talking to you. We're going to keep going."

They stepped closer. Then, as they reached the boat, a couple of the SWAT officers fanned out from the stack. They now had a clear view of Dzhokhar, whom negotiators had coaxed onto the side of the boat, to a spot where the tarp had been ripped away. "I'm saying, 'Holy shit, this is the kid on TV. This is him,'" Correale said. The same mop of dark hair, the hoodie with blue and orange lettering, the college-boy look that seemed so incongruous with his violent acts. Mike Trovato, a SWAT officer from the city of Revere who was part of the team, remembered his thoughts flashing quickly to his wife and his daughter, who was just a few months old. It was that kind of moment—police were trying to adhere to their training, trying to do their jobs, to follow orders, to focus. But their hearts were pounding. The climax had arrived.

Dzhokhar, illuminated like a stage actor by lights police had trained on him, was draped along the edge of the boat's port side, blood trickling down like rain on a storm window. His left leg hung over the side, and he was slumped over. He raised his shirt as SWAT officers approached, seeming to offer himself in surrender. But he kept rocking left to right, his right hand dipping out of view inside the boat. He seemed to be falling in and out of consciousness. He was a mess, a bullet round having left a wound on his head, his ear all ripped up, a gash on his neck.

"Show me your hands! Show me your hands!" Correale yelled at him. Brian Harer, a SWAT officer with the transit police, shouted similar instructions. One of the officers was calling him by name.

"All right, all right," Dzhokhar said back, his voice woozy, lethargic.

"Get off the boat," Correale said. "Get off the boat."

"But it's gonna hurt," Dzhokhar replied.

He had a point. The side of the boat was maybe seven feet off the ground. It wouldn't be an easy fall.

This was the tensest moment for the SWAT team. They couldn't see Dzhokhar's right hand and right leg. They feared what he might be holding, what he might be reaching for. Maybe the groggy voice was a ruse. Maybe he was just pretending to be out of it. Maybe this was all part of the plot. They'd heard all kinds of things about what weapons he had. And they were only a couple feet away from him. As he began to bring up his right hand, Correale thought, *Here it comes, here it comes.* Powell was thinking the same thing as he watched the hand slowly rise: *Pay attention to his hand. Pay attention to his hand.* Finally Dzhokhar's hand came into sight. He had nothing. They kept telling him to get off the boat, but he didn't. The time had come to pull him down.

In a flash, the SWAT officers, including transit officer Jeff Campbell and Revere Police chief Joseph Cafarelli, reached up from the ground and flung Dzhokhar down, the first hands anyone had laid on him since the bombs exploded at the finish line Monday afternoon. Dzhokhar landed on the ground, and not gently. The officers swarmed, immediately frisking him for explosives and weapons. They pulled up his shirt. They patted down his legs. Trovato put his knees on Dzhokhar's arm and checked his hands for triggers or cell phones that could detonate a remote bomb. They flipped him onto his stomach. Dzhokhar offered no resistance. Trovato, who wore only a T-shirt under his armor, had Dzhokhar's blood all over his forearms. Two transit cops, Saro Thompson and Kenneth Tran, each grabbed an arm. Thompson snapped handcuffs on his wrists. Around 8:45 P.M., the radio crackled with the words everyone had been waiting for: "He's in custody! He's in custody!" A cheer went up in the command trailer back at the mall. Amid the police radio traffic, Menino's voice cut in: "People of Boston are proud of you." Boston Police commissioner Ed Davis added his own congratulations, saying over the radio, "It's a proud day to be a Boston police officer."

In Henneberry's yard, the officers' priorities shifted to a new urgency: saving the life of a terrorist who had killed and maimed so many. "It was a real possibility that he could die without medical aid," Trovato said. "I very much wanted him to live." Like many other cops, he wanted to see Dzhokhar stand trial, to face justice for what he'd done. "Let's move him away from the boat," the FBI leader said. He was concerned an explosive device might be on board. Trovato grabbed Dzhokhar by the belt. Transit officers grabbed his arms. They dragged him across Henneberry's yard, fifteen or twenty feet away from the boat. "Okay, that's good," the FBI leader said. Another FBI agent ran up and began emptying Dzhokhar's pockets, to inventory things for evidence. Trovato and other officers yelled for EMTs. Two medics from the federal Bureau of Alcohol, Tobacco, Firearms and Explosives came running over and began working on him. Two Boston paramedics jumped in, too. The medics provided oxygen. Dzhokhar was lifted into a waiting ambulance and brought to Beth Israel Deaconess Medical Center, the same hospital where his brother had been taken. Dzhokhar was in rough shape: fractured skull, multiple gunshot wounds, including one from a bullet that went through the left side of his face, and injuries to his mouth, pharynx, and middle ear. He was battered and bloody, but he was alive.

At 8:45 P.M., the BPD tweeted the three words the city badly wanted to hear: *Suspect in custody.* The news swept through the crowd of media at the scene like wildfire; within minutes, Anderson Cooper and Diane Sawyer were repeating it on CNN and ABC. The instant Dzhokhar's capture was made public, Greater Boston erupted in euphoria. All the pressure that had been building since the bombing, all that anxiety and uncertainty, evaporated. Revelers streamed into the streets near Fenway Park. They flooded Boston Common. They ran out onto the sidewalks. They waved American flags and shouted teary thank-yous to police. They belted out "God Bless America." In Watertown, they cheered as Dzhokhar's ambulance sped toward the hospital. In the center of town, a crowd gathered outside the H&R Block and hollered attaboys at the cops, whose blue lights swirled in the darkness. Unlike the night before, those lights now cast a reassuring glow. The sense of relief was overwhelming, and it was everywhere. Police officers who'd been at the scene exchanged hugs, high fives, and emotional reflections. Some shed tears of joy. It had been one hell of a week. Adrenaline dissipating, they felt pride, exhaustion, and grief for the damage that remained. All the cheering felt good. As they left Franklin Street, Cox said, it looked "like if the Red Sox had won the World Series." Not everyone follows baseball, though. Everyone was following this. Everyone had a stake in it. In an era of social and political fragmentation, it was perhaps the closest Boston would come to a shared, unifying moment.

Correale, Powell, and Cox stayed at the scene a few minutes, then started the unhurried walk back to their van. It didn't take long before the gravity of it all began to sink in. *That's probably going to be a piece of history right there*, Powell thought. His fiancée called as he walked away from Franklin Street. She had just seen him on TV. She was proud but a little piqued—Powell had told her only that he would be helping out that night. It wasn't exactly untrue. He'd just left out the part about being on the front lines. "The drive back, we're like, we can't believe we were involved in that," Correale said. "What are the odds?" It's possible that commanders on the ground initially assumed they were a Boston SWAT team, because of the similarity of the Boston and Malden uniforms. But it had hardly mattered in the end—they were trained to do the job, too, and they had done it. "We took one of the most wanted men in the United States into custody— we were part of that," Correale said. "And that's something."

One of the state troopers who took part in the operation at the boat was a member of Deval Patrick's police detail. He told the governor afterward that any one of the officers there would have gladly put a bullet in Dzhokhar. But when Dzhokhar was wheeled to the ambulance right in front of them, the restraint was striking. No one made even a gesture of disrespect. "Is it my place to kill him? If he posed a threat to me and my officers, in a second," Cafarelli said. "But I'm not the instrument—and my guys aren't the instruments—of vengeance for anybody. Bring him to justice and let the courts do what they gotta do."

When it all ended, Patrick was relieved but still concerned that there might be more to the story than they knew. The investigation, in many ways, was just starting. Was the crisis really over? He wasn't sure. "So personally, it felt like a triumphant moment, but not a conclusive moment." At 10:05 P.M., President Obama spoke at the White House. He thanked law enforcement for their work. He promised a thorough examination of the Tsarnaev brothers' backgrounds, motivations, and associates. He paid homage to the fallen. And he praised Boston's spirit for carrying the city through one of the most trying weeks imaginable. "Whatever they thought they could ultimately achieve, they've already failed," the president said of the terrorists. "They failed because the people of Boston refused to be intimidated." Back in his temporary quarters at the Parkman House on Beacon Hill, Menino cracked his bedroom window and heard the party on the Common. He felt proud of the city, and happy as hell.

The sense of liberation Friday night was real, and in many ways deserved. The week had indeed been hard on just about everybody. Since 2:50 P.M. on Monday, Boston had been in terror's grip. The sense of release could hardly have been more welcome. It was easy, though, for most of the celebrants to shout, and to sing, and to broadcast their civic pride in the BOSTON STRONG T-shirts that were suddenly everywhere. It was easy for them to crack open a Sam Adams that night or pour a shot of Jack. It was easy to go to bed knowing that they could wake once again to a peaceful city, restored to its rightful sense of order. It was easy to look forward to the next morning's Starbucks ritual, thankful that your son's baseball game was back on.

But for Heather Abbott, for Billy and Patty Campbell, for all the wounded and the grieving families still reeling from Monday's attack, there would be no such unburdening. There would be no luxury of exhalation. The week had ended for everyone else. Not for them. In many ways, it never would. As Krystle Campbell's brother put it, "I'm happy that nobody else is going to get hurt by these guys. But it's not going to bring her back." The only thing to do was to move forward, one day at a time, in hopes that tomorrow would be better than yesterday.

In the early months of 2013, Heather Abbott felt ready for a change. She had built a successful corporate career and had close friendships and a busy social life in Newport, Rhode Island, but new opportunities were right around the corner.

A marathon runner, Army Reservist, and trauma surgeon at Massachusetts General Hospital, Dr. David King had begun to feel more at home in Boston. He and his wife, Anne, moved back north with some trepidation after years spent studying and working in Miami.

Krystle Campbell (right center, patterned dress) was a Boston girl with a big presence, who loved the life of her city. Nearing her thirtieth birthday, she was looking to settle down and take on a new project in the restaurant or hospitality business.

Over the past twenty-five years, Dave McGillivray (right) has become synonymous with the Boston Marathon. As race director, McGillivray is the marathon's public face, spirit guide, and minute-by-minute micromanager.

Shana Cottone was in high school in New York on 9/11; when she came to Boston to attend Northeastern University, she loved how safe she felt in her adopted city. A few years later she joined the Boston Police Department, thriving in her role reaching out to troubled people.

Tamerlan Tsarnaev (center, rear) was the oldest of four children, which included sisters Bella and Ailina and a younger brother, Dzhokhar. Together with their parents, Anzor and Zubeidat, the family immigrated to America in 2002 and 2003.

The Tsarnaev family had high hopes for Tamerlan, but after his once-bright future in the boxing ring dimmed, he had little else to turn to, instead spending hours watching Islamic videos on his computer.

After arriving in the United States as an elementary school student, Dzhokhar Tsarnaev seemed to have assimilated successfully into American society. His life, however, was also on a downward spiral.

Bill Iffrig, a seventy-eight-year-old marathoner from Lake Stevens, Washington, was running down the left side of the course when the first explosion threw him to the ground. With police officers scrambling all around him, Iffrig thought, *This might be it. This will be the end of me.*

Shrapnel from the first blast ruptured the femoral artery of Sydney Corcoran, a seventeen-year-old from Lowell, north of Boston, whose mother, Celeste, lost both legs. Two bystanders, Zach Mione (right) and Matt Smith, helped save Sydney's life by fashioning a tourniquet.

In a matter of seconds, the celebratory holiday atmosphere of Boylston Street transformed into a chaotic, bloodstained crime scene, with first responders and volunteers working urgently to save lives.

Police and race officials stopped the marathon on Commonwealth Avenue, less than a mile before the finish line. Thousands of confused, cold, and exhausted runners remained on the course.

An emergency responder and volunteers, including Carlos Arredondo, in the cowboy hat, raced Jeff Bauman to an ambulance after the explosion outside Marathon Sports ravaged his lower body. Bauman lost both legs in the bombing.

Many runners cherished competing in the Boston Marathon above all other races. They were devastated to learn of the tragedy unfolding ahead.

Police and medical personnel waited outside the Boston Medical Center emergency room on April 15, 2013, for more bombing casualties to arrive. The city's hospitals were inundated with patients in the hours after the explosions.

This photo of Martin Richard, taken at his school in 2012, quickly became an Internet sensation—and a poignant symbol of the city's losses—after the bombing. NO MORE HURTING PEOPLE. PEACE, read the sign held by the boy who became, at eight years old, the youngest person killed at the marathon.

Boston University graduate student Lingzi Lu, twenty-three, who had gone to the marathon with friends, was killed by the second bomb. A native of Shenyang, China, she was close to completing her statistics degree.

On Tuesday, April 16, barely twenty-four hours after her daughter, Krystle, was killed on Boylston Street, Patty Campbell struggled through a brief statement to reporters from the porch of her home in Medford, north of Boston. "We can't believe this has happened," she said.

Dozens of running shoes were left behind in sympathy and solidarity at the makeshift memorial to the bombing victims. The memorial began in the street where metal barricades blocked off the crime scene, and was later moved to a corner of the park in Copley Square.

The day after the bombing, children held candles during a twilight vigil in Boston's Dorchester neighborhood for Martin Richard and other bombing victims. The gathering in Garvey Park, near where Martin lived, drew more than one thousand people, many of whom knew the boy and his family.

Posters hung at the memorial attracted thousands of signers from across the world, who scrawled messages of love, strength, and solidarity with Boston.

President Barack Obama addressed two thousand people inside Boston's Cathedral of the Holy Cross during an emotional interfaith service on April 18, 2013. "Your country is with you," Obama said. "You will run again."

04-15-2013 14:37:40

Chilling security footage showed Tamerlan and Dzhokhar Tsarnaev, each carrying a bag, walking behind unsuspecting marathon spectators perched along the race route. The video provided the key break in the case.

Sean Collier, a twenty-seven-year-old who had wanted to be a cop all of his life, was assassinated by the Tsarnaevs as he sat in his MIT police cruiser on the night of Thursday, April 18, in what would be a violent prelude to a violent night.

During a chaotic firefight with the Tsarnaevs in suburban Watertown, a bullet severed the femoral artery of Richard "Dic" Donohue, a thirty-three-year-old police officer with the Massachusetts Bay Transportation Authority. Donohue's fellow officers and firefighters raced to save his life.

A SWAT team assembled on deserted
Nichols Avenue in Watertown during the
manhunt for Dzhokhar Tsarnaev on
Friday, April 19.

Under lockdown as
police combed their
neighborhood for
Dzhokhar Tsarnaev,
Watertown residents
spent much of Friday
watching the drama
unfold on TV and
peering warily out of
their windows, hoping
for a successful ending
to the search.

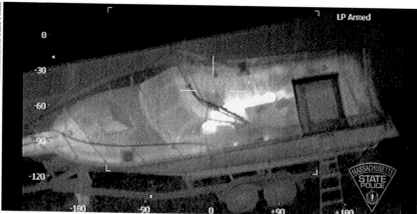

A Massachusetts State Police helicopter equipped with a thermal-imaging camera captured this image of Dzhokhar Tsarnaev hiding in a boat, the *Slipaway II*, in the backyard of David Henneberry. Henneberry discovered Dzhokhar after going out to check on his boat, rushing back inside to call police.

Dzhokhar Tsarnaev left Franklin Street in Watertown in an ambulance on the night of Friday, April 19, after being pulled from the boat by police and taken into custody.

Celebrations erupted in the streets after the capture of Dzhokhar Tsarnaev. Relieved residents crowded Watertown sidewalks to cheer police as they left the scene; others gathered that night on Boston Common to sing and chant "USA!" and "BPD!"

A week after her death, Krystle Campbell's friends and family gathered at St. Joseph Church, in her hometown of Medford, to bid her good-bye. The church had to turn mourners away.

Bombing victim Jeff Bauman, who had locked eyes with Tamerlan Tsarnaev right before losing both of his legs in the first blast, pointed at Carlos Arredondo, the bystander who helped save his life, while being honored at Fenway Park on May 28, 2013.

Heather Abbott threw out the ceremonial first pitch at a Boston Red Sox game at Fenway Park on May 11, 2013. Discharged from the hospital that morning, she returned home to Newport, Rhode Island, later that day, her first time back since the bombing.

Nearly six weeks after the bombing, marathoners, spectators, and first responders came together under a spring rain to rerun the course's final mile, in an event organizers dubbed #onerun.

Samantha Herwig broke down while crossing the finish line of the Run to Remember in Boston, on May 26, 2013, which honored fallen police officer Sean Collier.

The June morning that the city began taking down the memorial in Copley Square, Krystle Campbell's parents, Billy and Patty, toured the site for the first time, taking a rosary as a memento. Many artifacts from the memorial were preserved in the city archive.

Jane Richard, seven, who was the youngest person to lose a leg in the bombing—and whose older brother, Martin, was killed—appeared at Fenway Park on October 13, 2013, with the youth choir from St. Ann Parish in Dorchester. The children sang the national anthem before Game 2 of the American League Championship Series.

Red Sox left fielder Jonny Gomes placed the 2013 World Series trophy on the Boston Marathon finish line during the team's victory parade on November 2, 2013. "This is for you, Boston. You deserve it," veteran Sox slugger David Ortiz had said, after the Red Sox defeated the St. Louis Cardinals three days earlier, earning a World Series title like no other.

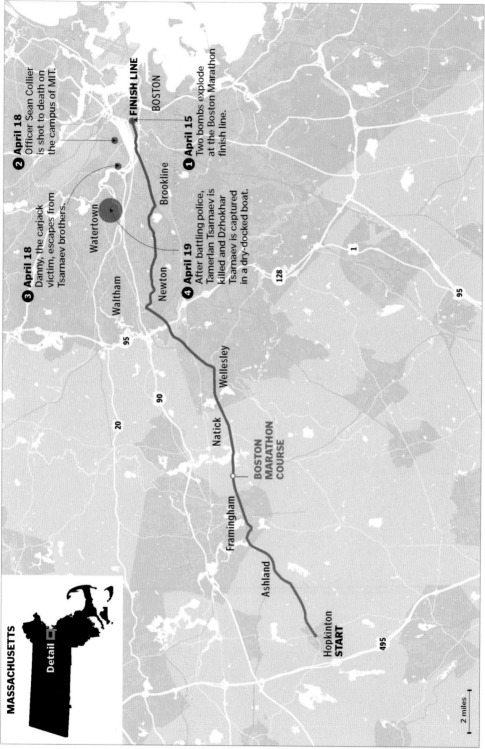

MASSACHUSETTS

Detail

FINISH LINE

BOSTON

2 April 18
Officer Sean Collier is shot to death on the campus of MIT.

3 April 18
Danny, the carjack victim, escapes from Tsarnaev brothers.

Watertown

Waltham

Newton

Brookline

1 April 15
Two bombs explode at the Boston Marathon finish line.

4 April 19
After battling police, Tamerlan Tsarnaev is killed and Dzhokhar Tsarnaev is captured in a dry-docked boat.

Wellesley

Natick

BOSTON MARATHON COURSE

Framingham

Ashland

Hopkinton
START

1

128

95

90

20

95

495

2 miles

Chiqui Esteban/*The Boston Globe*

Detail

BOSTON

DALTON ST.

COMMONWEALTH AVE.

NEWBURY ST.

Hynes
Convention
Center

Prudential
Center

BOYLSTON ST.

Heather Abbott
Amputee

Martin Richard
Victim

Lingzi Lu
Victim

Dzhokhar Tsarnaev
dropped his backpack
outside Forum restaurant
and set off the second
explosion 12 seconds later.

Shana Cottone
Police officer, was between the two blast
sites and rushed toward the second to help.

RING RD.

Lord & Taylor

Krystle Campbell
Victim

Tamerlan Tsarnaev
dropped his
backpack outside
Marathon Sports
and set off the first
explosion.

Old
South
Church

EXETER ST.

Boston
Public
Library

Marathon
finish line

DARTMOUTH ST.

The Westin
Copley Place

COPLEY
SQUARE

Chiqui Esteban/*The Boston Globe*

PART 2

CHAPTER 15

A CITY REBORN

Starting toward normal

t began with a handful of small American flags tucked into the barriers that blocked off Boylston Street. Almost by the hour, in those first uncertain days after the bombing, the makeshift memorial grew, becoming strangely powerful and enduring, a place of pilgrimage and reflection for the thousands of people who flocked to Copley Square. It was as if by getting close, by breathing the air, they might understand what had happened there. Many felt compelled to leave a token, some symbol of their grief or solidarity. And so the bouquet of flags became, too, a rising pile of race medals, candles, and rosary beads. It swelled with running shoes and baseball caps and arrangements of fresh spring flowers, purple irises and yellow daffodils and white lilies. It became, as the days went by, a free-form shrine, adorned with hockey pucks, a bag of Boston Baked Beans candy, and clamshells bearing messages like "Boston will run again." Everything had its place—the stuffed Wisconsin badger, the quartet of elf figurines with *B*s scrawled on their pointy hats, and the quilt of handwritten note cards, left by visitors from around the world:

Houston Loves Boston
Greece Loves Boston
Tibet Stands with Boston
Colombia is with Boston
We will not submit
May the light outshine the darkness

Kevin Brown first saw the memorial on Thursday, three days after the bombing. The fifty-eight-year-old carpenter had tried to get into the Cathedral of the Holy Cross for the interfaith service with President Obama, drawn there by heartache and a love for the city of Boston. The big stone church was full, all of its seats taken, so he joined the milling crowd outside. After the service, Brown walked to Back Bay, where he came upon the memorial. He spent hours there that day, at the eastern edge of the cordoned-off crime scene, in the quiet company of hundreds of others seeking solace. He returned the next day, and again the day after that. When the police ordered the sprawling memorial moved out of the street, he was one of dozens of volunteers who formed a human chain and passed the items down to their new home on a wide swath of plaza in front of the Bank of America at the corner of Boylston and Berkeley Streets. Later, when the city moved the memorial to its third and more lasting home in Copley Square, Brown dutifully followed. It had become, for him, a kind of calling.

The square, named for the colonial portrait painter John Single-ton Copley, is in many ways the heart of Boston. The memorial to the bombing victims lay between the Boston Public Library, the oldest publicly funded library in the country—with its Beaux-Arts façade, interior murals by artist John Singer Sargent, and the motto FREE TO ALL carved above its doors—and the rustic stone profile of Trinity Church, a Romanesque tour de force by the architect H. H. Richardson. Both buildings are on the National Register of Historic Places, as is Old South Church across the street, its Venetian Gothic tower rising above a congregation first established in 1670. Even in a place as history-steeped as Boston, it was hard to find another square boasting three such landmarks. Over the centuries, it had hosted many more. Copley was home to many of the city's best-known institutions before they moved elsewhere: Harvard Medical School, MIT, the Museum of Fine Arts, Boston University, Emerson College, and Northeastern University all started there. It was a remarkable run of history for a swath of land that began the nineteenth century as an 850-acre tidal marsh, part of the Charles River estuary, and was filled in with sand and gravel to relieve overcrowding in the city in the 1850s. The massive job of creating the new neighborhood took decades—the work went on even in the middle of the Civil War and, at its peak, saw some four hundred train car loads of fill delivered to Back Bay daily. The landscape that arose on that hard-won foundation became a thing of beauty, an elegant embodiment of the city's loftiest ambitions.

The week following the bombing, Brown spent hours there, day after day, helping to organize the maze of mementos on the pavement at the edge of the square. He felt a welcome sense of purpose; the simple routine gave him comfort. Three weeks before the marathon, Brown had lost his mother. Isabelle Brown was ninety when she died, after a long, full life, and he hadn't expected it to hit him like it did. His mother had been a pillar of strength—she raised eleven children while working two jobs after Brown's father became disabled—and she and her fourth son had enjoyed an unusually close relationship. "We were exactly alike," Brown said. "We clicked. I made sure she was treated like a queen." His careful work at the memorial became, in part, a tribute to her.

Soon Brown was spending twelve hours a day at the site, taking on the role of unofficial caretaker. It comforted him to see the reverent crowds who gathered at all hours, to hear them saying prayers and singing hymns, to watch them unlace their sneakers, leave them there, and walk home barefoot. He loved the children who approached to ask, ever so politely, where to hang the drawings they had made. It gave him peace to light the candles on the ground as darkness fell, to replace the dead flowers with fresh ones, and to talk with those who wanted company. He met the governor and the vice president's wife, Jill Biden, a runner who stopped by to leave her shoes beside the others. People brought him cups of hot coffee and fresh rolls of tape. They passed him cash and told him to buy what was needed: more flowers, more candles, sheets of plastic to cover the place when it rained. He served at their will; they had made the place together. It was hard to explain what it meant or why it mattered, but one visitor, Sally Graham of Dorchester, came close: "In some ways, it says to me [that] good does outweigh evil."

A carpenter from Indiana had built three wooden crosses for the memorial, one each for Martin, Krystle, and Lingzi, the victims who had been killed at the finish line. Visitors draped rosary beads over each one; every day, Brown carefully rearranged the heavy, tangled necklaces so the name on each cross could be easily seen. After people began asking about a cross for slain MIT police officer Sean Collier, Brown built a fourth cross just like the others, roughly three feet tall. He carried it to Boston on the bus and subway from his home in Brockton, a blue-collar city twenty-five miles to the south. Brown's daily trek to the memorial took ninety minutes each way; the commuter train would have been faster, but it cost twice as much and he could not afford it. A serious back injury had prevented him from working much in recent years.

The same day Brown brought the fourth cross to Boston, Collier's father showed up and stayed at the memorial for hours, helping the caretaker paint his son's name on the cross. "Boston needed a place to heal," Brown said later, reflecting on the outpouring he witnessed. "I never thought it would grow so big and last so long." His family didn't understand what he was doing in a far-off Boston park, but he believed his work there had clear purpose. If the memorial became an eyesore, the city would take it away, leaving people—leaving him—with no place to grieve.

On Saturday, the day after the citywide lockdown and the capture of Dzhokhar Tsarnaev, residents woke to a perfect spring day, buds in the trees and forsythia blooming brilliant yellow. They reveled in the leisurely routine of a normal—or almost normal—Saturday: pancake breakfasts and kids' soccer games; dog walks and birthday parties. Boylston Street was still closed, and David Henneberry's Watertown backyard was still teeming with FBI agents, as it would be for more than a week. But elsewhere it was possible to begin moving on from the harrowing five-day ride that had just ended. The day felt like a gift, and to some, a celebration of endurance and resilience. "Yeah! We're alive!" one resident, Roberta Nicoloro, shouted, greeting her neighbors with hugs after emerging from her home in Watertown.

The assault that began with two backpacks on the sidewalk had inspired, from the start, a posture of defiance. A few hours after the explosions, two Emerson College students opened up a laptop and designed a simple T-shirt they could sell to raise money for the victims, a way to transform helplessness into useful action. For a slogan, they chose BOSTON STRONG, a local adaptation of the LIVESTRONG campaign made famous a decade earlier by cyclist and cancer survivor Lance Armstrong. It was simple, more about the place than the event, and it struck the right tone, the two students thought. They ordered 110 blue-and-yellow shirts and hoped for the best. Within a day or two, their rallying cry had struck a chord, becoming universal shorthand for the way the city wanted to be seen—and to see itself—after the tragedy: unbroken and unbowed. It appeared on city buses and on billboards, on stickers and wristbands, on baseball hats and storefronts. Mayor Menino embraced it, and beloved Red Sox slugger David Ortiz did, too, in his own memorable way. "This is our fucking city, and nobody is going to dictate our freedom," he told the cheering crowd at Fenway on Saturday. "Stay strong." Within two weeks, the Emerson students, Nick Reynolds and Chris Dobens, would sell more than forty-seven thousand T-shirts, raising $716,000 for the victims.

Boston's embrace of the slogan was not without backlash. Critics of the way the city had handled the day of the capture, with its sweeping shutdown of just about everything, mocked Bostonians for calling themselves strong. "Last time I saw them they were cowering indoors," observed one unimpressed out-of-towner in an online post. Mental health experts voiced concern that widespread use of the term "Boston Strong" might marginalize those traumatized by the attacks, making them feel weak or discouraging them from seeking help. But if some people wore the T-shirts as a display of strength or defiance—an easy proposition for anyone not directly touched by the bombing—far more were drawn to the "Boston Strong" campaign as a way to publicly support the victims. There was the donation they were making—of the $20 paid for every shirt, $15 went to the victims' fund—but there was also the unified message they were sending to the wounded men and women watching from the city's hospitals: *We stand behind you.* The victims heard, and signaled their appreciation. Heather Abbott wore a personalized "Heather Strong" T-shirt. The Richard family wrote in a statement that "Martin was 'Boston Strong,' and now we all must be, for him and for all of the victims." Billy and Patty Campbell later toured the memorial in Copley Square clad in the iconic blue-and-yellow T-shirts.

That impulse to help, which had inspired both the bystanders improvising tourniquets and the college students selling T-shirts, swept the city in the days after the attack, a philanthropic wave that surged over the most optimistic projections. The calls had begun flooding the mayor's office and the governor's office early Tuesday morning, the day after the bombing. They came from corporations and from individuals in Boston and around the country, asking what they could do to help and offering money. Menino and Patrick spoke briefly before the morning press conference that day at the Westin and agreed they must act fast to set up a fund for the victims. Menino gathered his team in his hospital room after the briefing and made a plan: They would recruit volunteers to run the fund, and solicit free office space, minimizing administrative costs. The mayor was adamant that it would be a single fund, an undivided pool of cash to provide the maximum benefit and equity. They would call it the One Fund; the website would be ready to go live that night. If they could bring in $10 million, Menino thought, that would be a success. But the calls kept coming, more than he ever imagined. By the end of the first week, they had reached $20 million; by summer, the total would climb past $60 million. "People wanted to give $1 million, half a million, matches," Menino said. "Everybody was saying, 'I don't need to be recognized.' I'd never seen anything like that." John Hancock Financial, the lead sponsor of the marathon, gave the first $1 million gift. Athletic shoe maker New Balance gave $1 million; other corporations lined up behind them. The Red Sox initially contributed more than $600,000, a figure that would grow, with help from partners, beyond $2 million. Millions more streamed in online from individuals around the world. Menino reached out to Ken Feinberg, the administrator of the 9/11 victims fund and a Massachusetts native, to ask for his help in distributing the payments.

The last thing Menino needed or expected at such a critical moment was the Internal Revenue Service getting in his way. The mayor had been firm from the start: that the money would go to aid, not administration, and that the setup would be simple and streamlined. He wanted a few volunteers in a donated room processing incoming checks as fast as they could. But the IRS was cool on his plan, Menino said, telling him, in essence, "Just a minute, Mr. Mayor." For reasons the mayor found utterly uncompelling, the IRS wanted donations channeled through a city or state agency. They wanted him to organize a fund-raising event. The mayor was furious at the interference. "Why?" he demanded to know. "We already have the money, and we don't need the bureaucracy." He started calling everyone he could think of who might intervene, all the way up to Vice President Joe Biden. Finally, something shifted—maybe it was all the phone calls; maybe it was the erupting IRS scandal over its screening of political groups—but in mid-May, the One Fund received its tax-free designation.

Barely two weeks before the marathon bombing, Menino had stood in Faneuil Hall and announced that he would not seek a sixth term in office. It was a deeply emotional moment for him, saying farewell to the city he loved and had served for a record two decades—a onetime insurance man, elected mayor after a decade as a little-known city council member from Hyde Park, a neighborhood on Boston's southern fringes. He was seventy, and despite his recent health problems, he vowed to use his remaining time well: "I have nine months left—just think of what I could do in nine months! We could have some real fun." In truth, his legacy was more or less cemented by this point: He was the fabled urban mechanic, focused on the little things that make city life work: the throwback pol with a long memory and reach into every neighborhood. He would never win eloquence awards—some had nicknamed him "Mayor Mumbles," fondly or not so fondly—but his twenty years in city hall had been untainted by scandal, and his stamina was unmatched. Polls showed that Menino had personally met more than half the city's residents, an incredible yet completely believable feat, given his near-constant visibility at parades, cookouts, ribbon cuttings, and tree lightings.

This was not exactly how Menino had envisioned the twilight of his term. He could not have foreseen a period so demanding and emotionally draining. In some terrible way, the bombing on Boylston Street seemed to complete a cycle that had begun a dozen years earlier, on a sparkling September morning at Logan Airport, when two planes roared down the runway, rose above the sunlit water, and turned south, headed for New York. That day, September 11, 2001, had been among the worst Menino had faced. Boston's connection to the attack on the World Trade Center towers was an enduring source of pain and frustration for him. At the time, he had wondered in private if his city would be next, and now, more than a decade later, his fear had finally been realized. There was no comparison between the scale of the events, but this one was his.

The bombing was an unprecedented moment, and yet Menino's read of it was characteristic, infused with his optimism and pride in his hometown. He saw a city that would be stronger for the experience. He lauded the teamwork among city, state, and federal agencies that had come together, more or less seamlessly, and he was moved by the actions of ordinary people, like the college students who raised more than half a million dollars selling T-shirts. He imagined keeping the spirit of collaboration alive, using it to fuel progress in other areas. "We're a big city, but we are also a small city," Menino said the day after Boylston Street reopened to the public, as he sat having lunch on the patio outside the Lenox Hotel. "Helping neighbors out: That's what this renewal is all about."

With money continuing to pour in for the victims, the end of Marathon Week brought another surge of feeling, this one for the first responders. The Boston Bruins invited twenty-six of them to their home game at the TD Garden on Sunday, and after the final buzzer, brought them onto the ice for an emotional ceremony. Most of those honored were police and firefighters, but David King was there, too, looking slightly uncomfortable in his sport jacket, holding his six-year-old daughter's hand as they waited for his name to be called. "Brad Marchand, meet Dr. King!" came the booming voice of the announcer. The Canadian forward skated over, pulled off his black-and-gold jersey, and handed it to the doctor as the crowd lingering in the seventeen-thousand-seat rink roared its approval. King was not an avid sports fan by any stretch, but in that moment, feeling the warmth of the gesture, it didn't matter. "That was the coolest thing that ever happened, at least to me," he said later, after the jersey had been signed and framed and hung in a prominent spot on the wall of his office at Mass General.

It was, for King as for many of the police there on the ice with him, a striking departure from everyday routine in a world where their efforts were not always appreciated. Caring for trauma patients was not like working in other specialties, where doctors sometimes built long relationships with patients. King's patients often appeared at 2:00 A.M. with gunshot or stabbing wounds, and it sometimes seemed to him that they expected to be saved, and took it for granted, no matter how many hours and how much effort it took. When he went to check on such patients the next day, introducing himself as "the doc who fixed you," it was rare to hear a word of thanks. "When's breakfast?" was a more common response. Looking back over the course of his trauma career, King could count on one hand the patients with whom he had connected deeply and stayed in touch. Never in his life, before the marathon bombing, had he felt such gratitude for the work he did, and the feeling was at times a little overwhelming.

Boylston Street, a place usually packed with people and life, remained desolate. Up close, it looked like a movie set: Gatorade cups strewn everywhere, folding tables, water bottles, and barricades left in disarray. As if bombs had gone off everywhere. On the weekend following the attack, Dave McGillivray and a small marathon team got their first chance to return. The city wanted to reopen Boylston as soon as possible, and the remnants of the marathon had to be swept away first. After getting permission from the FBI, they put on full-body hazmat suits and began the messy work of cleaning up, of restoring Boylston to its normal state. On Saturday, they worked on the street, clearing away the race debris. On Sunday, a couple of McGillivray's deputies cleaned the medical tent. It was not a pleasant task. They were surrounded by the evidence of Monday's trauma and by reminders of the hasty exits, like the unclaimed bags with runners' bib numbers attached. They tried to remain stoic, to stay focused on the work. "I'm as emotional as anyone, but I also gotta get beyond it and get the job done," McGillivray said. "That's my calling. That's what God put me here for."

It had not been easy, for anyone, to put the street back together. The evidence—the ball bearings and nails shot by the bombs with lacerating force; the fragments of the brothers' backpacks—all of that was gone, collected and sorted and labeled and sent to crime labs for processing. The blood and the orange FBI spray paint had been removed from the sidewalks, steamed away in the wee hours of Tuesday morning, eight days after the bombing. But residents and business owners let back in later that Tuesday had found a street frozen in time. Hotel workers had to sweep up broken glass and mop up blood from tiled floors, left behind by injured people who had run inside seeking safety. "I'm just trying to pull it together," said Mark Hagopian, operating partner of the Charlesmark Hotel. "It's eerie.

It just feels haunted a little bit." Employees at other businesses found more shattered windows and bloodstained carpets, half-eaten pizzas and half-empty bottles of beer, swarms of fruit flies and rodents that had moved in. The losses to Boylston Street businesses were staggering, with early estimates in the tens of millions of dollars and little clarity about how much would be covered by insurance.

In the midst of the mess were countless poignant reminders of the joyful way Marathon Monday had unfolded until 2:50 P.M. GO LAURA GO, read a small sign tucked into the corner of one store window. Sharon Maes returned to her apartment near Forum wearing the same bright green pants and orange sweater she had been wearing when the second bomb exploded, as she cowered in her doorway a few feet away. She had left without her wedding ring; her husband had left without his wallet. "We don't even know if we locked the door," she said. Coming home triggered conflicting emotions. "I'm happy, but I'm sad," she said. "I'm very confused about how it will feel." There would be one last private gathering on the Boylston sidewalks before the street's strange separation from the city ended. As darkness fell on Tuesday, Mayor Menino, under a cold rain, escorted a few dozen family members of the victims to the two blast sites. They huddled together beneath a tent, looking out at the place where their loved ones—who had gathered there to celebrate—had instead faced death.

If there was one moment that most powerfully symbolized the promise of better days ahead, it came before dawn on Wednesday, April 24, nine days after the explosions left their mark. At 3:35 that morning, police officers lifted the barricades blocking Boylston Street and stacked them on the sidewalk. With no further ceremony, the street reopened to cars and pedestrians, its empty stores and restaurants and sidewalks ready to return to business. As the sun came up, coffee shops hummed with activity. Two panhandlers got back to work at the corner of Exeter Street. Everything looked normal from a distance, except for some boarded-up windows, but if you watched closely, you could see it: hitches in the foot traffic past the bombing sites, people pausing to absorb the new significance of the two places on the sidewalk. Up the street at the victims' memorial in Copley Square, a new sign had appeared in the days just before Boylston reopened, asking: CAN YOU FEEL A BRAND-NEW DAY? It was the feeling that the city had been longing for, and with the crime scene gone, it seemed to finally be a possibility.

At Marathon Sports, right where the first bomb had gone off, manager Shane O'Hara had gone back in with the store's owner on Tuesday, at the eight-day mark. A crew from ARS Restoration Specialists—experts in reclaiming places where bad things had happened—had already done the worst of the cleanup, ripping up the rug, removing the tiles, and ridding the storefront of bloodstains. Even with the progress, the place in many ways looked as it did when they'd left—nearly full beer bottles, empty apparel racks, broken hangers. O'Hara felt uncomfortable in there, like he was snooping around in his own store. His sense of unease was amplified by what they all now knew about the first bomb's toll, the young life—Krystle Campbell's—that had been taken right outside their door. "It was just a disgusting feeling that day," he said. The next day, Wednesday, O'Hara and his staff tried to rebuild; the owner was eager to reopen. They straightened up the front of the store. O'Hara scrubbed his office. He put away an extra register they had taken out for the weekend of the marathon, typically a peak time for sales. *I'm starting all over again*, he thought.

When Thursday came, emotions among the staff ran high. They took a group picture. They had pizza together. They made some speeches. They shared tears. Then they were finally ready to face the world again. After the bombing, O'Hara and some of his colleagues had made a pact that they wouldn't go out the front door of Marathon Sports again until the store was open—that they would use only the back entrance until customers were allowed inside. The last time O'Hara had been through the front door was a week ago Monday, when he'd been tending to the wounded on the sidewalk. Afterward, using it just didn't feel right. Around 2:00 P.M., the staff tore down the paper covering the front of the store, walked together to the front door, and threw it open. Outside, a crowd of people had gathered, maybe two hundred strong. O'Hara and his staff formed a line to welcome them in. At first, no one moved. Someone started clapping, and then everyone started clapping. O'Hara and the others led customers inside. It was gangbusters from the opening minutes. The support from the public that day, and in the days that would follow, was cathartic. The outpouring would never erase the tragic memories that O'Hara and his colleagues carried. But it was a start.

CHAPTER 16

LETTING GO

The only way forward

All week long, Heather Abbott had been waiting.

She had been waiting with her friends to get into Forum when the second bomb exploded a few feet away. Then she had waited on the ground for someone to help her, and for an ambulance to make it down the street. After doctors at Brigham and Women's Hospital saved her badly damaged foot, Heather had waited to see if the transplanted blood vessels would take, and what her prospects of a normal life would be. Finally she had made her decision, the hardest she had ever faced. She was ready to move on, yet here she was, waiting again. Her fourth and final surgery—the surgery that would set her new course—had been scheduled for first thing Monday morning, one week after the bombing. The morning had been busy, though. Her surgeons had fallen behind. They kept postponing the time of her operation, first by one hour, then again. This delay was excruciating. Now that she had made up her mind, she wanted it all behind her. She needed to stop dwelling on what was about to happen and start figuring out how to deal with it.

Heather had decided to amputate her left leg below the knee. In the end, after long consultation with doctors, and with people who had faced the same choice, she had felt surprising clarity. The pain she had fought all week was almost unbearable. Living the rest of her life that way, in discomfort and on medication, was not something she was willing to accept. Neither was the likelihood that she would be unable to walk normally, or run. If she kept her mangled foot, doctors told her, it would never look the same. With a prosthetic leg, she could look almost like herself. Heather knew she had to be honest about what mattered to her. She wanted to live an active life; she wanted to look healthy and normal and attractive. If she couldn't do those things, could she be happy?

Her friend Jason had been with her the night before, on Sunday, when a nurse came to mark her left leg for the surgery. The below-the-knee amputation meant her loss would be easier to cope with than those of some other victims, whose legs had been amputated higher up. To give her a full range of prosthetic options, though, doctors would take some healthy tissue, higher up on Heather's leg, as well as her devastated foot. She could have opted to lose just the foot, but her doctors and other amputees explained that the highest-tech, most lifelike new prosthetics—those that would allow her the greatest range of motion and activity—were designed to replace the foot, ankle, and lower leg. As more advanced prosthetics were developed, some amputees who had lost a foot were even opting to go back to surgery and give up part of their leg, in order to gain a higher quality of life. Heather didn't want to go only halfway and then regret it. But the thought of her losing more than just the foot pained Jason; he had struggled, from the start, with the thought of any kind of amputation. Heather tried to reassure him that the choice was for the best, and that she had made her peace with it.

After he had gone and she was alone in her hospital bed, the finality of what was coming hit her with full force. Heather was almost always collected and rational, strikingly so. The young doctor who had taken her into surgery the night of the bombing told her later he had never seen a patient stay so calm with injuries so severe. But the week had been cruel. The rising hope of its early days—when it had looked like her foot could be saved—had collapsed. In the nighttime quiet of the hospital, Heather broke down and cried.

Medford was the city where he'd grown up, the city where he'd learned to love running and launched his career in race management. Dave McGillivray had returned many times since. But never for something like this. It was Sunday evening, six days after the marathon bombing. Krystle Campbell's parents were holding their daughter's wake at Dello Russo Funeral Home on Main Street. McGillivray had grown up with the Dello Russos. When McGillivray's father died a few years earlier, the family had held his wake there. It was surreal to be back on this day, for this reason, but he knew he needed to make an appearance. With his presence, the marathon itself was sharing the family's grief. McGillivray planned to meet a couple of colleagues from the Boston Athletic Association at the funeral home. One was Amy Dominici, a consultant who'd worked on the race for years. McGillivray called Dominici when he arrived, asking where she was. She told him she was already in the line, which snaked down the block and all the way around a corner. McGillivray parked his car and went to find her. When he did, he couldn't believe where they were standing. It was the street where he'd lived as a young boy. His childhood home, the two-family his grandfather had built, with the basement playroom his father had added for the kids, stood only a few houses away.

The line moved glacially. Dominici went to the front to see if they could get in quickly ahead of the others. McGillivray hated to cut lines, but he wasn't wild about spending two or three hours waiting, either. The funeral director then ushered Dominici, McGillivray, and Tom Grilk, the executive director of the BAA, inside. In a room near the entrance, photos from Krystle's life were arrayed on poster board—Krystle in a New England Patriots jersey; at Fenway Park; in a wedding party on a beach. In nearly every shot, her signature smile radiated. McGillivray was nervous about meeting her family. He didn't know what to say. He let Dominici take the lead.

"We're all here from the BAA," she told Krystle's mother, Patty.

"I'm sorry," Patty said, "I don't know what that is."

It was a humbling moment for McGillivray. He realized how much bigger than the Boston Marathon this was. He grew uneasy, wondering if Krystle's family would hold him responsible somehow. All of this had happened at *his* race, after all. Without the marathon, there would have been no bombs. Their daughter would still be alive.

Dominici explained that the BAA was the organization that staged the marathon.

"Oh, how nice of you to come," Patty said, and then she and Dominici shared a laugh about how young Patty looked. McGillivray was relieved. It had gone okay. Dominici had successfully broken the ice, and he had paid his respects. They left soon after.

With hundreds of mourners still in line, Dello Russo had to keep its doors open beyond the four hours set aside for the wake. One of those waiting, Melanie Fitzemeyer, thirty-nine, was a former babysitter of Krystle's. The skin on her forearm was still pink from the tattoo of Krystle's name she'd had inked into her flesh the night before. "I'm here because my heart hurts," said another woman in the line, Barbara Moynihan, fifty-six, who had gone to school with Krystle's father. "I have two daughters, and if I lost one of my daughters—there are just no words." When the sun set, the wait to get into the funeral home grew windy and cold. Few, if any, gave up. As the first wake or funeral for any of the Marathon Week victims, the night had become a vessel for public grief, the first opportunity to shake a hand, give a hug, offer words of condolence. For hours, Patty and her family gamely received the goodwill, much of it from perfect strangers. Krystle, they understood, was a symbol of a city's sorrow, but she was more than that to them. She was a daughter, a granddaughter, a sister, a niece.

The next morning, under a bright blue sky, hundreds of friends, family, neighbors, well-wishers from Medford, and dignitaries packed into St. Joseph Church in the center of the city to bid Krystle goodbye. About two hundred people were still waiting to get in when the church hit capacity. Police and spectators lined High Street. An honor detail of firefighters formed a corridor leading up to the church doors, snapping to attention and saluting as pallbearers passed with the casket. A solitary church bell tolled as the crowd fell silent. When the service was over, the pallbearers carried Krystle's casket back outside and into a waiting hearse. Krystle's mom, dad, and brother walked out behind it, her seventy-nine-year-old nana, Lillian, whom she had nursed through ill health, following closely behind.

The funeral procession journeyed a mile or so up the road to Medford's Oak Grove Cemetery, the place where, as it happened, Dave McGillivray had mowed the grass as a kid. There, too, not everyone could fit, so they cut off the flow of cars. At first, before Krystle's family got there, mourners stayed back from the grave. When the family arrived, the crowd filled in around them. A hush fell over the gathering. "Our citizenship is in heaven," said the Reverend Chip Hines, the pastor of St. Joseph Church, reading from the Letter of Saint Paul to the Philippians. In the months ahead, Krystle's final resting place would be marked with a reddish gravestone bearing her photograph within the outline of a heart. It would blossom with red, pink, and orange flowers, a faded blue Red Sox cap, an angel figurine with shamrocks. On this day, a week after her death, her friends had trouble leaving her for the last time. Krystle had always surrounded herself with people. She had loved good company more than anything. She had been a devoted confidante, a beloved coworker, a big piece of everyone's sunshine. But her friends also knew that Krystle would want them to move on, to seize the promise of their own lives. As her friend Tim Getchell later explained, "She'd kick our asses if we just sat around and cried."

Brian Fleming spent the week making lists of names. From the moment the bombs had exploded, the director of the Boston Police Department's peer support unit had been focused on one task: figuring out which officers could be at psychological risk from what they had witnessed that day. He started with those working at the finish line, in what he called "the bull's-eye"—the center of the mayhem. They were the ones most likely to suffer traumatic stress. From there he moved outward, to the police in the surrounding rings of impact: one step, two steps, three steps removed from the action. The research took days. Together with his tiny staff, Fleming interviewed first responders who had been on Boylston Street and studied photographs and video clips, trying to make sure he didn't miss anyone. All of them would be summoned to a debriefing, a meeting to talk about what they had seen and felt and done. It didn't matter if they thought they needed it or not. The group sessions would start Monday, a week after the bombing, and they were mandatory.

The scale of the undertaking was unprecedented. A typical stress-inducing "critical incident"—a shooting or the death of a child, for example—might involve half a dozen officers out of a force of two thousand. They would gather for a single session to talk about it. Fleming's team normally ran two or three such meetings a month, including some for members of police departments elsewhere. When the list of marathon responders was finished, it included 650 people. It would take nine days and fifty-seven sessions to reach them all. Some of the discussions lasted two hours; others stretched to five or six. Sitting together in classrooms at a union training center, they reviewed what had happened when the bombs went off, filling in the blank spots for one another. They discussed their own reactions. They learned about the most likely symptoms of stress—anxiety, insomnia, tics—and how to handle them in a healthy way, without becoming isolated or obsessed. "We try to get it out so they don't bury it," Fleming said.

The discussions were led by a special team of forty BPD officers, who worked regular police shifts but were also trained to help their peers. In addition, the New York City Police Department sent eighteen retired and active officers, all similarly trained, to assist. The added manpower was appreciated, and so was the message that their presence sent. If anyone came in thinking the meetings were overkill or a needless formality, the sight of the NYPD changed their attitude. "Then they knew it was serious business," said Fleming. "No one has the experience they did." When the New York officers talked about how 9/11 affected them, it gave the Boston officers permission to open up.

Everything that happened in the rooms was confidential. Still, the push for honesty was an uphill battle. "Cops don't want to bare their souls," said Fleming. Despite the heavy emphasis on protecting privacy, some worried that something they said would leak out. Some were afraid of being seen as weak, in a job where strength was everything. *I'm okay, I'm fine* was their default position. Sometimes Fleming thought "fine" ought to be a red flag. So his team kept at it for weeks and months, chipping away at the resistance over time, making phone calls and meeting people for coffee. After the mandatory sessions were over, as he kept making the rounds, he sometimes found a cop he thought should go for counseling. Just try it once, he would suggest. If you don't like it, okay. Months later, in the fall, there would be calls from officers who had just begun to connect their symptoms to the bombing. The calls could keep trickling in for years.

The events at the marathon finish line had been tough for everyone, veterans and rookies alike, but the more experienced responders at least had previous experience with trauma. There had been a lot of young officers at the finish line that day; some of them saw their first dead body on Boylston Street. After it was over, the youngest, greenest cops were the ones most likely to rush back to work. They were eager to prove they could handle it: to show the world that they were fine, whatever they had seen.

Shana Cottone knew she needed some time off. On Saturday, the day after the dramatic capture in Watertown, she packed up her car and her pet beagle, Monkey, and headed south to New York, where she had grown up. She had yet to make sense of what had happened at the finish line. She badly needed a change of scenery and a few days away from TV. When she drove onto the ferry that would take her to Long Island, it was clear to her how much the week had seeped into her head. She was anxious the moment she got on the boat, hypervigilant in a way she had never been before on this easy homeward trip across the water.

Working her regular beat in East Boston the previous day, Shana had been riveted by the manhunt. She flipped on the radio while driving to work at 5:30 A.M. and discovered what had happened overnight. The death of Sean Collier hit her hard. *That could have been any one of us*, she thought. Two of her friends lived in the zone that was locked down; imagining how nervous they must be, she called one of them to offer reassurance. She sent a text message to a fellow police officer, a good friend, to remind him to wear his bulletproof vest. All week she had been waiting for something to happen. Even as the door-to-door searches dragged on all day, Shana felt in her gut that some resolution was coming. She had promised Roseann and her family that the bombers would be captured, and she felt a personal responsibility. At one point she stepped into a bar on her beat to check for the latest updates on TV. Later, she heard some other police officers discussing possible outcomes; one said the cops should kill the suspect when they found him. Shana could not resist interrupting. "Keep your opinion to yourself," she said sharply. "Some people want to see him tried in court." When police finally surrounded Dzhokhar Tsarnaev on the boat, Shana's adrenaline surged. She watched the standoff on the TV in the lunchroom at the station, jumping around like a kid in her excitement, sending updates via text message to Roseann's sister. She felt almost giddy with relief when it was over.

The next morning, though, the giddiness was gone, and the weight of the week resettled on her shoulders. She just wanted to get out of Boston and see her dad. The phone call she had made to him from the van right after the bombing had been one of the worst moments of her life; she believed then that she might never see him again. It was strange and sad to think how abruptly things had changed: When Shana first moved to Boston from New York, not long after 9/11, it had been her new city that felt safe. Now a shadow lay over both places. She hoped when she got to Long Island, she could stop thinking about Monday. Her mind kept traveling back to those minutes in the street. As she drove south, she kept picturing the victims. She wondered when the memory would fade. It would not be soon, she was sure of that.

At Boston Medical Center, Celeste Corcoran was one week ahead of Heather. The mother of two had lost both her legs in the bombing, and now, as the haze of medication lifted, the reality of her situation was settling in. It was impossible for her to see how her life could ever be normal. On Sunday, as Heather was summoning her resolve and counting down the hours until surgeons would take her leg, Celeste was in tears in her hospital bed. She wiped her eyes with tissues, clutching her daughter's hand, as a marine with two prosthetic legs stood before her. Hospital monitors beeped in the background as he spoke with clear conviction, on a mission to convince her she would walk again.

"I can't do anything right now," Celeste said, her voice shaking.

"Right now, yes," the young man allowed. "But I'm telling you with all my heart, you are going to be more independent than you ever were. . . . This isn't the end, this is the beginning."

None of the amputees could know what was coming. Everything was still ahead of them, and some of it would be unimaginably painful. In the lull before the months of hard work started, visitors like these marines delivered motivation. "We knew that everyone had had a very rough week, and we knew that these guys would walk in and just give them hope," said Karen Guenther, president of the Semper Fi Fund, the nonprofit group that sent the marines, Gabe Martinez and Cameron West, to visit amputees at four Boston hospitals that weekend.

The city and the nation, also craving reassurance, seized upon the hope the visit offered to the Corcorans. A video of the bedside interaction, uploaded to YouTube by a relative and then posted on Celeste's Facebook page, was viewed more than 100,000 times in less than two days. *Progress, one day at a time*, her cousin wrote online. All the amputees—sixteen in total, all of them now missing one or both legs—would work toward the same milestones. One by one, they would leave the hospitals where the ambulances had first taken them. They would move to Spaulding Rehabilitation Hospital in Boston, a gleaming new facility on the waterfront near historic Bunker Hill. There they would be fitted with their first prosthetic legs, and then, over grueling weeks of therapy, learn to stand up, balance without crutches, and to walk. They would learn how to get out of bed, how to shower, and how to care for the remaining portions of their trun-cated limbs. Some would be haunted by "phantom pain" that seemed to come from the leg that was gone, a phenomenon poorly under-stood and hard to treat. Doctors would try to strike a delicate balance in managing pain, blocking it enough for them to start rehabilitation, while keeping the fog of the narcotics from getting in their way. Some who had lost one leg to amputation were left with a remaining leg that was badly damaged. The "good" leg could slow their progress, and in the most serious cases, the threat that they could face a second amputation lingered. The last patient to remain at Spaulding, Marc Fucarile—the man Shana had escorted to Mass General in the police van—would not go home until late July, one hundred days after the bombing.

They had all lost their limbs at a time of growing interest in the plight of amputees. More than 1,500 American soldiers had lost limbs in combat since the wars in Iraq and Afghanistan began a dozen years earlier, drawing attention to the two million people in the United States living with amputations. Scientists like Hugh Herr at MIT, himself a double amputee, had begun developing more so-phisticated prosthetics: computer-controlled knees and robotic an-kles. There were prosthetic legs that contained microprocessors and motion sensors, and legs with custom-made silicone skin and sculpted toes that looked astonishingly real. Increasingly, wounded soldiers had begun choosing to have their severely damaged legs amputated and replaced with high-tech prosthetics—sometimes months or years after being injured—to achieve a higher quality of life. The amputees in Boston didn't realize it yet, but the international attention focused on their suffering would bring another burst of momentum to the field. It would also spur debate about the high costs of better prosthetics, as survivors discovered they had limited insurance coverage for artificial limbs that could cost $1 million over the course of a lifetime.

For Celeste Corcoran, the way forward may have begun with the marine at the foot of her bed. As he encouraged her, she grew more composed. She stopped crying and talked about her sister Carmen, how proud she had been to go and watch her finish her first-ever marathon. She told the marines how her sister didn't get to cross the finish line, because of the bombs, and how Carmen planned to run again next year, for Celeste. Warming to the conversation, she even joked about becoming a runner herself. "Running's never been my thing, because I always get the most horrible shin splints," she confessed. "Now," she said, gesturing down at her missing legs, "I don't have shins anymore. I'm not gonna be having shin splints. I can do this."

"That's the attitude right there," one marine told her approvingly.

As she wept in her hospital bed that Sunday night before her surgery, Heather's distress lit up the monitors in the nurses' station. A nurse who came to check on her sat down by her bed. The woman knew what Heather was facing, and she stayed at her side for an hour, reviewing all the reasons for choosing amputation. It helped, and Heather was finally able to sleep. On Monday, her resolve returned. She would make this final trip to the operating room, and then she would start working, day by day, to get her life back. The bombing had left her with a terrible, complicated problem, one that seemed almost insurmountable. But solving problems was her specialty. Somehow, she felt confident she would find a way.

The doctors made their final preparations for the operation. They warned her about a needle that was coming, but assured her that they would sedate her first. She started to nod off, the drugs making her sleepy. Then she felt the needle stab her in the thigh, a piercing pain that jerked her to alertness instantly. "Wait, I can feel it," she gasped. No one else seemed alarmed or surprised. Finally, then, the anesthesia swallowed her. She would not wake again until it was all over. When she returned to her room that afternoon, her friends were lined up in the hallway waiting for her. Exactly one week earlier, they had been with her at the marathon. They had stayed by her side, waiting to see if her foot would be saved, and now they were here for the start of the next phase, when she would learn to navigate the world anew. Her friend Jason found himself crying. He couldn't believe they had ended up here. He held on to Heather's arm and couldn't let go.

Jason couldn't yet see what Heather already knew: She was going to fight her way back, whatever it took. The very next day, she would get out of bed and stand up using a walker. Two days after that, again leaning on the walker, she would will herself to somehow move ten feet. The nurses and family watching her beamed. Heather, unimpressed, thought, *Oh boy . . . If they're that excited about ten feet, this is really going to take a long time.* She was still in constant pain—now at the site of the amputation instead of her foot—but at least the pain would end someday, when the leg was healed. "This is the situation I'm faced with, and it's not going to change," she would say three days after the surgery, facing a room full of reporters at her first hospital press conference. "To dwell on the negative would be a waste of time."

CHAPTER 17

MISSING THE SIGNALS

Radical views and unsolved murders

With every day that passed, the questions burned brighter: What had driven two brothers, one married to a Rhode Island girl, the other a college kid who'd been well liked at his Cambridge high school, to kill and maim at the Boston Marathon? What had pushed them to this place—was it disaffection with their adopted country? Resentment at their station in life? Some faint identification with foreign jihadists? As Marathon Week receded, no clear answer emerged. There were plenty of reasons why it didn't matter—and plenty of people who made it clear they didn't care. But along with the anger and dismissal there was longing for a way to make sense of it, a box to put it all in. What the Tsarnaevs had done was evil enough. The lack of clarity about their motivations only made their disregard for life more difficult to stomach.

What was clear, within minutes of Dzhokhar's capture, was that this was not the first time that US authorities—from local homicide investigators to federal intelligence officials—had heard the name Tsarnaev. Not even close. Shortly after the chase ended that Friday night, the FBI acknowledged that its agents had investigated Tamerlan for suspected terrorist inclinations two years earlier. Within days, it came out that the CIA had, too. In Boston and in Washington, news of the government's past probes sparked pointed questions: Could the bombing have been prevented? Would a more vigorous investigation have saved lives?

In March of 2011, Russia's Federal Security Service, the agency that had grown out of the Soviet-era KGB, sent a letter to the FBI through the US embassy in Moscow. The Russians reported that Tamerlan had, apparently while living in the Boston area, become a radical Islamist bent on joining militant groups abroad. Tamerlan, the letter said, had first sought to team up with "insurgents in Palestine" but had difficulty learning the language. Instead he hoped to link up with militants within Russia. The Russians' concerns, the *Wall Street Journal* reported, were based at least in part on intercepted text messages between Tamerlan's mother and a relative, in which she indicated Tamerlan hoped to join fighters in the Caucasus region. The letter asked the FBI to share any information it had on Tamerlan and his mother, whom the Russians believed had also become radicalized.

So, two years before the Boston bombing, FBI counterterrorism agents in Boston searched for Tamerlan in government databases. They looked for records of his phone communications, whether he had visited websites promoting radical activity, his travel plans, and any associations he might have with militants. Agents even interviewed Tamerlan and his parents. They didn't find much, at least not enough to trigger further action. Under its own guidelines, the FBI must close a domestic investigation of an individual after ninety days unless it finds "derogatory information" that justifies reasonable suspicion of a terror threat. The FBI reported its inconclusive findings back to the Russians in August 2011, and had Tamerlan's name added to a US Department of Homeland Security watch list. That way, any time Tamerlan exited or entered the United States, customs officials would be alerted. Tamerlan's name would remain on the list for a year.

Russian authorities still had misgivings. In September 2011, they went to the CIA with the same concerns. The CIA investigation, though, also found no evidence that Tamerlan had ties to violent extremism. Still, CIA officials had his name added to a second watch list, the Terrorist Identities Datamart Environment. Known as TIDE, the list is US intelligence agencies' catchall for anyone connected to a terrorism investigation, a database of hundreds of thousands of names. Tamerlan was among those on the lowest rung of suspicion, so he wasn't barred from air travel or subjected to additional screening at airports. When he then went to Russia in January 2012, US customs officials got an alert. But after his trip ended that July—after he had traveled to Dagestan and reportedly sought to make contact with militants, just as Russian authorities had feared—his return to the United States did not trigger any notifications. The customs list had stopped tracking his travel after a year, and the TIDE database didn't flag him because his travel documents had an alternate spelling of his name and a different birth date. Without even trying, the would-be terrorist evaded the systems designed to monitor his movements, proving that the nation's antiterrorism firewall still had holes. Boston would pay the price.

The week after Dzhokhar was captured, Congress launched high-level hearings to determine whether the government should have done more. "We learned over a decade ago the danger in failing to connect the dots," Republican US representative Michael McCaul of Texas, chairman of the House Committee on Homeland Security, said at his panel's hearing. "My fear is that the Boston bombers may have succeeded because our system failed." McCaul's reference, of course, was to September 11, 2001. After the largest terrorist attack in US history, Washington took significant steps to improve intelligence sharing, even creating a new cabinet agency, the Department of Homeland Security, and new collaborative groups in every major US city called Joint Terrorism Task Forces, composed of federal, state, and local law enforcement officials. Those measures were informed by a key conclusion of the 9/11 Commission: that if government agencies had shared intelligence about terror threats facing the United States, they may have disrupted Al-Qaeda's devastating attack.

In the weeks after the marathon bombing, deficiencies in communication came under the spotlight once again. When Boston Police commissioner Ed Davis testified before Congress, he said he hadn't known that the FBI and CIA had investigated Tamerlan prior to the bombing—even though Boston police officers sit on the city's Joint Terrorism Task Force. Davis said he wasn't sure he would have done anything differently than federal investigators, but he would have liked to have known. "If there is information that comes in about a terrorist threat to a particular city, then local officials should have that information," he said. "There should be a mandate somewhere that the federal authorities have to share that with us so that we can properly defend our community."

There were communication lapses between countries, too. When Russian authorities first queried the FBI and CIA about Tamerlan in 2011, they asked US officials to alert them if Tamerlan ever traveled there. But US officials apparently never informed their Russian counterparts about Tamerlan's 2012 trip. FBI director Robert Mueller III told Congress that while he did not believe such a notification would have prevented the bombing, he acknowledged the communication breakdown. For its part, the FBI had repeatedly asked Russian authorities for more information on Tamerlan, but none ever came. In a May 2013 meeting in Moscow, members of Congress asked two top Federal Security Service officials about the Russians' failure to respond. "Why is it that three times our government has asked for more specific info regarding Tamerlan Tsarnaev, and you refused to do it?" Representative Bill Keating, a Democrat who represents a US House district south of Boston, said he asked Russian authorities on the trip. Russian officials said they never saw those requests.

In the months after the bombing, the FBI declined to send anyone to public congressional hearings, saying it couldn't divulge anything while its own investigation into the attack was ongoing. And that self-scrutiny would in the end yield little. In August 2013, the *New*

York Times reported that the FBI had determined that the agency could not have done anything more than it did to avert the bombing. Keating wasn't persuaded. "Until they give us facts that we can review as an independent branch of government," he said, "I don't think that's particularly useful what they think." McCaul said that US officials receive only about two dozen letters from foreign countries every year about specific individuals like Tamerlan. That makes such warnings fairly extraordinary, he said, so the FBI and CIA should have performed a more thorough investigation. "What the Russians said was right," McCaul said. "What they said came true."

On September 11, 2011, three men—Raphael Teken, Erik Weissman, and Brendan Mess—were murdered in the city of Waltham, just west of Watertown. They were found the next morning in Mess's second-floor apartment, on their stomachs, throats slashed, heads tilted to the right, their bodies covered in marijuana. Murders were rare in Waltham. In the decade before the three were killed, the city had seen five. This triple homicide appeared to be drug-related, and not just because of the marijuana. Weissman, thirty-one, had founded Hitman Glass, a bong manufacturer. Mess, twenty-five, a martial arts instructor, had told a friend he was considering getting into a marijuana-growing venture. Investigators thought he was running a drug operation. All three, including Teken, thirty-seven, a graduate of nearby Brandeis University, had been selling drugs for years, according to their friends. But they were known for low-level deals; friends could recall only one episode of violence, when Mess was beaten up for not paying a drug supplier in full.

The ritualistic array of the bodies suggested these were no ordinary killings. Other evidence indicated the violence wasn't random, either. There were no signs of forced entry into the apartment, nor any marks of a struggle, even though both Mess and Teken practiced martial arts. Still, investigators found few other clues. For more than eighteen months, no suspects were named. Then, in the wake of the marathon bombing came a chilling revelation: One of the Waltham murder victims, Brendan Mess, had been Tamerlan Tsarnaev's "best friend"—or at least that's what Tamerlan had told John Allan, the owner of the Wai Kru mixed martial arts gym in nearby Allston, where Mess and Tamerlan occasionally worked out. Tamerlan often ate with Mess and Weissman at a nearby diner, Brookline Lunch, and had been a regular visitor to the apartment where Mess and Weissman lived. Mess's girlfriend recalled Tamerlan and Mess making plans there a week before the murders. "Tam asked Brendan, 'Are we going to do that thing?'" she recalled. "And I asked Brendan what that was, and he told me not to worry about it."

More troubling, Tamerlan, despite their friendship, wasn't visibly perturbed by Mess's grisly death. He didn't show up to the funeral or memorial service. He didn't tell his wife that Mess had been killed; she learned of the murders through local news reports. When she asked Tamerlan what might have happened, he suggested that it might have been a drug deal gone bad. Others, too, found Tamerlan to be strangely nonchalant. "He laughed off the fact that he was murdered," said Allan, the gym owner who had known them both. "Like, 'Aw, man. It's crazy, right? I guess if you do that, that's what's going to happen.'" Friends of the victims said they told homicide investigators about Tamerlan's relationship to Mess. Investigators, however, never followed up. After the marathon bombing, that became an easy decision to second-guess: Would a more aggressive murder investigation have stopped Tamerlan before his violent spree in April 2013?

The question became much less academic after authorities began, following the marathon attack, to take a hard look at Ibragim Todashev, whose phone number the FBI had obtained by analyzing Tamerlan's phone. Todashev, whom Allan had mentioned to investigators, had also trained with Tamerlan at the gym, and he was someone who stood out. "He's got a bad temper, he clearly has anti-American sentiment, a radical-style Muslim," Allan said. Todashev and Tamerlan sometimes prayed together. Todashev had graduated college in Chechnya, where he was from. He had come to the United States in 2008, hoping to improve his English, and the US government granted him asylum from Russia later that year. In April and

May 2013, FBI agents interviewed him at least three times at FBI offices in Florida, where he lived.

On May 21, Todashev sat down for a fourth interview, this time at his Orlando apartment. The interrogation, with an FBI agent from Boston and two Massachusetts State Police troopers, started at 7:30 P.M. and lasted five hours. Investigators questioned Todashev about the Waltham murders. Todashev admitted he had been involved, implicated Tamerlan in the killings, and started to write a statement describing what had happened, according to the FBI; a court filing by federal prosecutors would later confirm that Todashev had asserted Tamerlan's participation in the murders. At the interrogation, Todashev was sitting at a table, across from one of the state troopers and the FBI agent. When the agent looked away, according to a law enforcement official's account, Todashev picked up the table and threw it at the agent, knocking him to the ground. The agent drew his gun and saw Todashev running at him, either with a metal pole or a broomstick. The agent shot Todashev, who fell backward. Todashev got up and charged the agent again. The agent fired more shots, killing him. The FBI initially released few additional details about the confrontation. The bureau even told the Florida medical examiner not to disclose its report on Todashev's autopsy, citing an ongoing investigation into the shooting. Todashev's family and civil rights groups, fearing a cover-up, called for more transparency from the FBI. The state prosecutor in Orlando, Jeffrey Ashton, said his office would conduct its own independent review.

Tamerlan's possible involvement in the Waltham slayings added a sickening coda to the story of the marathon bombing. The murders—on the tenth anniversary of 9/11—had come at a turning point in his life, his isolation deepening, his views increasingly radical, his family falling apart. Only weeks before, his parents had sought a divorce. Had the killing of Teken, Weissman, and Mess been Tamerlan's first violent strike against America? Had it been a warm-up, of sorts, for the marathon attack, and for murdering Sean Collier—the race and the cop both symbols of everything he wasn't and would never be? Maybe all this cycled through his head that Thursday night of Marathon Week, not long after he and his brother had gunned Collier down. When they kidnapped Danny and commandeered his Mercedes, the route they drove took them right past the street where three men had been slain.

For two days after being yanked from the Watertown boat, Dzhokhar Tsarnaev lay unconscious in a hospital bed at Beth Israel Deaconess Medical Center. FBI agents trained to interrogate "high-value" detainees waited outside the room for him to wake up. When he finally did, the agents began to pepper him with questions—and they did so before reading him his Miranda rights; a public safety exception to the procedure allows investigators to conduct limited interrogations of suspects before informing them of their right to stay silent. On April 21, Dzhokhar began to talk, providing investigators with their first details straight from the mouth of one of the men who had planned the assault on the marathon.

Dzhokhar, nursing a serious gunshot wound to the mouth and neck, provided some answers by nodding and by writing on a piece of paper. Talking was difficult. But he communicated quite a bit. He told investigators that he and his brother had considered other schemes, including mounting suicide attacks and setting off bombs at another large public celebration beloved by the city—the traditional Fourth of July concert along the Charles River, where hundreds of thousands gather every year to watch a massive fireworks show set to the music of the Boston Pops. When the brothers, working in their Cambridge apartment, assembled their bombs faster than expected, they began looking for a place to strike sooner than the summer. They had cased police stations—several in Boston and one in Cambridge—seeking law enforcement officers to target, before settling instead on the Boston Marathon. They had drawn motivation, Dzhokhar said, from the US invasions of Iraq and Afghanistan, and they had acted on their own, without any direct assistance from Al-Qaeda or another terror network. Though the date in mid-April coincided with tax day, and fell close to Adolf Hitler's birthday and the anniversary of the Columbine High School massacre, both April 20, those events did not appear to influence their timing.

In mining Dzhokhar's laptop, investigators had found books and a magazine promoting radical interpretations of Islam. The books included *Defense of the Muslim Lands*, *The First Obligation After Iman*, and *Jihad and the Effects of Intention Upon It*, which promotes martyrdom. Dzhokhar had also downloaded one book, noteworthy less for its long title—*The Slicing Sword, Against the One Who Forms Allegiances With the Disbelievers and Takes Them As Supporters Instead of Allah, His Messenger and the Believers*—than for the author of its foreword, Anwar al-Awlaki, a New Mexico–born Muslim cleric. Awlaki, whom counterterrorism officials had tracked for years, was an apparent source of inspiration for Dzhokhar and Tamerlan, who likely watched Awlaki's influential Internet videos.

Awlaki was once seen as a moderate Muslim voice but became infamous for his anti-Western screeds, which his followers posted on the Internet. YouTube removed clips of his sermons in 2010, after a British student said that watching them inspired her to try to assassinate a member of Parliament—he survived the attack. By then, US officials viewed Awlaki as a major source of inspiration for militants trying to strike against the United States. The 9/11 Commission found that three of the 9/11 hijackers had seen Awlaki preach and had met with him. Nidal Malik Hasan, a US Army major and psychiatrist, e-mailed extensively with Awlaki before shooting and killing thirteen people and injuring more than thirty at the Fort Hood military base in Texas in November 2009. Umar Farouk Abdulmutallab, who confessed to trying to set off explosives hidden in his underwear while on an airliner headed to Detroit on Christmas Day 2009, stayed at Awlaki's house and got Awlaki's approval for the bombing attempt, according to prosecutors. And Faisal Shahzad, an American citizen with an MBA, said his May 2010 attempt to detonate a car bomb in Times Square was inspired by Awlaki's call for holy war against the West. Thus when a US drone strike killed Awlaki in Yemen in September 2011, President Obama called his death a "major blow to Al-Qaeda's most active operational affiliate."

Whether linked to Awlaki or not, these smaller, self-contained terror plots—perhaps financed or inspired by Al-Qaeda but carried out by a quiet few—had increasingly worried US homeland security officials since 9/11. These attackers didn't necessarily have to find a way into the United States; some were already here, concealed, in effect, within ordinary-looking families. Their weapons of choice, including crude bombs and automatic weapons, could be acquired with relative ease or created using Internet recipes and widely available materials. "These extremists have no formal relationship with Al-Qaeda, but they have nonetheless adopted the Al-Qaeda ideology," Matthew Olsen, director of the federal National Counterterrorism Center, told a high-level homeland security conference in June 2011. "And what makes them especially worrisome is that they're really difficult for us to detect and, therefore, to disrupt." The Tsarnaevs seemed to fit the profile—homegrown terrorists seemingly assimilated in America but harboring a latent hatred for it.

In August 2011, the White House warned in a policy paper of a growing number of American citizens and residents just like the brothers who were moved to act by the ideology of extremists abroad. "The number of individuals remains limited, but the fact that Al-Qaeda and its affiliates and adherents are openly and specifically inciting Americans to support or commit acts of violence—through videos, magazines, and online forums—poses an ongoing and real threat," the paper said. President Obama, in the paper's introduction, called on Muslims to help root out these threats. "Communities—especially Muslim-American communities whose children, families, and neighbors are being targeted for recruitment by Al-Qaeda—are often best positioned to take the lead because they know their communities best," he said. Another necessary step, according to Olsen and the White House, is that federal, state, and local authorities communicate and share what they know—exactly what Ed Davis and others said should have happened before the Tsarnaevs brought deadly explosives to Boylston Street. Tamerlan, after all, had set off alarms years before, and there were troubling intimations about his intentions. The lack of knowledge of any specific intentions, however, meant they failed to attract more than a piecemeal response from law enforcement.

While back on the campus at UMass–Dartmouth the Wednesday after the bombing, Dzhokhar hung out, federal prosecutors said, with two friends he had entered college with in 2011: Dias Kadyrbayev and Azamat Tazhayakov, nineteen-year-olds who were born in Kazakhstan to well-off families. The three friends were among the few Russian speakers on campus. Classmates said they often spent time together, and with other international students. Kadyrbayev and Tazhayakov shared a black BMW, which Dzhokhar would sometimes borrow. The car had a fake license plate on the front, a gift from Spanish friends, that read TERRORISTA #1. Tazhayakov's father would explain later that the plate was supposed to be a joke, a nod to a lyric from "Harlem Shake," a popular dance track. "Terrorista #1 doesn't mean Osama bin Laden, doesn't mean 'terrorist,'" Tazhayakov's father told a Kazakh television station. "In their slang, it means 'happy-go-lucky,' 'a leader of the pack,' that sort of thing."

On that Wednesday, two days after the bombing, Kadyrbayev drove over to Dzhokhar's dorm. The two chatted outside as Kadyrbayev smoked a cigarette. Kadyrbayev noticed that Dzhokhar's hair had been trimmed. Later on, Dzhokhar drove to the apartment Kadyrbayev and Tazhayakov shared in New Bedford and stayed until around midnight. The next day, Thursday, April 18, Dzhokhar gave Tazhayakov a ride home after class. It was just another week at college. Until suddenly it wasn't.

On Thursday evening, after the FBI images of the bombing suspects led every news report in the country, a third friend, former UMass–Dartmouth classmate Robel Phillipos, who had gone to Cambridge Rindge & Latin with Dzhokhar, allegedly called Kadyrbayev as Kadyrbayev drove back to the New Bedford apartment. Phillipos was nervous. He told his friend, "Turn on the TV when you get home." The face of one of the suspects was a little too familiar. Here, in grainy pixels on the screen, was a man who looked an awful lot like Dzhokhar, a man now being described as one of the most wanted criminals alive.

The three men's accounts of what happened next diverged somewhat, but not long after the FBI put out the pictures, Kadyrbayev, Tazhayakov, and Phillipos went to Dzhokhar's dorm room. His roommate told them Dzhokhar had left an hour or two before. So the three friends put on a movie. As they watched, they noticed a backpack full of hollowed-out fireworks, the powder gone. At one point, Kadyrbayev texted Dzhokhar, saying he looked like one of the suspects, Kadyrbayev told investigators.

lol, Dzhokhar replied—"laughing out loud" in text-speak. *You better not text me.*

Kadyrbayev got another text from Dzhokhar that he showed to Tazhayakov. It included a bizarre invitation plus a traditional Muslim greeting: *If yu want yu can go to my room and take what's there :) but ight bro Salam aleikum.*

In Dzhokhar's dorm room that night, Kadyrbayev, Tazhayakov, and Phillipos allegedly picked up Dzhokhar's laptop and his backpack, which contained, among other things, fireworks and a jar of Vaseline. They brought the items back to the New Bedford apartment. As they watched the continuing news coverage, Phillipos would tell investigators, the friends began to "freak out." Kadyrbayev wondered aloud whether they should get rid of the stuff they'd taken from Dzhokhar's room.

"Do what you have to do," Phillipos said he replied.

Kadyrbayev then allegedly put the backpack with the fireworks into a black garbage bag and deposited it in a trash bin outside the apartment. The next day, Friday, April 19, after Dzhokhar had been identified by name as one of the bombing suspects, Kadyrbayev and Tazhayakov watched as a garbage truck took the contents of the trash bin away.

Investigators soon interviewed and then arrested the three friends, accusing them of trying to help Dzhokhar cover up the bomb plot. Kadyrbayev and Tazhayakov were each charged on two counts of obstruction of justice. Both pleaded not guilty. Kadyrbayev's lawyer contended that he had not, in fact, recognized Dzhokhar on the news and thus didn't know his friend was a bombing suspect; Tazhayakov's lawyer said his client was shocked Dzhokhar could have committed an act of terrorism. Phillipos faced two counts of making false statements in a terrorism case, following misleading accounts he allegedly provided to investigators. Phillipos's lawyers said that he had nothing to do with removing the backpack or destroying potential evidence. Less than two weeks after the marathon attack, more than thirty federal agents combed through a New Bedford landfill looking for the discarded items. After hours of searching, they finally came upon Dzhokhar's backpack. Inside were fireworks, Vaseline, a thumb drive, and something that spoke to Dzhokhar's more mundane concerns before April 15, 2013: a homework sheet from the university.

The more the media drilled into the Tsarnaevs' background, the more their relatives came under the spotlight. On the Friday morning after Tamerlan was killed, with police still hunting for Dzhokhar, investigators and reporters found their uncle Ruslan Tsarni, a corporate lawyer living outside Washington, DC. Tsarni first spoke with FBI agents inside his home. When he emerged, he walked up to the television cameras and reporters gathered outside looking for the latest in what had become the biggest story in the world. In an impromptu press conference, aired live on network television, Tsarni offered condolences to the bombing victims, denounced his nephews, and ordered Dzhokhar to turn himself in. Asked to explain what provoked the brothers to attack, Tsarni said: "Being losers. Hatred to those who were able to settle themselves. These are the only reasons I can imagine of. Anything else—anything else to do with religion, with Islam—that's a fraud. It's a fake." He was asked how he felt about the United States. "I respect this country, I love this country," said Tsarni, who moved to the United States in 1995 and became a US citizen. "This country, which gives [a] chance to everybody else to be treated as a human being and to just be a human being."

An opinion writer for the *Washington Post* called his words "inspiring" and said his press conference was "a moment we all needed." The *New Yorker* said he "looked like he might hunt his nephew down himself." Two aunts of the Tsarnaev brothers, Maret Tsarnaeva and Patimat Suleimanova, had a very different view of things. Both expressed disbelief that their nephews could have set off the bombs. "I'm suspicious that this was staged," Maret Tsarnaeva told reporters in Toronto. "I just do not believe our boys would do that." Suleimanova, living in Dagestan, said that Tamerlan may have been religious, but he wasn't an extremist. "A man who takes Islam cannot do this," she said. "They are not terrorists. I have no doubt that they were set up."

Tamerlan and Dzhokhar's mother, Zubeidat, was the most insistent that her two sons had been framed, claiming, the week after the bombing, that it was all "lies and hypocrisy." Her defiance was hardly surprising—US officials had her on a terrorist watch list, too. "They already want me, him, and all of us to look [like] terrorists," she said at an April news conference in Dagestan with Anzor, her ex-husband and Tamerlan and Dzhokhar's father. This was the family that had once come to the United States seeking a better life, settling in Cambridge, raising two boys whose lives became flecked with American influences. This was the family who had chosen this place, who had wanted it. Now, as they stood dismissing the overwhelming evidence of their sons' horrendous crimes, they seemed as distant from American soil as they could possibly get.

CHAPTER 18

RUNNING AGAIN

The marathon man finishes the race

He had to run. No question. Dave McGillivray had made the commitment forty years ago in honor of his late grandfather: He would complete the Boston Marathon every spring, until his body wouldn't let him. He'd kept the promise, one way or another, all these years. Nowadays that meant heading out to the starting line later on Marathon Day, once he had satisfied his race-director duties. This year, the bombing had complicated things. The phone call had come as he was about to start down the course. His personal mission was suddenly the last thing on his mind.

He couldn't just walk away from his promise, though. Especially not now. It was a question of timing—when would it be appropriate to get back out to Hopkinton, to keep his streak alive? In the days immediately following the attack, there was far too much to do—helping the Boston Athletic Association contend with the fallout, ensuring that runners were accounted for, supporting crestfallen volunteers. He was conscious, too, of appearing respectful, of not wanting to seem self-absorbed. So he waited for the funerals to pass, for the crush of care at the hospitals to ease, and for the city to reopen

Boylston Street; he felt like he shouldn't be the only person with access to the finish line. And yet he was anxious to get going. The demands of overseeing the marathon made it difficult to train adequately. Year to year he was never sure he could go the distance. "Emotionally and physically, I wanted to get it done," he said. "It was on my nerves."

He settled on a Friday, eleven days after Marathon Monday. He contacted his running partner Josh Nemzer, who was the course director for the race, and asked if he was available. Nemzer was. They made plans to go to Hopkinton early that morning, but they kept their intentions quiet. They didn't tell the media, didn't alert the cops, didn't inform any race executives except Tom Grilk, the head of the BAA, who understood their desire for discretion. Nemzer's son Aaron drove them out to the starting line. McGillivray's son Ryan met them out on the course. There was something special about the small group—just McGillivray and Nemzer running the course and their sons trailing in cars. It would be a moment for them alone.

Around 8:30 A.M., they prepared to set off. They tied on their running shoes. Nemzer's son took a picture. They had done this so many times together that their prerace routine was automatic. "It's almost like two people who don't have to speak," Nemzer said. Then they were gone, heading east down the sidewalks and the sides of roads—unlike on Marathon Monday, the streets this day were not closed to traffic. Aaron, driving his dad's Honda CR-V, and Ryan, driving his pickup truck, shadowed them, stopping every once in a while to offer the dads water, Gatorade, bagels, and pretzels. "It felt good to take these first steps back toward Boston," Nemzer said.

About halfway down the route, McGillivray's cell phone rang. It was Ed Jacobs, the technical producer for the marathon, whose company, Interstate Rental Service, held the contract to build the bleachers and other finish-line infrastructure. McGillivray was breathing heavily—breathing like he was running. Jacobs picked up on it.

"Where are you?" Jacobs asked.

"I'm in Wellesley," McGillivray responded.

"You're not doing your run, are you?" Jacobs asked.

"Well . . . well," McGillivray stammered, not wanting to divulge the secret. He didn't want to lie, either.

"You are, aren't you?" Jacobs said. He told McGillivray he would meet him at the finish line.

What McGillivray didn't know was that Jacobs would alert a Boston police officer that McGillivray was out on the route and would soon enter the city. The officer got on his radio and made the announcement. McGillivray's annual running of the course was part of marathon legend. It wasn't something police would let go unnoticed. When McGillivray reached Hereford Street, the final road before the route curves around to Boylston, he saw a Boston police cruiser. An officer got out. "Are you McGillivray?" the officer asked. And with that, McGillivray's plan to quietly run the marathon came apart.

A police officer on Boylston flipped on his sirens and began moving cars to the side of the road. Other officers began cheering him on— "Go Dave, Go!" The commotion drew people out of the stores. The news had also broken on Twitter. The media, which had often covered McGillivray's postmarathon runs and were now hungry for fresh stories, converged. A news helicopter appeared overhead. *I'm in deep trouble*, McGillivray thought to himself. The attention, the fanfare, the spectacle—this was exactly what he had hoped to avoid. The last thing he wanted was to be the guy who brought sirens to Boylston Street so soon after the bombing. *Who is this clown?* he imagined people in their cars thinking. At the same time, he didn't want to appear ungrateful. He knew that everyone's intentions were good. So he went with it.

Crossing the finish line was emotional, there in the sunshine in the middle of a bustling Friday, at the very spot where evil had visited his beloved race. Because of all the hoopla, though, it wasn't quite the cathartic experience he had envisioned, or needed. "That special moment never came," McGillivray said. He was too busy trying to shrink from the spotlight, fending off requests for interviews from the TV cameras. He slipped into the front seat of Nemzer's car, the cameras trained on the passenger window as if he were a criminal or misbehaving starlet. The memory was one he would not soon forget. He was usually accessible to the press, but not today, not like this.

And yet the act of running, of completing the marathon course once again, just like he had done for more than four decades, had still been important. With this run, this personal feat in defiance of the bombing, Dave McGillivray wanted to make a statement. "I felt, I can't let this act of violence deter me from doing what I usually do," he said. Much of Greater Boston felt the same.

Even with panic and fear still fresh, runners vowed, soon after the attack, to return for the next Boston Marathon, on April 21, 2014. Indeed, it was hard to find any who planned to stay away. NPR host Peter Sagal articulated the prevailing conviction this way: "Goddamn it, I'm not going to let these guys ruin the marathon." More than one political leader promised that the next year's race would be "bigger and better" than ever. It was easy for them to say, though. They weren't the ones who had to pull it off.

To McGillivray, Grilk, and other race organizers, it was clear immediately that staging the 2014 marathon would be a massive undertaking. The number of prospective entrants would spike. The crowds would swell. Security would have to be tighter than ever. Amid all these demands, organizers would need to strike a delicate balance. How would they both pay tribute to everyone affected by the bombing and preserve the essential character of the Boston Marathon—the competition and athletic excellence, the remarkable spirit of inclusion? In other words, how would the 2014 race at once look back and ahead? "We want to do the best job we can to give appropriate recognition to everyone who was affected," Grilk said. "And then move on." In practice, the task was monumental, and much of it lay at McGillivray's feet.

One of the first things he and other race organizers did, a month after the stunted marathon, was to grant automatic entry to any 2013 runner who hadn't finished but had made it to the halfway point or farther before the race was stopped, around 5,600 people in all. More than 80 percent of them chose to re-up. "That's a strong statement to me," McGillivray said. "They're saying, 'We're coming back, we got invited, we will not be denied.'" That sentiment drove Amy Formica, a runner from near Pittsburgh, to reserve her hotel room for 2014 within weeks of the attack. Not having made it across the finish line nagged at her. The kindness she experienced from strangers amid the panic and confusion only strengthened her desire to come back. "You're not going to scare me or my family away," she said. Formica, her husband, and their two sons planned to stay in Boston even longer this time. The BAA ultimately announced that it would allow an additional nine thousand runners in 2014, raising the cap from twenty-seven thousand to thirty-six thousand entrants. At the starting line, instead of three waves of nine thousand runners each, there would be four. The only other time the Boston Marathon field had been this big was in 1996, for the one hundredth anniversary race. Race organizers also announced in November 2013 that they would open the 2014 marathon to a limited number of nonelite runners who could show that they had been "personally and profoundly" affected by the bombing.

Not that it was ever easy to put on the Boston Marathon, but when the field size, course, and security blueprint stayed more or less the same year to year, it was a little bit like "add water, you got soup," McGillivray said. After 2013, race organizers and public safety agencies had to almost start over. Everything had to be reevaluated, from spectator access along the 26.2-mile course to how the finish line layout would look. One of the biggest changes they began planning for was a prohibition on bags. If the early plans held, runners would no longer be able to bring bags out to Hopkinton. Spectators would no longer be able to get near the course with bags, at least not in areas where big crowds gathered. Adding nine thousand runners presented a host of new considerations, too, including how to handle more trash, where to put additional portable restrooms, and keeping roads closed longer to accommodate the fourth wave of competitors.

The most delicate planning involved the tributes, the emotional cornerstones of what was sure to be the most poignant Boston Marathon ever. McGillivray, Grilk, and their team envisioned a series of special events leading up to Marathon Day, beginning with a large gathering on April 15, 2014, six days before the race, perhaps at the same time that the bombing had happened. The event, likely at the nearby Hynes Convention Center, would draw in victims, family members, police, firefighters, and other first responders, and probably a host of political leaders. Afterward, according to the early plans, guests would join together in a procession down Boylston Street to the finish line. Then, on the Saturday before the marathon, the BAA would host its typical premarathon 5K race, but with a bigger field, maybe ten thousand runners in all, to accommodate those taking part as an act of healing or remembrance. Following that race, an invitation-only run or walk—perhaps a modest loop around Back Bay—would bring bombing victims, their families, first responders, and hospital staff to Copley Square.

After that, the focus would shift to putting on a stellar marathon, to restoring its glory. There might be a moment of silence at the start or another acknowledgment of the tragedy, but race organizers hoped to leave much of the sentiment for the tribute events. What they couldn't control—and, to a degree, what they feared—were well-meaning but misguided attempts along the sidelines to honor the bombing victims. Would spectators try to write messages on the course using paint that became dangerously slick in the rain? Would they hang balloon arches over the road but not anticipate high winds bringing them down? Would novices set up new water stations in dangerous locations? The list of unknowns was endless.

For many other marathons, including Chicago and New York, making big changes is easier because the course lies within a single city. The Boston Marathon snakes through eight communities; only the final leg is actually in Boston. That means race organizers must coordinate with eight different municipal police departments, eight different public works departments, and so on. Emerging from the early planning meetings for the 2014 marathon, McGillivray was struck by how much work it would take to bounce back from 2013. "The magnitude of it just hits you in the face," he said. He became so caught up in the next year, in fact, that he lacked the time and space to reflect on the bombing and everything it meant. That would have to come later.

In the running community, it's widely believed that McGillivray is the man you want in charge of the marathon; Grilk said he doesn't know if anyone else even has the capability. McGillivray likes to joke that he's never had to worry about someone taking his job, because no one else would want it. But more than ever, as they looked ahead toward 2014, McGillivray and Grilk were feeling the weight of expectations. They would never please everyone. Not everything would be perfect. They were buoyed, though, by all the expressions of support from around the world. "When that many people are pulling for you, it matters," Grilk said. "The challenges have been severe, but it really helps you get past all that stuff, and it leaves you with a very strong sense of stewardship, of privilege, for being at the center of something that has so many people's attention. And you want to get it right."

Before they turned to 2014, race officials had to carry out one of their most important postrace rituals. Every year after the marathon is over, they pull up the 3M adhesive strip that's laid across Boylston Street for the finish line; it's not the kind of thing that can just be left there year-round. The finish line is such a Boston landmark, though, that they paint it on the road for show, typically the day after the race. With Boylston closed for days after the attack, that wasn't possible. But on the night of April 29, two weeks later, they were finally able to bring out the stencils and the blue and yellow paint, giving the iconic band a fresh coat that it needed more than ever.

McGillivray is often asked: Why are so many people running these days? His answer is that the sense of intimidation has fallen away. They see that running is not just for the smug kale-buyers at Whole Foods, that being a runner requires little more than decent shoes and the discipline to get out the door. They see the value in leading a healthy life. They want to feel good about themselves. They see their neighbors doing it. More a lifestyle than a sport, running satisfies a craving for physical, mental, and emotional lift. McGillivray figured that out as a kid—his first race came at age five or six—and he's been a running evangelist ever since. "It gives you so many things that you can go out and do other things as a result—be a better parent, be a better teacher, be a better worker, be a better tuba player," McGillivray said. "It's just like, 'I can run a marathon? I can do *this*.'"

Naturally, the more people who took up running, the stronger running communities became, in Boston and around the world. The spike in interest spawned all manners of running clubs and just about every themed road race imaginable, from Ontario's sweet-filled Chocolate Race to the James Joyce Ramble outside Boston, in which costumed actors read Joyce's work throughout the route. Almost four months after the 2013 marathon, McGillivray oversaw the cherished Falmouth Road Race on Cape Cod, a seven-mile competition among 12,800 entrants along a stunning seaside course. Shortly before it started, he watched two acquaintances and running enthusiasts get married on a little patch of land near the starting line. When they were officially man and wife, McGillivray yelled, warmly, "Congratulations, now get out!" With that the wedding party, decked out in wedding-themed running gear, took off down the course. Seven miles later at the finish line, the groom picked up the bride and carried her across to wild applause.

Around the country, that spirit, following the Boston Marathon attack, proved to be stronger than fear. Even with security at unprecedented levels, road races were selling out at record pace. Not only was there no retreat, runners appeared to be flocking to mass public events. Runners even had their own "Boston Strong" uniforms—their marathon jackets. On April 16, the day after the Boston race, marathoner Vicma Lamarche and her husband left the city for Mexico's Isla Mujeres; she had promised him the trip for putting up with her five-month-long training regimen. Lamarche, part of a running club called Black Girls RUN!, grabbed her marathon jacket as they left. Her husband was a little unnerved. He worried that she was making herself a target—and they were headed to an airport, no less. Lamarche didn't care. It was a badge of pride. When they got to Logan Airport, it was full of runners. They all had their jackets on, too, a small but meaningful expression of unity. Peter Sagal was moved to do the same. That first week after the bombing, he wore his jacket everywhere. "Because I wanted people to see it."

CHAPTER 19

GIANT STEPS

Standing tall, Heather forges ahead

It had been almost one month since the marathon. Heather Abbott was back at Fenway Park, standing on crutches at the edge of the storied ball field. She wore a Red Sox jersey, her last name emblazoned on the back in red, the middle letters hidden by her long blonde hair. Waiting to be waved forward to the pitcher's mound, she struggled to calm her nerves. She hadn't been this anxious since the first moments after the bombing: In another minute, the thirty-eight-year-old would crutch across the grass in front of more than thirty thousand people. Then she would balance on one crutch, raise her right arm, and throw out the ceremonial first pitch. Sox catcher Jarrod Saltalamacchia would try to catch it. There was no guarantee she wouldn't fall. Or that she could throw it far enough. Instinctively, she understood the weight of the moment—not just for her, but for the city. Television cameras would capture her appearance and deliver it to a world craving proof of hope. Everyone in the park was willing her success on this overcast Saturday in May. It was a feeling she would come to know well in the months ahead, a potent blend of expectation and goodwill.

Heather had practiced for this day. At Spaulding Rehabilitation Hospital, where she had been since leaving Brigham and Women's on April 29, she had gone outside in the sunshine with her friend Roseann Sdoia—whom she had known before, coincidentally, but who had also lost a leg in the bombing. Together, they practiced hopping across the spring grass on their crutches. Heather tossed a ball to Roseann, coached by their physical therapist. The transition to Spaulding had been hard for Heather—leaving the nurses she knew and enduring three or four hours of painful, strenuous physical therapy each day. The rehabilitation hospital, newly opened on the Charlestown waterfront, was sparkling, but the staff was still smoothing out rough edges. It could be hard to find a pillowcase or a water pitcher. And the attitude was no-nonsense: no relenting, no taking it easy, no cutting corners. You were supposed to work through the pain. When Heather was seized by doubt about her Fenway invitation, and suggested rolling out to throw the first pitch from her wheelchair, therapist Samantha Geary was adamant. "Don't you dare," Geary told her. "You take your crutches and you hop out there. Everybody needs to know you're okay."

Now another physical therapist, Dara Casparian, was beside her as she started forward across the soggy infield. The Fenway fans were on their feet, cheering and yelling her name. She stopped at the appointed spot, handed one crutch to her therapist, and took the baseball in her hand. She threw it at once, before she had a chance to lose her nerve or her balance: arm up and back, then the forward motion, then the release. For a split second, the stadium held its breath. Then the ball was snug in Saltalamacchia's glove, and the crowd emitted a roar, a sudden wall of noise that enveloped her. It was the sound of affirmation: *See there, it's just as we thought—she will, they will, we will all be okay.* It wasn't that simple, of course, but the leap was hard for people to resist. It felt good. Back on the edge of the field, Heather's parents were waiting, beaming, along with her friends from Newport who had been with her at the marathon. She let herself be swept up in the collective embrace. The biggest star on the team, David Ortiz, had signed a ball for her. The team's manager of pregame ceremonies, Dan Lyons, would e-mail her later and call her appearance one of the best moments of his thirty-year career. Heather knew she would always remember this feeling. It felt like a celebration, and it was. She had checked out of Spaulding that morning. When she left Fenway, she was finally going home.

She was happy and excited on the drive to Newport, still feeling the warm approval from the Fenway crowd. And there was more to look forward to—she couldn't wait to be home again. She had not anticipated the mix of feelings it would bring, though, or the memories. Her apartment was like a time capsule. Everything was just where she had left it on the morning of Marathon Monday, rushing out the door to catch the train to Boston. The last minutes of her old life, perfectly preserved. She looked around, taking it all in. Then, in her bedroom, she saw a waiting stack of packages. It took her a minute to figure out what they were, and when she did, it felt like a punch in the gut. Before the marathon, Heather had ordered some new spring clothes. Sometime in the past month, they had been delivered. Someone, her parents or friends, had carried them inside for her. There were several pairs of stylish high-heeled shoes in boxes, and a couple of short dresses for the beach. The sight of them gave her an unexpected jolt. It had been just weeks ago that these things had been so natural and easy: shopping for shoes, looking forward to spring, dreaming of summer. It would never be that way again. She sank onto her bed and wept for everything that had ended.

"Heather! You're Heather, right? You look great!"

Some people rushed right up to her on the streets of Newport. They had seen her on TV; they wanted to wish her well. Others stared at her from across the room, studying her face, her leg. "Yes, it's me," she wanted to say. On good days, the attention was strange but nice. On bad days, it could feel intrusive and overwhelming. Some people didn't think before they greeted her, and then they froze, unsure how to proceed. It was up to her then to end the interactions gracefully. She tried to remember that they all meant well.

Her mother stayed with her at the apartment for six weeks. It was helpful, but also challenging, for someone so accustomed to living on her own. She was still getting used to her prosthetic leg. It was a temporary one—the socket would be recast again and again during the first months, to ensure a good fit as her leg, still healing, continued to shrink and change shape. The first time she tried it on, her disappointment was keen. In the hospital, experienced amputees had given the bombing victims pep talks, telling them how they would one day do everything they had done before. Putting on her first prosthetic leg would be a life-changing moment, Heather had thought, a leap toward normalcy. Then she stood up and felt how hard and painful and uncomfortable it was. *It's not my leg*, she thought. *My leg is never coming back*. It was obvious, yet somehow the surreal and hectic early weeks had blurred the permanence. For someone in recovery, she was surprisingly busy. She had hired a financial adviser, who was going to project how much her disability would cost over her lifetime. She had interviewed nearly a dozen companies before deciding which one would make her prosthetics. She was weighing whether to accept any speaking engagements. There was lots of mail still coming in, and invitations. There was a homecoming party in the ballroom at Newport's Rosecliff mansion, organized by friends and attended by both Rhode Island senators. There was physical therapy and doctors' appointments. It was almost like a full-time job. How she would balance it with her real job, once she went back to work, she wasn't sure.

She went out again in Newport with her friends, but it wasn't the same. She was still taking painkillers—the pain and throbbing in her leg still woke her up at 2:00 or 3:00 A.M. on many nights—and she didn't want to drink when she was medicated. The places she loved, where she had felt at home, had turned into obstacle courses. One night at SpeakEasy, one of their regular haunts, she tried to get upstairs to the bathroom and couldn't. Her friend Jason offered to carry her. "Just leave me alone," she told him, the darkness in her voice surprising everyone. The well-intentioned offer had touched a nerve. Heather's independence was her most prized possession. She remembered how she used to walk home alone from bars in the wee hours, never worrying that anyone would try to hurt her. Now she couldn't run away if someone did. When a noise awakened her in the middle of the night, she was struck again by her own helplessness. If someone broke into her apartment, there would be no time for her to put on her other leg and get away. Such thoughts had not come to her in the hospital, when she had been surrounded by people. It was only now, on her own with time to think, that the stark reality of her limitations started to sink in.

And she was truly on her own now: The ex-boyfriend who had come back to her after the bombing, pledging to be there for her—he was gone again. It had been a gamble from the start, Heather had known that. Their history had left her with no illusions, but still, she had wanted to—maybe she had needed to—believe him when he asked her in the hospital for another chance. For a while, it seemed like he had meant it. He drove her home from the hospital; he helped her parents and pitched in at her fund-raisers. By late July, though, she could see he had not changed. He had let her down—again. It was over, and this time, there would be no second chances. Heather was hurt and angry, but grateful at least for the clarity, if not the timing. She had never needed someone more. Of the bombing victims Heather had gotten to know, she was now the only one completely on her own. Soon enough she would drive herself, carry her own bags, change her own lightbulbs. Months later she would wonder if her self-reliance had sped up her progress.

Even with all this pressing down on her, though, it was possible, for a few seconds, to forget about her leg. It happened at home one day when the doorbell rang. She was sitting on her bed, not wearing her prosthetic, and she leapt toward the door at the familiar sound. Her movement was an act of memory and instinct, but it was an outdated memory. She had only one leg now to land on, and she landed badly, falling on the floor. It hurt, and it was humiliating. It was like she was being punished for forgetting. Such rebukes came without warning. At the end of May, three weeks after going home from the hospital, Heather went to Boston for a One Fund concert. The five-hour benefit show brought together a dozen well-known bands and musicians, some with Boston ties, to raise money for the victims. Many of the marathon amputees were there in front-row seats. Jeff Bauman attended, and Carlos Arredondo, the bystander who had helped him. Heather sat next to Mery Daniel, another woman who had lost a leg. Her friend Roseann came, too. It was the first time all of them had had a chance to talk.

For weeks, Heather had been focused on her own ordeal. She had not watched the news; her knowledge of the other victims had been limited. Sitting now with others who had gone through the same thing, she felt herself part of a new community. Together, they welcomed hugs from members of New Kids on the Block and reveled in their proximity to Aerosmith. James Taylor and Carole King serenaded them with "You've Got a Friend." Heather was surprised to find herself crying, for the first time, in public. It felt okay. The other victims were mostly strangers, but in one important way, she knew them better than anyone. When the show was over, Heather and one of her friends stopped in a restroom before leaving the TD Garden. The floor was wet, and her crutch slipped out from under her. She fell hard onto the concrete. Pain ricocheted through her leg; all the joy of the night drained instantly away. *Don't forget*, the pain seemed to say. *Nothing will be easy for you now.*

She had been with Mery earlier that day, at a photo shoot for *People* magazine. Adrianne Haslet-Davis, a dancer who had suffered an amputation, was there, too. The shoot, at Spaulding, made them laugh. The magazine stylists had dressed them in "Boston Strong"–themed T-shirts; Heather couldn't believe she was going to be in *People* wearing a T-shirt. The photographer had called for "wind" to blow their hair, so an assistant stood in front them waving a piece of cardboard. The three women, each one missing a leg, stood on a platform with a slightly tilted surface. Adrianne wore her brand-new prosthesis; she had just gotten it that day. Frightened of falling, trying not to lose their balance, they held on to one another as the camera clicked and clicked. It was nerve-racking and ridiculous; how could it possibly produce a decent picture? They could not believe it when the photo landed on the cover, their smiling faces radiating confidence. The contradiction cut through her new life—the public snapshots, with their airbrushed theme of triumph, and the complex private realm where fear and strength and pain were all tangled up together.

On a Tuesday morning in mid-August, Heather stood in her bathroom blow-drying her hair. She spritzed herself lightly with perfume, finished a container of yogurt, and turned off the TV, where a weatherman was forecasting fog. She wore small hoop earrings, a mint-green and lemon-yellow sweater, and white Top-Sider loafers with navy trim. She also wore her prosthetic leg. It was her second day back on the job at Raytheon, the defense contractor where she worked in human resources. After the bombing, Heather had known the time wasn't right for a new job in Boston, or anywhere else. She needed her friends and family nearby—for now—so she had made her peace with staying where she was. There were moments, though, when it was hard. Back in June, a call had come from a company down south, asking her if she was interested in a job. No, she had told them, feeling a pang of loss. Instead, she would immerse herself in what she knew. She had started slowly the previous day, working for only five hours, sorting through the six hundred e-mails in her inbox. There had been a small party, with a cake, to welcome her back. Today would be more like a regular day: seven hours, with conference calls and stacks of files awaiting her review. She needed to be there at 9:00, but she would squeeze in an hour of physical therapy first.

She drove across Newport, past the long gray sweep of Easton's Beach, to the office building where she did her therapy. The large, open room was already humming with people stretching, exercising, lifting weights, trying to bounce back from all kinds of injuries. Heather stood on a spot where strips of tape made a star pattern on the carpet, and practiced tapping the heel of her prosthetic foot on each point of the star. It was dull, repetitive work, and surprisingly hard. She switched legs, trying it with her good foot. "It's the calf muscles," she said, quickly figuring out what was missing. "I don't have the calf." She moved through a series of deep knee bends; they seemed to be getting easier. Her therapist placed a block on the floor in front of her, and Heather stepped forward, bending low to pick it up. "We want to give her back her gliding, graceful motion," said Bert Reid, an owner of Olympic Physical Therapy, who had come over to greet her. "She's come a million miles, and she's got a million more to go." Heather made a face: a *million* more? The previous week at PT, she had loped down the back hallway in a half run. It had been slow and halting and extremely painful, but it had given her a flash of breathless belief: She would run for real again someday. Now she returned to the hallway. Facing the buttermilk-colored wall, she sashayed down one side, taking small, quick sideways steps, then reversed direction and came swiftly back, past exam room doors and a row of framed Little League photos. Her leg was starting to ache.

"From the pounding? That's okay," the therapist said. "We have to train it to absorb the pounding."

In the past, Heather had ended her sessions by icing her leg. But it was 8:45, almost time for work. "I don't think I have time to ice it," she said. Back in the car, she brushed out her hair and reapplied her lipstick. She headed for the Dunkin' Donuts drive-through, waiting to order a medium hot with skim milk and Splenda. The line was long and slow. It felt, at last, like a typical Tuesday morning. She was finally getting back to her old routine—exactly what she had wanted—but it felt less satisfying than she had expected. There was no way around it: She was different—her perspective on the world, not just her leg—and she wasn't sure she wanted the same things as before. The vividness and intensity of those days after the bombing had been like nothing she had ever known. Painful, yes, but also urgent and meaningful. It was almost inevitable that her old life would seem less gripping by comparison. Heather was deeply grateful to her employer; she knew she was lucky to have a job to come back to, good health insurance, and the flexibility to work part-time for now. She just didn't know if she still aspired to be a human resources VP. Even with all she had lost, she felt an expanded sense of possibility. Before the bombing, she had been ready for a change. The change that had come, violent and unexpected, had transformed her in more ways than one. Maybe it had prepared her, too, for some purpose she could not yet see.

Turning into the driveway to the plant, she pulled out her employee ID card and hung it up on her rearview mirror. A blinking red sign beside the security checkpoint proudly announced the number of days without workplace injuries. Heather drove slowly through the gate. It was 9:00 A.M. Time to get to work.

Another day, another stretch of open hallway. Another group of medical professionals watching her walk. It had been four months since Heather's leg had been amputated. She was back at Spaulding to see her doctor. As always, she had lots of questions: Would she ever stop shifting weight onto her good leg? Would her good ankle ever stop getting so swollen? What about the pain—would it ever go away? Her doctor, David Crandell, knelt in front of her as she removed her prosthetic leg and rolled off the soft protective sleeve she wore underneath. He held the stump of her leg in his hand, palpating it gently. Heather squirmed. It was still tender.

"So I'll always have some pain?" she asked.

"Well, no," the doctor said. "Not if you get to a certain level of activity. The tissue is getting used to bearing weight where it hasn't had to. . . . It's still only been a short period of time."

She was almost afraid to ask her next question: "Will the limp go away?"

"Yes. Yes," the doctor said without hesitation. "In several months, people will not know."

Heather longed to believe it. Most of what she still endured, no one else could see. But the limp announced to the world that she was different. That type of red flag, marking her as a victim, was what she had been trying to avoid when she had decided not to keep her foot.

Now the doctor had a question: What were her goals going forward?

"To get rid of this limp," Heather said firmly. "To get running like I used to run."

. . .

The morning felt like fall, damp and cold and gray, as Heather drove north from Rhode Island to New Hampshire. She was going to see the people who had made her prosthetic leg, to check on another one they were making now. Waiting for her there, with the new prosthetic, was a pair of four-inch high heels, platform pumps in a pale beige. They were the shoes Heather had ordered online before the bombing, the ones that had made her cry the day she came home from the hospital. Now she was getting ready to wear them for the first time. It had not taken Heather long to decide that she would wear heels again. She was known for her love of beautiful shoes; dressing up was part of who she was. To give that up would be a kind of surrender, and she refused. Plenty of things worried Heather about her situation, but walking on a prosthetic leg in four-inch heels—that didn't scare her a bit.

A few days before, near her home in Newport, she had stood up on a paddleboard in the ocean. It was the first time she had tried it since before the bombing, and she had been nervous. She had asked her friends to take her to a secluded spot where there would be fewer watching eyes, but somehow they ended up smack in the middle of a busy beach. She was self-conscious about her water leg—a waterproof prosthetic—but with an ACE bandage wrapped around the top, it was a convincing substitute. "Wow, that's risky!" a stranger had remarked at the beach. Heather had assumed he meant her paddleboarding. Then she realized he was talking about her friend, who had carried an expensive camera into the water. The outing felt like keeping a promise to herself—she had vowed to make it onto the board by summer's end, but she hadn't quite believed that it was possible.

In the old brick mill that housed the headquarters of Next Step Bionics & Prosthetics, she rolled her jeans above her knee, removed her everyday prosthetic, and pressed her weight into the high-heel leg, waiting for the click of the pin that would hold it in place. The quick switch was becoming familiar routine. Like other twenty-first-century amputees—at least those blessed with generous insurance coverage—Heather had, in place of her human leg, a tool kit of specialized synthetic options. She had her regular leg and her water leg for showering and swimming, and she hoped to get another high-tech leg designed for running. She had bought a big bag to tote her growing collection of prosthetics, a quilted duffel in a pink-and-green paisley print. She would not be taking home the new high-heel leg today. It had to be sent to England for a final step: the manufacture of a custom-designed cover that would resemble her real leg as closely as possible, right down to the color of her skin and the shape of her toes. First, though, she needed to make sure the shape of it was perfect. She stood before a mirror in her four-inch pumps, her gaze shifting from one leg to the other. The calf, she observed, looked kind of flat. "Let me give you a little more muscle," offered Dave Newman, a Next Step technician. He would add a little more ankle bone, too, while he was at it. It was easy to do, by heating up strips of lightweight foam and layering them on the prosthetic calf and ankle. Then he would sand it down again, sculpting and smoothing out the surface.

Down the hall in another room, a knot of reporters and six TV cameras were waiting. The company had invited the media to come see the work it was doing; the crews showed up, of course, because of Heather. It was time for her to make a brief appearance. She headed down the hall in her high heels, with the company president, Matt Albuquerque, holding her hand to steady her. Camera flashes lit up her face as she stepped through the door. Emerging from the room a few minutes later after answering every question, Heather turned to walk back down the hall. This time when Albuquerque reached for her hand, she pulled it away. "I can probably do it," she said. Her eyes were bright and she was grinning.

CHAPTER 20

WINS AND LOSSES

Living with the memory of April

The woman, a stranger, walked in and handed him a Starbucks gift card. "You might need this," she said. It was a small act of generosity, but it helped. The gift of hand-knit blankets helped, too, and the letters from schoolchildren in Kentucky and West Virginia. So did the wind chimes and painted ceramic hearts from the people of Newtown, Connecticut, still badly bruised from their own tragedy just months earlier. For Shane O'Hara and his staff at Marathon Sports, these and other gestures of kindness had helped them recover in the weeks after the first bomb exploded outside the front door. Their progress had been halting, but it had come. Focusing on the positive things seemed to hasten the pace.

There had been setbacks, too, including some insensitive comments from less conscientious visitors to the store. One of the first weekends after they reopened, a kid asked if the bombing had left limbs inside. O'Hara found the crassness shocking. At the end of June, he took a much-needed vacation with his family to their friends' place on Hilton Head Island in South Carolina. When he returned to work, he felt recharged and ready to go. Then, his first day back, someone came in and asked: "So, where did the bomb go off?" Just like that, his sense of peace and distance evaporated. It wasn't that O'Hara and his colleagues refused to talk about what they had gone through that April afternoon. They just wanted people to show the tact and respect the subject deserved.

Every day, the Marathon Sports staff came to work on Boylston Street knowing the memories could be stirred up at any time. If it wasn't a customer's remark, it was the TV trucks that gathered outside when the attack was back in the news. It was the curious tourists, visible through the store window, pausing at the site of the blast. O'Hara knew the bombing had changed him. He had become quieter, his appetite for jokes and pranks not what it used to be. Maybe all that would come back, but a few months after one of the hardest days of his life, he couldn't be sure. "I just want it to be over," he said. "And it never is going to be over."

Boston, six months out from the bombing, had begun to move on, too. The passage, though, would be long. The marathon attack of 2013 would not fade easily, promising to linger indefinitely in the city's consciousness. Later, it would surely take its rightful place in history, on the timeline of local events that had shaped the world beyond: the launching of the 9/11 terror attacks from Logan Airport; the red state–blue state convention speech by Barack Obama in 2004; the racial tensions and school desegregation battles of the 1970s; the gangland killings under the reign of James "Whitey" Bulger; the ascension of the Kennedys to near royalty; the agitation of local abolitionists and revolutionaries; the midnight ride of Paul Revere; and the shot heard around the world that heralded American independence.

Remembering offered some choices. April 15, if you let it, could be defined by a heartless attack. Or it could be defined by the selfless work of Samaritans and first responders. It could mean cowardice, but it could also mean bravery. It could mean unimaginable losses, but it might also mean an unexpected breakthrough—a new perspective on what was important in life, a new kinship forged in a time of fear. Of course, concentrating on the good stuff—the humanity and the strength—came easily for those not badly hurt or in mourning.

The most severely wounded remained on their own distinct paths, each with his or her own unique map to recovery. Celeste Corcoran, Jeff Bauman, Roseann Sdoia, Lingzi Lu's family and friends—they and all the others would have to negotiate many ups and downs, hoping to reclaim, one day, a life that felt like their own again. Some would find peace; some would struggle. Others would dwell somewhere in between. There was no justice in any of it.

An hour before the bombs exploded on Boylston Street, the Red Sox had celebrated their walk-off win against Tampa Bay, courtesy of slugger Mike Napoli's double off the Green Monster in the bottom of the ninth inning. What the Sox couldn't have known then, in their twelfth game of 2013, was that this kind of win would define the season, a season of improbable comebacks, good humor, steady management, and unruly beards, ending with the most unlikely feat of all: winning the World Series on a cool Wednesday night in late October. It was the team's third championship in ten years but its first won on home soil in nearly a century. Few had ever felt so right. Fireworks shot into the night sky, players soaked up the acclaim, champagne was prepared. But first, hearts turned to the April tragedy that had unfolded blocks away from Fenway Park. "This is for you, Boston," World Series MVP David Ortiz said over the public address system, hoisting the shiny trophy to the sky. "You deserve it." The celebration carried into Thursday morning. Hundreds gathered on Boylston. Traffic stopped as fans knelt down in the darkness, touching and kissing the blue-and-yellow finish line.

Two days later, on a brilliant Saturday morning, the Red Sox climbed onto amphibious duck boats and rolled through downtown for their victory parade, hundreds of thousands of fans rejoicing along the route. When the procession reached Copley Square, left fielder Jonny Gomes climbed down onto Boylston with the World Series trophy, set it gently on the finish line, and draped it with a jersey that said 617 BOSTON STRONG. The crowd joined together in singing "God Bless America." Shane O'Hara stood with the Sox players, tearfully accepting one of the jerseys. Initially he'd had misgivings about taking part in the brief ceremony. He wasn't entirely comfortable being

a public face of Boston's healing. He recognized the moment's impor-
tance to the city, though, so he accepted his role. He was glad he did.
Gomes pounded him warmly on the chest. Jarrod Saltalamacchia
gave him a sincere hug. The support felt good. In his slow recovery
from April, another page had turned.

After Dzhokhar Tsarnaev was captured, after the TV cameras
moved on, the crime scene in David Henneberry's Watertown backyard remained active for nine days and nights. FBI agents stayed
there around the clock, working under floodlights after darkness fell.
Inside, Henneberry and his wife, Beth, joked that they were sleeping
in the safest house in America. When the investigators finally departed, they took the couple's beloved twenty-four-foot powerboat,
the *Slipaway II*, with them. It had been totaled, battered by bullets
and stun grenades. There was very little insurance and, remarkably,
no government recompense. After that fateful Friday night when he
stood on a ladder and spotted Dzhokhar hiding inside, Henneberry
never touched his boat again. "I never even patted her good-bye," he
said. He liked to think they might be reunited someday: maybe at the
Crime Museum in Washington, DC, where other bullet-riddled exhibits include the car used to film the final death scene in the 1967
movie *Bonnie and Clyde*.

The first week after the capture, the Henneberrys received 575
phone calls. Most were from reporters, but there were a few real es-
tate agents, too, who seemed to think they might want to sell their
house. The mail began arriving soon after, piles of cards and letters
from all over. A single stuffed envelope from Lincoln, Nebraska,
contained 130 notes from Pound Middle School students; they had
been studying ancient Greece, and heroism, at the time of the marathon. "Please, sir, know what an impact you made on their lives,"
their teacher wrote. A woman named Liz from Trenton, New Jersey,
wrote of how the drama in Boston had triggered terrible memories
of 9/11. "You reminded our nation that good people can make a difference," she said. Henneberry was touched and baffled by the grat-

itude. All he had done was call 911—wouldn't anybody in his shoes have done the same?

Their neighborhood had become famous, too, and for a time the traffic past the house was constant. Henneberry was recognized—he was "the boat guy"—when he went out. He and Beth vowed to get another boat as soon as they could. "This guy took a lot from us," Henneberry said. "He won't steal our passion away." Sun-drenched summer Sunday mornings came and went with no lazy, meandering journeys down the Charles River. Passing time made that night in April seem less real, the bullet holes in their fence the only proof. "It's true, but you can't quite believe it's true," he mused. He still wondered why it had to be *his* backyard: "What kind of coincidence? What kind of fate?"

In September, Henneberry traveled north of the city, to Marble-head, to pick up his new boat at last and steer it home. He and Beth had accepted the money appreciative strangers had raised for them online: $50,000 in three days after the capture. The new boat was much like the old one, a twenty-four-foot fixer-upper in need of all the meticulous care he could provide. He had decided to call it *Beth Said Yes*, retiring the *Slipaway* name forever. Cruising up the river into Watertown, Henneberry came around the bend and saw Beth waiting at the dock. He pulled the boat close and she climbed aboard. It had been a long, strange trip, but he was home.

Initially, Danny didn't tell his parents a thing—not about the carjacking, nor the frightful ride with the Tsarnaev brothers, nor his dramatic escape. Finally, a week or so later, he shared the wild tale with his dad, who promptly relayed it to his mom. His mother didn't mince words. She asked Danny to come home to China. But he wasn't going to leave the life he'd found in America, which, outside of one bizarre night in April, he felt pretty good about. He got another Mercedes, a silver one this time. His heroism earned him a break on the lease payments. That girl in New York he liked? Well, they were still, six months later, just friends. But they had met a few times since Marathon Week and had gotten to know each other better. Both were happy he had survived, so they could still talk to each other. And that was something.

In the days after his adventure, Danny had found it almost impossible to believe that it all had really happened. It read like a fictional story, a scene ripped from a novel or a movie script. At first, he stayed home and didn't venture out much. Then he found solace in exercise. He had just begun running a week or two before the carjacking—he credited the conditioning with helping him flee that night. A couple of weeks after it was all over, he started running again, almost every day, finding that it calmed his nerves. Danny felt, as the drama receded, like his life had more or less returned to normal. There were small ways, though, in which he had changed. He still liked to drive, for example, but he wasn't sure he would ever again roll down his window or pull over if he saw someone asking for help. When he stopped to reflect on that night, he felt conflicting emotions. He had learned that he could be brave and strong, that he possessed the courage required to confront difficult situations. But he wasn't sure his nerves could handle going through something like that again. He knew he was alive because of luck and the decisions he'd made. It could easily have gone a different way.

It started before they even got out of the city. The second bomb had just exploded a few feet away; Brighid Wall and her husband Brendan had scooped up their two children, ages four and six, and their nephew, five, and fled through the Starbucks next to Forum into the alley. They made it to a church on Newbury Street and sat on the steps. Wall's son Declan hadn't spoken since the bomb went off, but now, on the church steps, he piped up with a request: Could his mother please call the babysitter, Marissa? "Tell her I don't want to go to the Swan Boats anymore," the six-year-old said. Later, on the drive home to the quiet beach town of Duxbury, Wall's sister tried to convince the boy that the blast had been fireworks. It didn't work. He remembered everything. So did his four-year-old sister, Fiona. She called the bombing "the storm" and drew pictures of it, overlapping circles of red and gray and yellow. In the middle she drew her prized pink-and-purple Red Sox hat. It had been knocked off her head in the chaos and lost on the sidewalk. Her father went to Fenway a few days later and got her a new one.

Wall took the children to the doctor and had their hearing checked. She got a referral to a children's therapist. She did her best to answer their questions, and she reminded them how brave they had been. "What if it happens again and I'm not so brave?" asked her son. "It's not going to happen again," she told him. The children heard that a little boy had died. "Did a six-year-old die?" Declan asked. He wanted to know if "that man"—Dzhokhar Tsarnaev—was going to hell. They talked about it less as time went on, but it was there, beneath the surface. "Did that happen from the bomb?" one of the children would ask when they saw someone on crutches or in a wheelchair. One day they went downtown for their swimming lessons. "Let's park at the playground," Wall suggested, "and walk to the pool." Her son refused. "We need our car at the pool," he explained, "so if an emergency happens, we can leave quicker." She reassured him again that there would be no emergency. Sometimes she worried he might always be afraid. She kept watching him, listening closely, waiting to see.

On the night of Sunday, October 13, the seven-year-old girl in a number fifteen Dustin Pedroia jersey walked confidently up to a bank of microphones behind the pitcher's mound at Fenway Park, laid her right hand across her heart, and led the packed stadium in singing the national anthem. Six months after the marathon bombing took her leg and her eight-year-old brother, Jane Richard stood on her prosthesis and belted out "The Star-Spangled Banner" under the lights alongside a children's choir from her church, St. Ann Parish in Dorchester. She basked in the resounding applause from the stands, and from the Red Sox players standing nearby. It was game two of the American League Championship Series against the Detroit Tigers. The Sox, having lost the first game at home the night before, badly needed a lift. More than a few citizens of Red Sox Nation believed, when the hometown team pulled off a dramatic come-from-behind victory later that night, that Jane's presence had been the catalyst.

Her willingness to put herself at the center of one of the most public places imaginable was an inspiring and hopeful thing, rippling well beyond the baseball stadium. It was a marker, too, of how far she had come. Jane had spent three months in hospitals and hundreds of hours in physical therapy. She had undergone at least twelve surgeries. She had returned to school, as her older brother, Henry, had done back in the spring. The Richard family's burden had been far heavier than any family should ever bear. Bill and Denise had nursed their own serious injuries while they mourned Martin's death and helped Jane adjust to life as an amputee. But, they reported four months after the bombing, "we are making progress on this long, difficult and painful road forward." For her parents, Jane was a source of wonder—and, at times, exhaustion. One thing she loved was Irish step dancing. From age four, she had attended a dance school near her house. The hope was that in time, she would be able to return to the school and continue the hobby. It wouldn't happen right away, that much was clear. But she was determined. She had already begun practicing at home. "Watching her dance with her new leg," her family said, "is absolutely priceless."

He sat alone, confined to a small cell in a federal prison hospital an hour northwest of Boston. It was a week after Dzhokhar Tsarnaev had been pulled from the boat in Watertown. A narrow window and food slot were now his only regular links to the outside world. US marshals had quietly transferred him there overnight from Beth Israel Deaconess Medical Center in Boston, where the ambulance had first brought him after his capture. The federal prison hospital, in the town of Ayer, sat on a sprawling former army base known as Fort Devens. Just days before, Dzhokhar had enjoyed the freedom of sleeping in his college dorm room. Now he was one of more than one thousand inmates and defendants locked away under the constant watch of guards. This was where he would stay—with severe restrictions on his access to mail, media, phone calls, and contact with other inmates and visitors, even his defense team—as criminal proceedings against him began.

In June, a federal grand jury handed up a thirty-count indictment against Dzhokhar, charging him with using weapons of mass destruction to kill and maim, as well as the fatal shooting of Sean Collier. Seventeen of the charges carried the prospect of the death penalty. The decision on whether to pursue a death sentence would ultimately be made by the US attorney general, Eric Holder. Dzhokhar's trial would then follow. In announcing the indictment, Carmen Ortiz, the US attorney in Boston, detailed how Dzhokhar and Tamerlan had bought fireworks for the powder, ordered bomb-making parts, and downloaded instructions on how to assemble their devices. She would not characterize the note Dzhokhar had scrawled in the boat as a confession, but she said the brothers' motive in attacking the marathon was apparently to protest US foreign policy. Ortiz also said that she had met with the relatives of the victims and with survivors. "Their strength is extraordinary."

At his first public appearance two weeks later, Dzhokhar offered no hint of remorse or contrition. Before his federal court proceeding, he sat in a holding cell with guards observing him through surveillance cameras. At one point, he decided he had a message to send: He lifted his hand toward a camera lens and flipped up his middle finger. Soon after, he came into the courtroom in ankle chains and an orange jumpsuit, his left arm in a cast and one eye swollen. During the seven-minute hearing, he fidgeted in his seat. He studied prosecutors as they talked. He glanced, at times, at the more than thirty survivors and family members watching the proceeding. When he finally spoke, in a climax both mundane and riveting, the accused terrorist leaned over a microphone and repeated, "Not guilty," as each charge was read—in a thick accent that startled his high school friends in attendance, who remembered him speaking perfect English. As he was led away afterward, he blew a kiss to his two sisters, one of whom was sobbing. The other held a child in her arms. John DiFava, the MIT police chief who had come to watch, said as he walked from the courtroom that Dzhokhar wasn't worth a single tear. "I'd like to grab him by the throat," he said.

With Dzhokhar awaiting trial under lockdown, the body of his brother Tamerlan would lie unburied for weeks, the subject of an ugly fight over whether a dead terrorist deserved the same decorum afforded everyone else. Tamerlan's wife, Katherine Russell, had decided not to take his body after his death; she would return to using her maiden name and move with her daughter back into her parents' home in Rhode Island. Dzhokhar was in custody and his parents were back in Russia. Tamerlan's uncle, Ruslan Tsarni, together with Tamerlan's sisters, finally claimed the remains from the state medical examiner more than two weeks after the bombing. The body was first transferred to a funeral home in North Attleborough, south of Boston, where about twenty protesters soon gathered. It was then taken to Graham Putnam & Mahoney Funeral Parlors in Worcester, whose owner, Peter Stefan, was known for providing burial services for the poor and unwanted. The body would remain there for six days while Tsarni and Stefan tried to find a burial plot. Tamerlan's mother, Zubeidat, wanted to bring her son's body back to Russia, but she lacked the money. Tamerlan wouldn't be laid to rest in Cambridge— the city manager preemptively denied him a cemetery deed, saying that his burial there would not be in the city's interest. Tom Menino took a similar stand in Boston. Protesters began picketing outside the funeral home, arguing that Tamerlan's body did not deserve traditional burial privileges. The standstill threatened to drag on for days.

Then Martha Mullen stepped in. A mental health counselor from Richmond, Virginia, Mullen had heard about the protests on NPR. "It portrayed America at its worst," she said. "Jesus says [to] love our enemies. So I was sitting in Starbucks and thought, maybe I'm the one person who needs to do something." Mullen researched Muslim burial traditions and requirements and contacted Islamic Funeral Services of Virginia, which responded within an hour that it could provide a plot for Tamerlan at Al-Barzakh Cemetery, in the nearby town of Doswell. Then she contacted the Worcester Police Department, which had been providing around-the-clock protection for Stefan. A plan was crafted to spirit Tamerlan's body out of Worcester in a rented van. Tamerlan was buried on his right side in an unmarked grave, facing toward Mecca.

They parked his truck in front of the church, the shiny black Ford F-150 he'd gotten two months earlier. The truck bed was filled with flowers. Bunting hung from the front bumper. A sticker with the MIT police insignia was affixed near the driver's door; another sticker on a window said REST IN PEACE OFFICER SEAN A. COLLIER. This was how Collier's family, friends, and fellow police officers said good-bye to the promising young cop ruthlessly murdered by the Tsarnaevs, at a private service in a town north of Boston. Officers from the Somerville Police Department, which Collier had been about to join, led the way out. A few months later, Collier acquired the municipal badge he'd always wanted. In front of family and police from around the state, he was posthumously made a Somerville police officer at a ceremony at city hall. "Sean has been called many things over the past four months," said Collier's brother, Andrew. "But one of the things Sean would be the most proud to be called is a great cop." His badge number, 310, would remain unused by the department, the slot standing vacant in his memory.

Around the country, total strangers—many of them runners—were moved by what they saw in Boston and sought ways to help. The month after the bombing, Marsha Strickhouser, a public relations manager from Clearwater, Florida, helped put on the Boston Memorial Run in nearby St. Petersburg. Runners held candles, heard from competitors who had taken part in the Boston Marathon, sang "Ave Maria," and then set off on an untimed 2.62-mile run through the streets. The run raised about $20,000 for the One Fund. "It was something that happened to our country, not just Boston," Strickhouser said. That same spirit drove the One Run for Boston, a 3,300-mile coast-to-coast relay run begun in June that raised tens of thousands of dollars. From Venice Beach, California, across Route 66, through the Ozarks, and eventually onto Boylston Street, the route involved 319 legs and more than one thousand runners, each carrying a baton with a GPS transponder. Marathoner Nicole Reis, whose father, John Odom, was badly injured in the bombing after coming to watch his daughter, capped off the benefit run by pushing her dad across the finish line in a wheelchair shortly before 1:00 A.M. one night in early July.

Allison Byrne was among thousands of marathoners, spectators, and responders who came together to rerun the course's final mile at a Boston event later in the spring known as #onerun. Byrne was one of the only runners seriously injured in the April bombing. She was nervous about participating, knowing she would have to pass the very spot where shrapnel had brought her down, where she'd lain on the ground fearing for her life. But that fear wasn't enough to keep her away. This was a woman who had been so determined to complete the race on Marathon Day that she had asked the nurse at her side, Nancy Shorter, if Shorter could carry her across the finish line. "We'd love to," Shorter told her. "Don't think that's going to happen." Nearly six weeks later, with her husband beside her in the cold rain, Byrne finally did make it across. She had finished the race.

These moments were triumphs, signs of continuing progress, and they could bring an overwhelming rush of emotions. A few weeks after the bombing, when the Boston Pops Orchestra opened its 128th season at Symphony Hall, David King attended the concert as the special guest. The trauma surgeon stepped onstage for the final encore, vigorously guest-conducting a rousing rendition of the orchestra's signature anthem, "Stars and Stripes Forever," played every July 4 on the Esplanade. Standing in the historic concert hall, arms pumping as the crowd rose to its feet and clapped along, King was overcome by the support from so many strangers. He had to fight back tears. At times it could seem like the city really had changed, its broken pieces somehow soldered back together more tightly than before.

. . .

Her friends weren't wild about the idea. Neither was Heather, at first. Forum, the bar and restaurant where she had been when the bomb took her foot, was finally reopening, and its owners had invited her to be there. It was the last business on Boylston Street to come back, a missing piece of the puzzle about to snap into place. The more Heather thought it over, the more she felt drawn to return. There were gaps in her memory that bothered her. As time passed, it got harder to ask others who had been there, to drag them back to that day against their will. If she saw it again, it might make the picture clearer. Her friends were wary, but they agreed to go with her.

The reopening was a spectacle, a pop-up party on the busy Boylston Street sidewalk in the middle of a picture-perfect late summer evening. A brass band from New Orleans kicked off the festivities, marching from the marathon finish line down the sidewalk to the restaurant's refurbished front door. They settled in under the brand-new brown-and-red-striped awning and played "When the Saints Go Marching In." Curious passersby paused to listen. People leaned out of passing cabs to snap photos. "Go, Boston!" someone yelled from a trolley. Traffic snarled; a helmeted policeman blew a whistle. The wait staff at L'Espalier, the acclaimed eatery across the street, gathered at a second-story window to watch the commotion. Heather appeared, wearing a long dress, and helped hold a blue-and-yellow ribbon across the front of the restaurant as the mayor cut it. Inside, the din of socializing filled the space that had been silent for so long. "Being here, I can see how the city is moving along with life," said Carlos Arredondo, looking down at Boylston Street from an upstairs window, wearing his familiar cowboy hat. "It's moving along beautifully. And I'm moving on, too."

Downstairs, Heather sat at the bar receiving hugs and kisses from an endless stream of friends and well-wishers. A glass of wine sat untouched on the bar behind her. She looked happy and peaceful. A photographer approached to take her picture, and her friends gathered around, arms looped around one another's shoulders. Earlier, she had ventured out to the back alley, where she had lain on the ground on Marathon Monday. She had stood at the back door looking down, searching for the grass she remembered lying on. Asphalt stretched in every direction. There was no grass, she realized. She had imagined it. A voice rose from the alley—one of Forum's managers, thanking her for coming back.

"I'm going to have a good memory now," Heather told him.

For weeks, people had been coming to Copley Square to pay respects, strolling quietly through the memorial that had grown there, studying the somber handwritten messages and photographing the rows of running shoes hung on metal barricades. In June, the city put out word that it was time to take down the weathered shrine and transfer everything to the archives. On the evening of June 24, a muggy summer night, the public gathered at the spot for one last time. Around 5:30 P.M., police began moving everybody out to make room for a special ceremony for bombing survivors, their families, and the relatives of those who had been killed. A little while later they began arriving—the Richard family, with Jane in a wheelchair; Adrianne Haslet-Davis, the dancer who had lost part of her left leg; and others. There was even a brazen imposter in their midst: Branden Mattier, twenty-two, who soon after would plead not guilty, with his brother, to charges that they had tried to defraud the One Fund of $2 million by falsely claiming that a long-dead aunt had lost a leg in the bombing. Tom Menino, Ed Davis, and other local leaders greeted the victims with hugs and words of encouragement. Menino, after climbing gingerly out of his SUV, pointed playfully at Jane Richard as he approached her family. He spoke gently to her surviving brother, Henry. As the family walked away, Henry's mom put an arm around his neck. The memorial, in its first days, had been christened as a place of mourning and healing. Its final night would be perhaps its most poignant, the survivors gathered to observe another milestone's passing while the city hummed on, duck boats and ambulances rolling by as always.

At dawn the next morning, about a dozen city employees and volunteers pulled on rubber gloves, unfurled rolls of plastic bags, and began picking through the tattered inventory, untying the knots on the many tangled shoelaces. The only sound was the ripping of paper as careful hands tore down signs and banners. In a letter he had written to the survivors and to victims' families, Menino had spoken of "a respectful closing," one that would "help us all look to the future." For Billy and Patty Campbell, who came early that morning in matching blue-and-yellow BOSTON STRONG T-shirts, that future felt a long way off. They remained mired in the present, trying to make it through each day, trying to understand why Krystle had been taken. It was their first visit to the memorial. Patty put on glasses and leaned in close to read the writing on a poster; she reached out to touch a stuffed toy, a polished rock. A reporter asked her what the memorial meant to her. "It's confusing," she said. "I'm still in shock." The Tsarnaevs had lived a quarter of a mile from her mother-in-law, Patty said; her sister's son had gone to school with Dzhokhar. "I just don't get it," she said, her voice trailing off. Before they left, the Campbells took a string of rosary beads, one of hundreds draped by strangers on the four white crosses at the memorial's center. Then they walked away slowly down the sidewalk, their arms wrapped around each other.

The dismantling accelerated after their departure. Workers cut away deflated balloons and sodden ribbons and started sweeping. Kevin Brown, the volunteer caretaker who had lovingly maintained the site, helped to lift the wooden crosses and load them into a truck. By 8:45 A.M., three hours after they had started, the pavement was bare. A city archivist hoisted a pile of brooms over his shoulder and turned to go. Behind him, the morning foot traffic easily, unthinkingly reverted to its normal pattern, flowing across the sunny pink-and-gray brick.

CHAPTER 21

MILE 27

The road beyond

At first Shana Cottone didn't recognize the feeling. She was at a Zac Brown Band concert, at an outdoor venue south of Boston, when she started to feel sick. She figured it must be the piece of sausage she had eaten; Shana never ate sausages at concerts. She wandered away from her friends toward the restrooms. The crowd thinned as she walked, and her stomach stopped hurting. It wasn't the sausage, she realized—it was the crowd, triggering some memory of Patriot's Day and the marathon. It was like that now: a well of anxiety lay hidden within her, and without warning her reflexes could tap it. One night her dog started barking in the backyard, and before she knew it, Shana was creeping outside ninja-style, senses on high alert—only to find a fallen tree branch on the ground. She slept with both an air conditioner and a fan humming; still she woke up at the slightest murmur. It made her mad. The places that had once felt safe didn't anymore.

After the marathon, to cope with the stress, she had gone back to the treatment program, the one that had helped her stop drinking. It had helped, just as it had the first time. She had taken time off from

work, and used it to plant a garden in her yard. She was growing veg-
etables and herbs—cucumbers, basil, peppers, zucchini, eggplant—
and roses in a soft peach color. The roses she chose in tribute to
Roseann Sdoia, the woman whose life she had helped save on Boylston Street. They were friends now; Shana saw her often. It went back
to those fateful minutes in the street: the connection she had felt to a
wounded stranger, and the desperate, overwhelming need to help her.
It had been an instant kinship, and she could not walk away. It was a
feeling she had never had before in her role as a cop, and it was difficult to explain. "I need to see it through," she said. "I can't have it any
other way." In her backyard, the roses bloomed through the summer.

Shana was deeply grateful for the changes she had made in the
months leading up to the marathon. If she hadn't stopped drinking,
if she had been hungover that day, would she have reacted differently? She would never know, but it convinced her there was some
larger purpose in the painful reckoning that she had faced. She was
grateful, too, that after the bombing she had not given in to the urge
to start drinking again. It had been so tempting to seek that easy
solace, at a moment when she knew no one would judge her for it. But
she would have judged herself, harshly, for breaking her promise.
Instead, she knew she had been tested, and she had been faithful.

A week or so before September 11, working her regular tour in
East Boston, Shana responded to a call about a suspicious package
on the sidewalk. Standing there waiting for the bomb squad, she
fought to keep calm. Was this a dry run, preparation for a real attack
planned for the upcoming anniversary? Was a would-be bomber
watching them right now, taking notes on their positions, all to fine-
tune some twisted plot? No one around her seemed concerned. But
it turned out the suspicious object really was a bomb—a cardboard
container roughly the size of a soda can, filled with explosive powder
and wired with a fuse. The bomb squad X-rayed it on the scene to
confirm what it was, then took it away in a blast-proof bag and detonated it at their remote test range. It seemed a case unlikely to be
solved. The knowledge that the bomb had been real raised the stakes
for Shana. It was one thing to be anxious and write it off as irrational.

But if people really were *inside their homes making bombs*, well, what then? It had to change the way you lived. You couldn't let your guard down ever, even for a single second. It was hard to imagine living that way and still living fully. How, for example, could she ever decide to have children in a world so fraught with hidden danger?

On the night of September 11, she attended a remembrance ceremony at John Hancock Hall, a few blocks from the finish line. The organizers, from a Boston charity, had invited Shana and other marathon first responders to be honored as part of their program. She wore her uniform and sat in the front row. It was the first time she had been singled out that way for recognition. There were a lot of speeches about heroes, a lot of talk about stepping up and making a difference. Finally, near the end of the night, somebody read Shana's name. She stood up and turned, shyly, to face the applause.

He'd done this hundreds of times, sharing the stories of his running feats, the self-deprecating jokes about his height, and the motivational life lessons he'd picked up in staging the Boston Marathon all these years. But this address by Dave McGillivray, to a group of hospital CEOs in Boston's Seaport District on an October afternoon, was different. "I wasn't sure I was going to make it here," he told them. The day before, he'd gone to the hospital to get checked out. He hadn't been feeling quite right lately. His breathing had been off. He'd undergone a CT scan and an angiogram, which shows blood flow in arteries and veins. The news had been worse than he expected. The tests had revealed some significant blockage. He was devastated. He'd been so fit his entire life. How could this be? "I always thought I was invincible," he told the hospital group. The room was silent as he spoke in a shaky voice. He offered sincere thanks for everything the medical community did—work that, in the past, he had known largely from afar. Now it was his well-being they were guarding, too.

All his life, McGillivray had been able to outrun almost anything. Discipline, self-assurance, a clear mind, and a willingness to put in the hard work—these were the essential ingredients to success, whether his end goal was running the Eastern Seaboard or managing an unwieldy road race for thousands. He had been a paragon of health and fitness, a promoter of active lifestyles who ran more miles than most people ever would. He left the hospital deeply chastened. Yes, he had been fit. But he hadn't always been healthy. He hadn't been eating right. After a long run, he might grab three or four cookies. He had fueled his famous cross-country trek with junk food. None of it, he had figured, would do much harm. "I thought I was out there burning it all up," he said. Partly it was genetics. His father had undergone quadruple bypass surgery at age sixty-five, then lived to ninety after changing his diet and hitting the health club. But McGillivray knew this was also his own doing, and that made him feel embarrassed and frustrated. "I cheated myself," he said.

Once the initial shock faded, he returned to the McGillivray Way, determined to apply the same zeal and same lessons of preparation and execution that had always served him so well. He began to see his diagnosis not as a sentence, but as a second chance, believing that he could beat it with the right diet, medication, and exercise. "I don't need two warnings," he said. He began eating red rice and other healthy foods to lower his cholesterol, finding success immediately. He joined the local YMCA and planned to start swimming and lifting weights. He sought out a trainer, a nutritionist, a masseuse, and a new bike. He got a heart rate monitor, knowing he had to limit his intensity when he ran. "It's a whole new beginning," he said.

The year 2013 had already been a stark reminder of the fragility of life. One minute in April, McGillivray had been ready to start down the marathon course; the next, he was racing back to Boston to see his finish line in disarray. Six months later, his personal brush with mortality was a heavy postscript. He considered his youngest children—he had a daughter who was only four—and thought about how he had to make it a while yet. There was a lot still left to see. In the immediate term, he had another Boston Marathon to plan, which, given all the security changes, all the expectations, all the sensitivities involved with the first anniversary of the bombing, was already going to be one of his biggest tests ever. He had no intention of giving it up, though. If anything, his diagnosis had made him more motivated to dive into his work and to stay busy. The race needed him, and he needed the race. He credited the one hundredth Boston Marathon, in 1996, with saving his life after his difficult divorce. He looked at the 2014 race in much the same way. "I am not even going to remotely consider pulling back on the throttle," he said. Assuming he still had control. About six weeks after the bombing, McGillivray's son Luke came up to him again.

"Remember I told you I didn't want you to direct the marathon again?" the seven-year-old said.

"Yes," McGillivray said.

"You know why?"

"Why?"

"Because I want to direct it."

McGillivray's cardiologist had talked to him about stress, telling him that he was always going a mile a minute. McGillivray believed that stress lay in the eye of the beholder. For him, working hard, focusing on big problems, taking on a heavy responsibility—those things didn't feel stressful. Even putting on the 2014 marathon, the most intense, most fraught staging of the event in its 118-year history, did not, for him, feel like a source of strain. Or at least it didn't feel as stressful as *not* putting on the Boston Marathon, sitting on the sidelines watching it all go off without him. "I would be stressed if I was lying on a beach," he said. "I would be so stressed that the clock is ticking and I'm not getting anything done." His doctor, when McGillivray told him this, rolled his eyes. A lot had changed, but some things never would.

David King hadn't written a speech, but he wasn't worried. He would think of something. The trauma surgeon brought his wife, Anne, with him, and their two little girls, three and six, wearing matching polka-dot party dresses. The dinner at the Ipswich Country Club, north of Boston, was a fund-raiser for families of police officers killed in the line of duty. The organizers wanted King to talk about the marathon. Four months had passed, but people were still interested, still appreciative. They wanted to thank him for what he'd done. It was unfamiliar territory for King, who saved lives all the time but was almost never celebrated for it.

The former Somerville police detective who had invited him to the dinner, Mario Oliveira, was one of the only patients with whom King had ever kept in touch. Oliveira had narrowly escaped death in a 2010 shoot-out. A bullet missed his heart by an inch; his heart stopped twice on the operating table, and both times King revived him. Afterward, the cop considered King a brother. When the surgeon was in Afghanistan, Oliveira checked on his family. When Oliveira's second son was born, he gave him the middle name David. It had been King's only brush with that kind of gratitude—until now. Since the marathon, the city of Boston had embraced him. It made him feel less an outsider, more a part of something. It anchored him here in a way he never expected. He was eager to run Boston in 2014, but he had also volunteered to help Dave McGillivray with medical response planning for next year. He wanted to be part of making everything go smoothly.

King and Oliveira sat together at the dinner. As the meal wound down, the event organizers stepped to the podium to talk about Sean Collier. Then they honored Richard Donohue, the transit police officer wounded in the shoot-out. Donohue leaned on a cane at the front of the room, looking embarrassed by the standing ovation. "I miss Sean every day," he said. Collier's brother Andrew offered words of solace. "It's easy to focus on the evil," he said, "but the good in people outweighs the bad." It felt like the right way to end. The room began buzzing, on the verge of breaking up. But there was one last speaker: Dr. King. He began to talk about that week in April. A hush fell over the dining room again. He talked about his patients, about Roseann Sdoia. He described Obama's visit to Mass General, and his own assignment from the White House in advance, to write down every patient's story for the president. He explained how it had changed him, taking time to talk with every person who was wounded.

"I realized I'd worked on these patients for days and I hardly knew them," he said. "I realized all those little details really mattered." He paused to collect himself, briefly overcome, and the room was silent, willing him to recover. Then he spoke of Mario, the cop he'd saved, and their lasting bond. "All of you inspire me," he said finally. He returned to his seat and took his six-year-old into his lap.

In November, he ran the New York City Marathon. He decided to try for the same time he'd run in Boston in April—3:12—to link this race to the one that still loomed so large. He had taken two months off from running, though, to let his bad back heal, and he wasn't sure how well he would do. He felt no anxiety, except for a single moment at the start, when a cannon boomed close by without warning, shaking the ground. Running felt great, and the race went well. He finished just two seconds off the mark, with a time of 3:11:58. One of his marathon patients, Kaitlynn Cates, who had suffered a serious leg injury but not an amputation, had come to New York to cheer him on; she was waiting at the finish line with a sign that said GO DR. KING—MY HERO—BOSTON STRONG. His wife was there, too, and his daughters. Before they had left Boston for New York, King's parents had offered to take the kids so he and Anne could enjoy a weekend away by themselves. For a split second King had calculated the risk in his head: Would his children be safer staying home? Then he recognized what he was doing and shook away the thought. *Nope*, he told himself. *I'm not thinking like that.* The race would be a celebration, and his girls would be there with him.

"You have to smile, babe," Billy Campbell had told his wife, Patty, in the weeks after their daughter's death. "You can't be in grievance twenty-four seven. You have to start thinking about the good things." The prescription was wise and level-headed, but it would prove hard to follow—not only for Krystle's parents, but for her extended family and the community she had built around her. The only thing they could do was to try to push through every day. "I was very lucky to have two great kids, and one of them was taken away," Billy said. "I believe my daughter really could have made a difference in this world, for the good. She was out to really leave a mark. She already had in a lot of people's lives. She was special, man. She was special." It was hard to get past how unnatural this was. Daughters weren't supposed to die first.

The Campbells were a private family. They hadn't asked for any of this attention. They understood, though, that Krystle had become an emblem of Boston's sorrow. And they understood the expectations that came with that. So they put on the strongest faces they could muster and began representing their daughter at public events. Patty threw out a ceremonial first pitch at a Red Sox game at Fenway Park—the first time, her husband said, that she had worn a broad smile since the bombing. They attended a benefit concert at an Irish pub not far from their house. They stood alongside other proud parents at the University of Massachusetts Boston graduation ceremony, watching as the chancellor presented Krystle's posthumous bachelor of arts degree to her brother, Billy III. They went to a New England Patriots game, where the team honored victims of the April attack. Throughout, they tried to reclaim their lives. They got out of town a little with friends and family. They doted on their grandson. In September, Patty returned to her job in food services at Harvard Business School. Billy worried about her all day, until she walked back in the door. He kept his phone in his pocket all the time. Some days went okay, and some didn't. Sometimes the days cut both ways, like when they went to a relative's wedding in Philadelphia, or when they received Krystle's friends at home to look through pictures. Every celebration of life was a reminder of loss.

One of the better days came on a gorgeous, cloudless Tuesday in late September, five months after the bombing. With the morning sun shimmering on the sea, Krystle's parents, brother, and nana boarded a private ferry at Boston's Long Wharf alongside dozens of other relatives and friends. After a short ride, the ferry pulled up to a dock on Spectacle Island, the beautifully restored former landfill out in Boston Harbor that had held a special place in Krystle's heart. The group walked off the pier and onto a path that led up a hill, through a meadow of wildflowers and chirping crickets. At the top sat a wooden gazebo, built on an overlook offering majestic views of the Atlantic off the back side of the island. Above the entrance, a new sign had just been hung, yellow letters on two varnished boards: KRYSTLE M. CAMPBELL GAZEBO. Krystle's work family on the islands, led by state park officials, had thought this a fitting way to honor her memory and her love of this place.

Billy came in a gray suit. Patty wore blue pants, a cream-colored jacket, and pink tennis shoes. They took their places in the front row of white chairs arranged in front of the gazebo. Friends and family filled in behind them. The flags of the United States and Massachusetts flapped in the salty breeze. Krystle was "the lady with the million-dollar smile," Medford mayor Michael McGlynn said during a brief ceremony. She represented the confidence Americans had in their way of life, McGlynn said, invoking the words of the Reverend Martin Luther King Jr.: "Darkness cannot drive out darkness: Only light can do that. Hate cannot drive out hate: only love can do that." Her friend Tim Getchell told of Krystle's role in building the islands community. "This gathering is a small reminder of the huge presence she had out here and always will," he said. Patty spoke last. She walked up to the lectern and tearfully thanked everyone for their heartfelt words. "God bless you," she said. "Thank you." In that moment, it was all she could manage. "I'm sorry," she said. Then Patty, Billy, and his mother, Lillian, walked together toward a big red ribbon stretched across the gazebo entrance. With a pair of giant green-handled scissors, they cut the ribbon together, officially opening the gazebo under its new name. They walked slowly inside, studying the plaque hung in Krystle's honor. The red ribbon danced in the wind.

On the boat back to Boston, the solemnity of it all seemed to recede. There would be hard days ahead—that was certain. But this day felt like a celebration of Krystle's life, a warm gathering of many who knew and loved her, who came out to cheer her exuberance, her fondness for blue eye shadow, her indelible Boston-ness. "It feels really good," Billy said as he walked among the guests on the ferry. "It really does." Nearby, Krystle's friends and relatives stood by the boat's makeshift bar, talking, laughing, and swapping hugs and stories. A few of them cracked open blue aluminum bottles of Bud Light. Patty stood among them, a bottle in her hand, too, gazing out a window at the sparkling waves.

The October weekend had been busy, progress mixed, as always, with reminders of her limits. In one quiet step forward—one she had not planned to take just yet—Heather Abbott had gone on a date Friday night. It was one of her biggest quandaries: how to reenter the dating scene; how to explain her story to new people. Standing at a bar in her high heels, Heather looked just like everyone else—that was the point. So when was she supposed to tell a potential suitor about her missing leg? And how would she handle it if he rejected her then? For months she had pushed the thought away. She wasn't ready. Then a friend offered to set her up with a guy who was also an amputee, having lost his leg years before in an accident. It seemed like a good way to start, so she accepted. They sat on bar stools side by side and talked. The conversation went well. At the end of the night, when they started to get up, they found themselves momentarily stuck. Their prosthetic legs had somehow become hooked together, and neither one had realized it until that moment. They couldn't help but laugh as they pulled the prosthetics apart.

The next night, someone pulled a fire alarm in her Boston hotel, and Heather was forced to walk downstairs from the twenty-first floor. Going down stairs was still not easy, and she was slow. There was a moment in the stairwell, people running past her, when she felt panic flare. By morning, it had become a rueful lesson: From now on, she would ask for a room on the ground floor. But Sunday morning brought a welcome revelation, too. She left her hotel room wearing her striking new blade prosthetic, the kind used by amputee athletes for running. Unlike her other prosthetic legs, which looked so real they were rarely noticed, this one, a high-tech, custom-made carbon-fiber blade given to her by the Challenged Athletes Foundation, couldn't be missed. She had been afraid that people would stare as she walked across the busy hotel lobby, but no one did. Blending in was liberating. She checked out and headed for the athletic fields at Harvard University.

Outside, a cold October rain was falling. On a soaked playing field at Harvard, Heather joined a circle of other amputees doing warm-up stretches. She wore the hood of her gray sweatshirt pulled up over her head to fend off the chill. "You're running your own race," Joan Benoit Samuelson, a two-time Boston Marathon winner and Olympic gold medalist, told the group on the field, participants in a clinic for disabled athletes run by the foundation. "You're showing us it can be done. . . . Go get 'em." Heather would have loved to make it look easy, the way Benoit Samuelson made it sound, but she knew better by now. Like just about everything else, this was going to hurt.

Heather and the others lined up on the edge of the field, standing on artificial turf stained dark green by the rain. When the trainer gave the command, they ran to the other side, passing rows of orange cones along the way. On the first trip across, Heather was the slowest, her movements tentative and awkward. She was having a hard time figuring out how high to lift her prosthetic leg; she didn't want to scrape it on the ground and trip herself. On the trip back across the field, the trainer said, they would go faster. "Pull back, reach out; pull back, reach out," he called as they started off. Heather tried to concentrate on his instructions, reaching with her new leg, planting it and pulling past it. She tried to set aside the fear of falling. They reached the starting line again, stopped and turned around. "We're going to work on speed from here out," the trainer told them. She was still moving slowly, feeling her way in the cold.

On the wet field, morning became afternoon. The rain faded into mist, but the damp persisted. Heather kept running back and forth across the turf. Down the field and back, a short rest, then again. The ache in her leg became a constant throbbing, the new prosthetic pounding on her flesh with every step. Still she kept at it. It was possible that running would get easier in time—there was no way for her to know for sure. She kept going anyway, ignoring pain and doubt. It was the only way forward that she knew.

AFTERWORD

A heavy spring rain fell on Boylston Street. Side by side, marathon bombing survivors, first responders, family members, and public officials filed into the Hynes Convention Center, a couple blocks west of the finish line. Heather Abbott was there, and David King. Dave McGillivray found his seat, and Shana Cottone. It was April 15, 2014. One year earlier, runners had filled the street outside. They had sprinted past cheering crowds under a sunny sky, eyes fixed on the blue-and-yellow stripe. Next week, they would run again. First, though, the city had to reckon with the past, to cast off the deep shadow on the day.

The memorial ceremony drew 2,500 invited guests, including the friends and families of Krystle Campbell, Martin Richard, Lingzi Lu, and Sean Collier. Vice President Joe Biden came in for the event, joining Governor Patrick, former mayor Tom Menino, and Menino's successor, Marty Walsh, who had been elected in November. Flashes of anger and defiance punctuated the speeches, as when Biden lauded Boston for not yielding to fear. "You're living proof that America can never, never, never be defeated," he said. Mostly, though, the mood was quiet, reflective, and unexpectedly grateful. Menino, his pace slowed by cancer, acknowledged the pain of returning to "that place where our lives broke apart." His voice was ragged. "Lean in if you have to," he told survivors. "I want you to hear this solemn promise: When the lights are dim and the cameras go away, know that our support and love for you will never waver." Patrick Downes, a thirty-year-old amputee whose wife, Jessica Kensky, had also lost a leg in the bombing, rendered the crowd pin-drop silent as he described humbling gifts of love and sacrifice. "Historians . . . will tell of the devastation that was brought upon our families," he said. "I also hope they will tell of the unfailing compassion and unity that followed."

The deepest grief in the room was silent. Inside the printed program for the ceremony, attendees found a tribute to Lingzi Lu, the twenty-three-year-old graduate student who had died on the sidewalk near Martin Richard. Her father, Jun Lu, had written her a letter. "Lingzi," it said, "Mom and Dad could not have asked for a better daughter. We were so lucky and honored to be your parents." Earlier that morning, Martin's parents, Bill and Denise, along with their two other children, Henry and Jane, had huddled near the finish line to lay a wreath. Krystle's parents, Billy and Patty, stood beside them, a year of suffering etched into their faces.

The luck of the calendar, as it happened, offered a blessing. Patriot's Day—Marathon Day—always fell on the third Monday in April. In 2014, the holiday wouldn't come until April 21, leaving five full days between the bombing anniversary and the race. That gave city leaders and marathon officials a natural way to separate things: Commemorate the pain and loss first, then put on a marathon for the ages, Boston's 118th—a kind of safe passage from grief to competition.

The tribute ceremony moved outside as the hour approached 2:49 p.m., to mark the moments when the bombs went off. Crowds were gathered on the sidewalks. Many huddled under golf umbrellas, some wearing race jackets and running shoes, others in workday attire. Carlos Arredondo flashed a thumbs-up as he walked up Boylston in his trademark cowboy hat. The Richards, the politicians, and Boston Athletic Association executive director Tom Grilk gathered together near the finish line. And then, after the bagpipes played, after Menino, leaning on his Louisville Slugger cane, sang with the others to Ronan Tynan's soulful rendition of "God Bless America," the moment of remembrance arrived, accompanied by a still and somber silence. All across the city, people paused—at South Station, at Massachusetts General Hospital, at the MIT chapel, near where

Sean Collier had been killed. On Boylston Street, Old South Church tolled its bell as the minute slowly passed, twelve peals piercing the quiet. Richard Donohue, the MBTA police officer wounded in the Watertown shoot-out, raised an American flag. Denise Richard wiped away tears. Her husband stood by stoically. When the moment passed, an honor guard led everyone away from the site with a military cadence. The street opened again to the public soon after. People tentatively filled the space, moving deliberately, as if over hallowed ground.

On Franklin Street in Watertown, a new boat sat in David Henneberry's driveway. Neighbors pointed it out happily, grateful for the return to normalcy. Henneberry had bought the boat in the fall, months after the manhunt, with money donated by sympathetic strangers. Every day that spring that it was warm enough, he had worked on the boat in his driveway, varnishing and revarnishing the woodwork. But he worked without his faithful partner at his side. His wife, Beth, had died of cancer in January. He had named the new boat *Beth Said Yes* for her. Henneberry was still easygoing and soft-spoken, tolerant when people recognized him as "the boat guy." But the year had left him with one lasting lesson: "There's no certainty in anything."

Some of his neighbors struggled with the memories. Some remained troubled by the aggressive police response, the tanks and gunfire and the orders to stay in their houses. Others locked their doors when they never had before. They wondered if they would ever get all the answers, or know why the Tsarnaev brothers had picked their neighborhood to make their final stand. As the 2014 marathon approached, they found themselves remembering, and wondering again.

In the meantime, the One Fund, originally envisioned as a short-term charity, continued to receive millions of dollars in contributions. In September 2014, the organization announced an additional $18.5 million in payouts, bringing its total distributed funds to about $80 million. In this round, the organization placed a greater emphasis on so-called invisible wounds like post-concussive syndrome and traumatic brain injury. Organizers also put $1.5 million toward a new One Fund Center at Mass. General, to assist bombing survivors over the next two years. For some, the toughest part of the journey was still ahead. In November 2014, after a long fight to keep her damaged leg, Rebekah DiMartino of Texas became the seventeenth person known to have undergone an amputation as a result of injuries suffered in the bombing.

One of the biggest questions—when Dzhokhar Tsarnaev would go to trial—wasn't answered until the fall of 2014. The government had decided to seek the death penalty, adding layers of complexity to the case. Ultimately, a federal judge in Boston set the trial date for January 2015. The specter of Tsarnaev in a courtroom inspired both eager anticipation and dread. His trial offered a chance to unravel the mystery of the brothers' alleged methods and motivations. But it would force survivors and victims' relatives to relive an awful chapter. They, as with many others in the city, would soon have to wrestle with whether to pay close attention or none at all.

The Friday before the 2014 marathon, Dave McGillivray spoke at a dinner at the Harvard Club of Boston before a group of charity runners, including members of Team MR8, who were running to raise money for a new foundation honoring the memory of eight-year-old Martin Richard. One of the other guest speakers that night was a thirty-eight-year-old elite American runner named Meb Keflezighi. Keflezighi had come to the U.S. as an Eritrean refugee at age twelve, his family fleeing poverty and war with Ethiopia. "My life would have been [as] a soldier," he said. The family settled in San Diego. Keflezighi knew no English and had never run competitively before. He went on to excel in school and athletics, earning a scholarship to UCLA. He became a U.S. citizen in 1998 and represented his adopted country at the Olympics three times, winning a silver medal in Athens in 2004. Five years later, he won the New York Marathon, the first American triumph in twenty-seven years.

Injured for the 2013 Boston Marathon, Keflezighi had watched
from the grandstands at the finish line. He'd left the area just minutes
before the blasts. Like so many runners, he vowed to return to Boston. As top contenders go, however, he was getting up there in age.
He had lost his Nike shoe sponsorship a few years back. His best time
was several minutes slower than those of the top Ethiopian and Kenyan runners. Few would have put money on him to win. After the
dinner at the Harvard Club, McGillivray, Keflezighi, and one of Keflezighi's brothers walked back toward Copley Square together. It was
clear to McGillivray that Keflezighi recognized how much it would
mean if an American won Boston in 2014. "It was all he was thinking
about," McGillivray said. McGillivray asked him what his strategy
would be come Monday. Keflezighi said he planned to go hard at the
start and never let up. "He knew he needed to just take it out, and set
the pace, and hold on for dear life," McGillivray said.

The morning of the race, McGillivray assumed command of the
starting line in Hopkinton, as he did every year. But this Boston
Marathon, of course, would be unlike any before it. "We're taking
back our race today. We're taking back the finish line," he told the
crowd of runners over the loudspeaker. Besides the emotional weight,
McGillivray was contending with two major shifts from the prior
year. The first was a far bigger field size. More than 32,000 runners
would fill the course, including thousands who were stopped just
short of finishing last year. The other change was the enhanced security. The National Guardsmen along the course were armed military
police officers, unlike in years past. More undercover officers were
strategically positioned in the crowds. Cities and towns along the
route parked heavy equipment at key intersections to block vehicle
access. Police set up checkpoints in the finish line area.

McGillivray tried to focus on the race, but he couldn't completely
shut out jitters about a potential copycat attack. "You're always looking over your shoulder, regardless of how much security there is," he
said. The 2014 marathon was going to feel different than it used to—
there was no getting around that. The goal was to amp up the safety

measures and vigilance without taking the fun out of Marathon Monday. The planning and preparation for this one had been more demanding than ever before, but McGillivray's team was ready, finally, to put last year behind them.

Before the starting gun, race organizers held a moment of silence. A year earlier, they'd paused to honor the victims of the Sandy Hook school shooting in December 2012. Never had McGillivray imagined they'd be in the same spot a year later commemorating their own loss. "How surreal this was, now that we were doing this for ourselves," he said. Then it was time to put all that aside and start the march toward Boston. McGillivray got on a scooter with the lead vehicles, the gun rang out, and they were off. It soon became clear how big the crowds were. The gorgeous weather helped, but the draw of this year's race—the desire to simply be there—was undeniable. Runners would report afterward that support for them along the course seemed louder and warmer than ever before.

David King was out there running again, the ritual infused with even greater joy. Shana Cottone was among those watching the finish, from a hotel suite above Boylston Street. It was only her second time back since the bombing; she had avoided the street for almost a year. Today she was with Roseann Sdoia, the woman whose life she'd helped save a year ago. Her only duty this year was to watch out for her friend. It felt, to Shana, like coming full circle—maybe not closure, but something almost like it. "It's a new day in Boston," said Menino, who spent hours watching the race at the finish line, as he'd been unable to do the year before, his last as mayor. This would be Menino's final Boston Marathon. He would lose his battle with cancer little more than six months later.

Heather Abbott had always known she'd go back to the marathon. She had made a vow, and she would not let it go; she would not let the bombing take away the things she'd loved. She had convinced her friends to spend the day at Forum, the bar they'd been at last year when the bombs exploded. Some were reluctant, but they soon gave in. It was understood by now: Heather was in charge. By late winter, her plan for the day had evolved. She was going to run the last stretch of the marathon. "People were talking about the race, about running, and I thought, I don't want to just watch," she said of her decision. She requested, and received, the BAA's permission: She would jump onto the course about a half mile from the finish, to run the final stretch with her friend Erin Chatham. They had first met minutes after the bombing. Erin had knelt to help Heather as she lay bleeding on the floor of Forum. Erin's husband, Matt, had carried Heather out the back door to safety.

Six months had passed since the rainy autumn day when Heather had run for the first time on her prosthetic blade. It was still a struggle; every step was painful. But she was determined, as she'd always been. She'd gone back to yoga and started weight training. She practiced on a treadmill, and her balance was improving. She didn't care if she was slow, but she had to run the whole way. She would not stop and walk—not on Boylston Street, not on Marathon Day. When the day came, she was too busy to be nervous. She tracked Erin's progress from Hopkinton toward Boston, waiting for the right time to put on her running blade.

Then it was time to go and she was running, past the sidewalks packed with cheering people, past her friends at Forum and the police in the street. She carried painful memories with her, as she always would, but bigger than those thoughts was the knowledge she would make it. The finish line beckoned, nearer and nearer, the bright, wide sky and a fresh start beyond it.

He had the course all to himself. That's how it looked, anyway. Meb Keflezighi, wearing knee-high white socks, blue shorts, and a red, white, and blue tank top, flew by the crowds along Commonwealth Avenue in Newton, near Mile 18. No one else was in sight. By Heartbreak Hill, he was almost a full minute ahead of the field. Then, into Brookline, Keflezighi started to labor. He turned and saw the orange singlet of Kenyan Wilson Chebet closing in. Keflezighi's lead dropped to forty seconds. Then twelve. Then eight. Near Kenmore Square, Chebet was poised to overtake him. "I was thinking, 'Oh man, maybe he made a critical mistake,'" said McGillivray, who watched the whole thing unfold from his scooter. Keflezighi prayed: "God, just get me to the finish line."

Then McGillivray noticed something. Keflezighi still had some gas left in his tank. He began accelerating coming out of the course's final turns, creating fresh distance and discouragement for Chebet, who started flagging. When Keflezighi reached the turn at Hereford Street, which would take him onto Boylston for the home stretch, the race seemed to be his. He looked again over his shoulder, just to be sure. But he knew. "This is it," he told himself. "Your dream is going to come true." A few blocks later, he plowed through the blue tape, his mouth wide-open, his arms extended like wings. At two hours, eight minutes, and thirty-seven seconds, Keflezighi became the first American to win the Boston Marathon since 1983. A surge of pride and patriotism filled the streets. The finish line area was full of people determined to help Boston reclaim its special day. "I wanted and needed to be here," said Andrew Thomas, a twenty-one-year-old student from suburban Franklin. Whoever had written the script for the Red Sox World Series title in the fall had also apparently written this. "It couldn't have played out any better than it did," McGillivray said.

After crossing the finish line, Keflezighi kissed the pavement. "God bless America," he said shortly after. "A glorious day." For inspiration, Keflezighi had summoned the memories of the four victims of last year's terror—Krystle, Martin, Lingzi, and Sean, whose names he had scrawled in the four corners of his bib. He'd run with the words "Boston Strong, Meb Strong" in his mind. Up on the winners' platform, he was in tears, overwhelmed by the moment's weight. Mayor Marty Walsh rested the wreath on his head. The national anthem played. Keflezighi, the embodiment of an immigrant story gone right, hoisted the silver trophy over his head.

Acknowledgments

This book would not exist without critical contributions from so many, starting with our colleagues at the *Boston Globe*, whose tenacious reporting, elegant writing, and thoughtful editing during a very difficult week in April—and in the long days afterward—built a strong foundation for *Long Mile Home*. We are deeply grateful to work alongside them each and every day. Never have their breathtaking skill and dedication been more apparent than in 2013.

Our editor at the *Globe*, Mark S. Morrow, was a constant source of wisdom and counsel, as he has been to each book under his direction. His insights and judgment were essential, as was his steadying presence. Brian McGrory pushed this project from the beginning, rightly seeing the story as the *Globe*'s to tell. We are thankful for his support and leadership throughout. Christopher M. Mayer again proved his unwavering commitment to in-depth, long-form journalism and his expansive vision of what that can be. Other senior *Globe* editors were partners as well, including Christine S. Chinlund, Jennifer Peter, and Doug Most.

A number of journalists within the *Globe* family deserve special mention, starting with Sally Jacobs, Patricia Wen, and David Filipov, whose deep reporting and captivating writing on the lives of Tamerlan and Dzhokhar Tsarnaev played a key role in the book; their careful review of the manuscript was also indispensable. Eric Moskowitz's story on Danny, the carjacking victim, was one of the unforgettable *Globe* pieces published after the bombing, and his assistance in getting that story right here was invaluable. Mike Bello and Liz Kowalczyk were especially generous with their time and guidance. We are grateful to David Abel for his firsthand account of the bombing, and to Bryan Marquard for sharing his own memories of the days that followed. Steve Silva's brave video of the scene on Boylston Street was an important resource, as were the searing images of John Tlumacki and David L. Ryan.

Many *Globe* reporters conducted vital interviews with key sources, including Andrea Estes, Shelley Murphy, Thomas Farragher, Jonathan Saltzman, Jenn Abelson, Sean P. Murphy, and Kevin Cullen. Thanks to Scott Allen for his considerable editing and reporting talents. Stephen Smith and the rest of the Metro editing and reporting staff worked tirelessly to cover every angle of the story, as did the *Globe*'s graphics, photography, video, and online teams. Special thanks to Mark Arsenault, Matt Carroll, Michael Rezendes, Brian R. Ballou, Todd Wallack, Kay Lazar, Maria Cramer, Maria Sacchetti, Andrew Ryan, Andrew Caffrey, Bill Greene, Michael Levenson, Stephanie Ebbert, Akilah Johnson, Jenifer B. McKim, Wesley Lowery, Milton J. Valencia, Evan Allen, Derek J. Anderson, Alli Knothe, Vernice Liles, Dina Rudick, Chiqui Esteban, Ryan Huddle, Lane Turner, Bryan Bender, Noah Bierman, Matt Viser, Christopher Rowland, Michael Kranish, and Tracy Jan.

Janice Page was integral in developing a vision for *Long Mile Home* and helping us fulfill it. Ellen Clegg has continued to be a strong advocate for the book and the paper. Our thanks go as well to the *Globe*'s literary agents, Lane Zachary and Todd Shuster, who championed this project from the start and stood by us the rest of the way. At Dutton, our editor, Jill Schwartzman, was a trusted voice and dedicated partner. She deftly helped shape the book with a strong hand but a gentle touch. Thanks also to Ben Sevier, Brian Tart, Christine Ball, Amanda Walker, Stephanie Hitchcock, and Linda Cowen for sharing our vision and for all their work to make *Long Mile Home* a success. Thanks to Janet Robbins for her sharp editing. Our fact-checking team of Matt Mahoney and Stephanie Vallejo was crucial to our endeavor. Their careful scrutiny makes everything they touch better. Researcher and writer Walter Alarkon filled a big role in chronicling the national response to the bombing and the intelligence shortcomings that preceded it. Thanks also to Lisa Tuite, Jeremiah Manion, Maria Amasani, and Jim Wilson for their photo and research assistance, to Peter S. Canellos for his sharp editorial input, and to Jonathan Albano for his close review of the manuscript. Thanks to Mary Zanor, for her enthusiastic collaboration, and to Susanne Althoff, Anne Nelson, Francis Storrs, and Veronica Chao for their support.

We are forever indebted to the many, many people who took the time to help us understand and accurately capture the events of April 15, 2013, and all that came after. A few deserve special recognition, beginning with those whose stories form the core of the narrative: Heather Abbott, Shana Cottone, David King, Dave McGillivray, and Krystle Campbell's parents, Billy and Patty. By letting us into their lives, they have given the world complex, personal, and otherwise unattainable perspectives on the marathon attack and its aftereffects. We always believed in telling this important story through the eyes of the people who lived it; they made that possible, and we are extremely grateful.

Our sincere thanks, also, to: Shane O'Hara, Allison Byrne, Alain Ferry, Brighid Wall, Pat Foley, Sean O'Brien, Danny, Michael Lawn, Timothy Getchell, Sean McLaughlin, Bryan Conway, Susan Kane, Edward Davis, Thomas Menino, Deval Patrick, Nick Cox, Mike Powell, Rich Correale, David and Beth Henneberry, Kevin Brown, Jim Davis, Carlos Arredondo, Jason Geremia, Anne King, Rekha Drew, Alma Bocaletti, Scott Grigelevich, Greg Comcowich, Ann Todd, Brian Fleming, Bob Leonard, Patrick Menton, Jimmy Caruso, Frederick Lorenz, Dennis Keeley, Daniel Conley, Daniel Linskey, William Evans, Timothy Alben, Edward Deveau, Raymond Dupuis, John DiFava, Jeff Campbell, Saro Thompson, Kenneth Tran, Brian Harer, Vicma Lamarche, Michelle Hall, and Amy Formica. Special thanks as well to Tom Grilk, Jack Fleming, and their team at the Boston Athletic Association.

Finally, we are indebted to our families for the unconditional support that has been essential to this project and all of our work. To Jessica, Jonas, and Eli, and to Kevin, Cadence, and Poesy: our boundless gratitude and all our love.

Notes

1 **What you see first:** Descriptions of the Boston Marathon are based in part on interviews by Scott Helman in 2013 of runners Vicma Lamarche, Alain Ferry, Michelle Hall, Christine Mitchell, Tom Mitchell, Nicole McGurin, Joann Kwah, Eduardo Kelly, and Amy Formica.

2 **"Running is an affirmative act":** Caleb Daniloff, "I'm a Runner," *Runner's World*, July 2013, 136.

8 **The race, begun in 1897:** Christopher L. Gasper, "Soggy conditions didn't dampen spirits," *Boston Globe*, April 17, 2007; Nancy L. Marrapese, "Morse is Boston's man behind the scenes," *Boston Globe*, April 15, 1990; John Powers, "Everything came up Rosie, until . . . ," *Boston Globe*, April 14, 1989; e-mail from Boston Athletic Association official Jack Fleming, August 2013.

13 **It was spring:** Descriptions of Heather Abbott based on interviews of Abbott and Jason Geremia by Jenna Russell in 2013.

14 **There was nothing like:** Descriptions of David King based on interviews of King by Jenna Russell in 2013, and with Anne King in September 2013.

16 **She was a Boston girl:** Descriptions of Krystle Campbell are based largely on interviews in 2013, by Scott Helman, of Billy Campbell Jr., Tim Getchell, Sean McLaughlin, Bryan Conway, Al Dugan, Susan Kane, Laurie Cormier, Jane Tuite, Robert Tarutis, Nelida Lepore, Tony Szykniej, Robin Gomolin, and David Nieto; and a memorial event held at Spectacle Island on September 24, 2013.

19 **This year's marathon:** Descriptions of Dave McGillivray are based largely on interviews in 2013, by Scott Helman, of Dave McGillivray, Susan West, Bob McGillivray, Josh Nemzer, Ron Kramer, and Tom Grilk; a speech McGillivray delivered to a corporate conference in Boston, October 10, 2013; and the following book: David J. McGillivray with Linda Glass Fechter, *The Last Pick: The Boston Marathon*

Race Director's Road to Success (Emmaus, Pennsylvania: Rodale, 2006).

21 **She was in the best shape:** Descriptions of Shana Cottone based on interviews of Cottone by Jenna Russell in 2013.

35 **The voice had begun speaking:** This chapter is adapted from "The Fall of the House of Tsarnaev," a lengthy *Boston Globe* investigation of the Tsarnaev family by Sally Jacobs, David Filipov, and Patricia Wen published December 15, 2013. The investigation contained extensive new and exclusive reporting on the Tsarnaev brothers. Additional reporting contributed by Jacobs, Filipov, and Wen.

36 **A few months later:** Andrew Tangel and Ashley Powers, "FBI: Boston suspect Tamerlan Tsarnaev followed 'radical Islam,'" *Los Angeles Times*, April 20, 2013.

43 **One of the few cracks:** Janet Reitman, "Jahar's World," *Rolling Stone*, July 17, 2013, http://www.rollingstone.com/culture/news/jahars-world-20130717.

45 **"all-out war against Islam":** Muhammad Hussain, "Dimensions of Multiculturalism: Killings, Bombings and Free Speech," *Veterans Today*, May 27, 2013, http://www.veteranstoday.com/2013/05/27/dimensions-of-multiculturalism-killings-bombings-and-free-speech.

45 **Tamerlan's apparent radicalization:** Eric Schmitt and Michael S. Schmidt, "2 U.S. Agencies Added Boston Bomb Suspect to Watch Lists," *New York Times*, April 24, 2013.

49 **"A decade in America already":** Reitman, "Jahar's World."

49 **ready to accept him anyway:** Michael Wines and Ian Lovett, "The Dark Side, Carefully Masked," *New York Times*, May 5, 2013.

49 **One day in early 2013:** Wines and Lovett, "The Dark Side."

49 **Tamerlan drove up to Phantom Fireworks:** Federal indictment of Dzhokhar Tsarnaev, June 27, 2013.

50 **"If you have the knowledge":** Reitman, "Jahar's World."

50 **One of her relatives asked:** Marc Fisher, "The Tsarnaev family: A faded portrait of an immigrant's American dream," *Washington Post*, April 27, 2013.

51 **The volume on his alarm:** King interviews.

53 **Obama had paid:** Jay Carney, "President Obama and Vice President Biden's 2012 Tax Returns," *The White House Blog*, April 12, 2013, http://www.whitehouse.gov/blog/2013/04/12/president-obama-and-vice-president-biden-2012-tax-returns.

53 **Dave McGillivray rose alone:** McGillivray interviews.

57 **The roots of the Boston Marathon:** Boston Athletic Association, *2013 Boston Marathon Media Guide*, 80; John Hanc, *The B.A.A. at 125: The*

Official History of the Boston Athletic Association, 1887–2012 (New York: Sports Publishing, 2012), 40.

57 **New Yorker John J. McDermott:** Boston Athletic Association, *The Race Through History*, 1996, 1–10.

57 **Bill Kennedy, a New York bricklayer:** Caleb Daniloff, *Running Ransom Road: Confronting the Past, One Marathon at a Time* (New York: Houghton Mifflin Harcourt, 2012), 18–19.

57 **Johnny "the Elder" Kelley:** Boston Athletic Association, *The Race Through History*.

57 **After World War II:** Boston Athletic Association, *2013 Boston Marathon Media Guide*, 36.

57 **The race's popularity grew:** Bob Hohler and Shira Springer, "Marathon qualifying is revised," *Boston Globe*, February 17, 2011.

58 **"When you ran Boston":** Amby Burfoot, "Just Imagine," *Runner's World*, July 2013, 118.

59 **In the first four miles:** Michael Connelly, *26 Miles to Boston* (Hyannis, MA: Parnassus Imprints, 1998), 34.

60 **"who aren't necessarily world-class":** Connelly, 35.

61 **where a local Dixieland band:** Tom Derderian, *The Boston Marathon: A Century of Blood, Sweat and Cheers* (Plymouth: John Hancock Mutual Life Insurance Company, 1996, 2003), 26.

63 **"Hey, you slug, the race is over":** McGillivray and Fechter, *The Last Pick: The Boston Marathon Race Director's Road to Success*, 39–40.

65 **Shana Cottone reported to roll call:** Cottone interviews.

66 **It was barely light outside:** Abbott and Geremia interviews.

66 **It pained Menino to miss out:** Interviews of Thomas Menino by Jenna Russell, August and October 2013.

67 **Deval Patrick never had days like this:** Interviews of Deval Patrick by Andrea Estes and Shelley Murphy of the *Globe* staff, April 2013, and by Scott Helman, July 2013.

68 **William Evans finished his eighteenth Boston Marathon:** Nick Weldon, "One Hell of a Week," *Runner's World*, July 2013, 112; Sean Flynn, "The Finish Line," *GQ*, June 2013, http://www.gq.com/news-politics/newsmakers/201307/boston-marathon-attack-july-2013.

68 **Edward Davis left the marathon for home:** Interview of Edward Davis by Andrea Estes and Shelley Murphy, April 2013.

68 **Krystle Campbell got a text message:** Interview of Liz Jenkins and John Colombo by Scott Helman, September 2013; Eric Moskowitz, "The Marathon wounded: Karen Rand," *Boston Globe*, May 19, 2013.

69 **Dzhokhar and Tamerlan Tsarnaev were captured:** Remarks of Special Agent in Charge Richard DesLauriers at Press Conference on

Boston Bombing Investigation, April 18, 2013, http://www.fbi.gov
/boston/press-releases/2013/remarks-of-special-agent-in-charge
-richard-deslauriers-at-press-conference-on-bombing-investigation-1.

70 **Firefighter Sean O'Brien was working:** Interview of Sean O'Brien by
Jenna Russell, July 2013.

70 **Pat Foley, another firefighter, reminded himself:** Interviews of Pat
Foley by Jenna Russell, April and July 2013.

70 **Frederick Lorenz, a Boston fire lieutenant:** Interview of Dennis Keeley and Frederick Lorenz by Andrea Estes, April 2013.

71 **Brighid and Brendan Wall had miscalculated:** Interviews of Brighid
Wall by Jenna Russell, April and July 2013.

72 **another family was waiting, too:** Interview of Stephen Lynch by Jenna
Russell, April 2013.

72 **Lingzi Lu was one of them:** Evan Allen, "Student's life ends in the city
that she had grown to love," *Boston Globe*, April 18, 2013; Leslie Friday,
"Lu Lingzi, Roommate Were Like Sisters," *BU Today*, April 23, 2013.

72 **Alma Bocaletti was still running:** Interview of Alma Bocaletti and
Rekha Drew by Scott Helman, October 2013.

74 **Tamerlan Tsarnaev continued walking:** Interviews with law enforcement officials, 2013; federal indictment of Dzhokhar Tsarnaev, June 27,
2013; Kathleen Ronayne, "Jeff Bauman shares Boston Marathon story,
encounter with suspect Tamerlan Tsarnaev," *Concord Monitor*, May 6,
2013.

75 **"God protect us":** Interview of Carlos Arredondo by Jenna Russell,
April 2013; David A. Fahrenthold, "Boston Marathon bystander Carlos
Arredondo says he acted instinctively," *Washington Post*, April 16, 2013.

75 **Bill Iffrig:** John Brant, "Back on His Feet," *Runner's World*, July 2013,
96.

76 **Perched near the finish line:** Interview of Vicma Lamarche by Scott
Helman, June 2013.

76 **Inside Marathon Sports:** Interviews of Shane O'Hara by Scott Helman, 2013.

77 **It was there:** David Abel, "Runners and spectators raced to save lives,"
Boston Globe, April 17, 2013; David Abel, "Amid shock at Marathon, a
rush to help strangers," *Boston Globe*, April 16, 2013; interview of David
Abel by Scott Helman, September 2013; Elizabeth Cohen, "Nurses relied on trauma experience," CNN, April 16, 2013.

77 **That's not a cannon:** O'Brien interviews.

78 **The first explosion had rippled:** Geremia interviews.

78 **Brighid Wall threw her six-year-old son:** Wall interviews.

79 **Searching in the smoke:** Sam Trapani, "Heroes among us," *Danvers*

Herald, April 25, 2013, www.wickedlocal.com/danvers/news/x1853931027 /Heroes-among-us?zc_p=0; interview of Matt Patterson by Jenna Russell, December 2013.

79 **Allison Byrne was so eager:** Interviews of Allison Byrne by Scott Helman, 2013; e-mails from Nancy Shorter to author, November 2013.

80 **After he heard the deafening explosions:** Sushrut Jangi, "Under the Medical Tent at the Boston Marathon," *New England Journal of Medicine*, May 23, 2013.

80 **Heather Abbott lay on the floor:** Abbott interviews.

81 **Shana Cottone reached for her gun:** Cottone interviews.

82 **Firefighters tried to revive her:** Chris Doucette, "Boston firefighter in midst of bloody carnage," *Toronto Sun*, April 18, 2013; O'Brien and Foley interviews.

82 **Standing where the second bomb:** Keeley and Lorenz interviews.

82 **"Gimme the belt":** Foley interviews; Sam Gardner, "Boston Marathon victims form bond," *FOX Sports*, July 4, 2013.

83 **A van pulled up beside them:** Keeley and Lorenz interviews; Jessica Heslam, "Desperate ride bonds survivors," *Boston Herald*, November 14, 2013.

84 **In the alley between Boylston and Newbury:** Abbott and Geremia interviews.

85 **Shana Cottone leaned all the way:** Cottone and Foley interviews.

87 **They were coming for Heather:** Abbott and Geremia interviews.

88 **The two firefighters had run:** Foley interviews.

91 **Ed Davis couldn't believe:** Davis interviews.

91 **he had barely hung up:** Interviews of Davis and Daniel Linskey by Andrea Estes and Shelley Murphy, April 2013.

92 **Alben had been at the starting line:** Interview of Timothy Alben by Shelley Murphy, April 2013.

92 **Davis felt fairly certain:** Davis interviews.

93 **Communication failures amplified:** Michael B. Farrell, "Cellphone networks overwhelmed after blasts," *Boston Globe*, April 17, 2013.

93 **Two runners of South Asian descent:** Interview of Michelle Hall by Scott Helman, June 2013.

93 **They blew up at least one bag:** O'Brien, Foley, and Keeley interviews.

93 **One of Davis's immediate tasks:** Farragher, Russell, and *Globe* staff, "102 hours in pursuit of Marathon suspects," *Boston Globe*, April 28, 2013.

94 **Katherine Patrick had only been:** Patrick interviews.

94 **Hadn't one caught fire:** Brian MacQuarrie and Brian R. Ballou, "Nearly all are out of dark," *Boston Globe*, March 16, 2012.

95 **"I was really resistant":** Interview of Peter Sagal by Scott Helman, July 2013.

95 **The governor knew:** Patrick interviews.

95 **Patrick also conferred:** Patrick interviews; Scott LaPierre, "Press conference about Boston Marathon explosions," *Boston Globe*, April 15, 2013, http://www.youtube.com/watch?v=oeTQRJL537E.

95 **His doctors had tried to stop him:** Menino interviews.

96 **Dave McGillivray had changed:** Interviews of McGillivray and Ron Kramer by Scott Helman, July, August, and September 2013.

97 **After a few hours:** Farragher, Russell, and *Globe* staff, "102 hours"; interviews with law enforcement officials, 2013.

98 **It was the largest crime scene:** Farragher, Russell, and *Globe* staff, "102 hours"; Maria Sacchetti, Michael Bello, Kay Lazar, and Andrew Ryan, "Investigators scour the area for any clues," *Boston Globe*, April 17, 2013.

98 **President Obama addressed the nation:** "Obama vows to find who's behind Boston blasts," Associated Press, April 15, 2013, http://www.youtube.com/watch?v=BBeaamkBGk4.

98 **The prospect of a bombing:** Brian Castner, "The Exclusive Inside Story of the Boston Bomb Squad's Defining Day," *Wired*, October 25, 2013, http://www.wired.com/threatlevel/2013/10/boston-police-bomb-squad/all/; Alben interview; interview with BAA executive director Tom Grilk, September 2013.

99 **diplomatically sensitive operations:** Massimo Calabresi, "Richard DesLauriers: The Special Agent in Charge," *Time*, April 17, 2013, http://swampland.time.com/2013/04/17/richard-deslauriers-the-special-agent-in-charge/.

99 **Governor Patrick would later describe:** Patrick interviews.

99 **One of the first people:** Amina Chaudary, "What Really Happened? The Bomb, the FBI and the Media," *The Islamic Monthly*, May 21, 2013; "Exclusive Interview: Boston Marathon 'Saudi Man' transcript," *The Islamic Monthly*, May 21, 2013, http://www.theislamicmonthly.com/exclusive-interview-saudi-man-transcript.

100 **As darkness fell on Monday:** Cottone interviews.

101 **Karen Rand had arrived:** Liz Kowalczyk, "Hospitals size up the lessons of Marathon attacks," *Boston Globe*, July 28, 2013; Stephen Rex Brown, "Boston Marathon victim's dad was told daughter was only injured, then he found out she'd been misidentified and had been killed in the blast," *New York Daily News*, April 16, 2013.

101 **"That's not my daughter!":** Brown, "Boston Marathon victim's dad."

102 **Back on Boylston Street:** Sally Jacobs, "Hardest-hit family conveys thanks and cautious hope," *Boston Globe*, May 10, 2013.

102 **These were the bags:** Interviews of McGillivray, and Boston Marathon officials Rich Havens and Matt Carpenter by Scott Helman, 2013.

103 **Heather Abbott opened her eyes:** Abbott interviews.

105 **most critically injured patients had been "red-tagged":** Dr. Paul D. Biddinger et al, "Be Prepared—The Boston Marathon and Mass-Casualty Events," *New England Journal of Medicine*, May 23, 2013, http://www.nejm.org/doi/full/10.1056/NEJMp1305480.

105 **the first patient from the finish line:** Liz Kowalczyk, "Hospitals size up the lessons of Marathon attacks," *Boston Globe*, July 28, 2013.

105 **Mass General took in thirty-one:** Biddinger et al, "Be Prepared."

106 **It made for a nightmarish scene:** Byrne interviews.

106 **"What we like to do":** Gina Kolata, Jeré Longman, and Mary Pilon, "Doctors Saved Lives, if Not Legs, in Boston," *New York Times*, April 16, 2013.

106 **The array of other injuries:** Marathon patient timelines provided by Boston hospitals to *Globe* reporter Liz Kowalczyk, June 2013.

107 **there were inevitable inconsistencies:** Byrne interviews.

108 **The underpinnings of Boston's medical infrastructure:** "Harvard Medical School: The Early Years," *Harvard University*, http://hms .harvard.edu/about-hms/history-hms/early-years; "John Collins Warren Papers: Guide to the Collection," *Massachusetts Historical Society*, http://www.masshist.org/findingaids/doc.cfm?fa=fa0183; Walter C. Guralnick, DMD, and Leonard B. Kaban, DMD, MD, "Keeping Ether in Vogue," *Massachusetts General Hospital*, 2010.

108 **largely due to recent training:** Bissinger et al, "Be Prepared"; Atul Gawande, "Why Boston's Hospitals Were Ready," *New Yorker*, April 17, 2013, http://www.newyorker.com/online/blogs/newsdesk/2013/04 /why-bostons-hospitals-were-ready.html.

109 **Three miles away:** King interviews.

110 **75 percent of injuries:** Gawande, "Why Boston's Hospitals Were Ready."

113 **An online campaign for Jeff Bauman:** Jennifer Preston and Christine Hauser, "Victims in Boston Marathon Bombings Turn To Crowdfunding for Support," *New York Times*, May 6, 2013.

115 **Patrick spent time:** Patrick interviews; *The Last Word with Lawrence O'Donnell*, MSNBC, April 18, 2013.

115 **Patrick arrived at the emergency department:** Interview of Erin McDonough by Scott Helman, September 2013; Patrick interviews.

116 **Heather's close friend Jason Geremia:** Geremia interviews.

117 **the wait for information Monday night:** Interview of Rosemary Abbott by Jenna Russell, September 2013.

118 **Even with his legs gone:** Kathleen Ronayne, "Jeff Bauman shares

Boston Marathon story, encounter with suspect Tamerlan Tsarnaev," *Concord Monitor*, May 6, 2013.

119 **Patty Campbell summoned all her strength:** Bryan Marquard, "Krystle Campbell remembered as ever reliable," *Boston Globe*, April 16, 2013; "Mother of marathon attack victim speaks," CNN, April 16, 2013, https://www.youtube.com/watch?v=SUtRmZvmhe8.

120 **Two blocks east of the finish line:** Carpenter and McGillivray interviews.

120 **race officials did their best:** Ibid.; Christine Fennessy, editor, "4.15.13: An oral history of the 117th Boston Marathon," *Runner's World*, July 2013, 90.

121 **marathon officials took the medals:** Neil Swidey, "Restart: The future of the Marathon," *Boston Globe Magazine*, May 10, 2013; Carpenter interview.

121 **he slipped over to BAA headquarters:** Patrick and McGillivray interviews.

122 **a thousand people gathered in Garvey Park:** Evan Allen and Jenna Russell, "Photo of victim Martin Richard now a symbol," *Boston Globe*, April 16, 2013; Paige Buckley, "Thousands attend vigil for Richard family, marathon bomb victims at Garvey Park," *Dorchester Reporter*, April 16, 2013; Nina Golgowski, "A cry for peace here and everywhere," *Daily Telegraph (Australia)*, April 18, 2013.

123 **"Lingzi, where are you now?":** Allen, "Student's life ends in the city"; Andrew Tangel, Barbara Demick, and Laura J. Nelson, "Slain Chinese student embraced life in U.S.," *Baltimore Sun*, April 18, 2013.

124 **"To deal with those emotions of shock":** Dan Bobkoff, "Medford, Massachusetts, Remembers the Girl with the Freckles," *NPR*, April 17, 2013.

124 **The Medford High School Lady Mustang softball team:** Allison Goldsberry, "MHS Girls Softball Team Dedicates Season to Krystle Campbell," *Inside Medford*, April 17, 2013, http://insidemedford.com/2013/04/17/mhs-girls-softball-team-dedicates-season-to-krystle-campbell/.

124 **Later that evening:** "Medford Holds Prayer Vigil for Boston Marathon Victims," *Inside Medford*, April 18, 2013, http://insidemedford.com/2013/04/18/medford-holds-prayer-vigil-for-boston-marathon-victims/.

124 **"Of all the people that were there":** Interview of Bryan Conway by Scott Helman, August 2013.

124 **"I would like to say":** Comment left on a Facebook page called "R.I.P Krystle Campbell," accessed September 2013, https://www.facebook.com/pages/RIP-Krystle-Campbell/160980664067079.

125 **Krystle, to her, was a striver:** Interview of Robin Gomolin by Scott Helman, August 2013.

125 **The minute he saw her picture:** Interview of Robert Tarutis by Scott Helman, September 2013.

127 **At 2:50 P.M. on Monday:** Farragher, Russell, and *Globe* staff, "102 hours."

128 **"We were very confident":** Alben interview.

128 **Within minutes of arriving at the scene:** Davis interviews; Farragher, Russell, and *Globe* staff, "102 hours."

130 **The Lenox had been fully booked:** Interview of Scott Grigelevich by Jenna Russell, September 2013.

131 **The repetition could be numbing:** David Montgomery, Sari Horwitz, and Marc Fisher, "Police, citizens and technology factor into Boston bombing probe," *Washington Post*, April 20, 2013.

131 **"He was not startled":** Juju Chang, "Caught; In the Company of Evil," *Nightline*, ABC News, April 19, 2013.

132 **Fellow student Zach Bettencourt saw him there:** Chris Lawrence, "Hiding in plain sight," CNN, April 2013.

132 **"He was just relaxed":** Sarah Coffey, Patricia Wen, and Matt Carroll, "Bombing suspect spent Wednesday as typical student," *Boston Globe*, April 19, 2013.

132 **"Some of the activity on reddit":** Leslie Kaufman, "Bombings Trip Up Reddit in Its Turn in Spotlight," *New York Times*, April 28, 2013; "Reflections on the Recent Boston Crisis," *the reddit blog*, April 22, 2013, http://blog.reddit.com/2013/04/reflections-on-recent-boston-crisis.html.

133 **The episode became:** Jay Caspian Kang, "Crowdsourcing A Smear," *New York Times Magazine*, July 28, 2013, 36.

133 **It wasn't just "new media":** Maria Sacchetti, "Mass. pair sues *New York Post* over Marathon bombing portrayal," *Boston Globe*, June 6, 2013.

133 **In the rush to figure out the real story:** Farragher, Russell, and *Globe* staff, "102 hours."

134 **It was early Wednesday morning:** Interviews with law enforcement officials, 2013.

135 **"It was right there":** Alben interview.

135 **Alben would later say:** Michael Norton, "MSP colonel: public must be diligent," *State House News Service*, April 23, 2013.

136 **He showed Patrick photographs:** Patrick interviews.

137 **The doctors and medical teams showed up in scrubs:** Lisa Wangsness, "Obama pledges Boston 'will finish the race,'" *Boston Globe*, April 19, 2013.

138 **"Every one of us":** Transcript of the president's remarks released by the White House, April 18, 2013, http://www.whitehouse.gov/the-press-office/2013/04/18/remarks-president-interfaith-service-boston-ma.

138 **the president wiped a tear:** Katharine Q. Seelye, Michael Cooper, and Michael S. Schmidt, "FBI posts images of pair suspected in Boston attack," *New York Times*, April 19, 2013.

139 **The mayor arrived at the cathedral:** Menino interviews; Adrian Walker, "Three secular ministers preach healing," *Boston Globe*, April 18, 2013.

139 **Many had waited in line:** Martine Powers and Wesley Lowery, "Thousands turn out for Marathon interfaith memorial service," *Boston Globe*, April 19, 2013.

140 **"The urgency and the national implications":** Weldon, "One Hell of a Week," 114.

140 **The roads surrounding the cathedral:** Wangsness, "Obama pledges Boston 'will finish the race.'"

140 **Shana Cottone filed out of the cathedral:** Cottone interviews.

142 **David King had been awake:** King interviews.

144 **"They were grateful for the care":** Patrick interviews.

145 **US Homeland Security secretary Janet Napolitano acknowledged:** Farragher, Russell, and *Globe* staff, "102 hours"; transcript of April 18, 2013, hearing of the House Committee on Homeland Security.

145 **Investigators initially tried:** Interview with law enforcement officials, 2013.

145 **Boston Police commissioner Ed Davis made his case:** Davis interviews; other interviews by *Globe* staff with law enforcement officials, 2013.

146 **"You always want to apprehend":** Farragher, Russell, and *Globe* staff, "102 hours."

146 **Around 6:00 Thursday morning:** Davis interviews.

146 **He had one hour of anonymity left:** Farragher, Russell, and *Globe* staff, "102 hours."

147 **DesLauriers strode to a podium:** C-SPAN video of FBI press conference, April 18, 2013, http://www.c-spanvideo.org/program/FBIP.

147 **Back at UMass–Dartmouth that night:** Farragher, Russell, and *Globe* staff, "102 hours."

148 **"There was no in between":** *The Lead with Jake Tapper*, CNN, April 30, 2013.

149 **"You've got to go talk to that lady":** Kevin Cullen, "MIT officer always looked out for others," *Boston Globe*, April 23, 2013.

149 **Sean was known, too:** Cullen, "MIT officer always."

149 **Collier studied criminal justice:** Kathleen Hennessey and Wes Vent-eicher, "Officer slain at MIT loved his role; Sean Collier of MIT saw police work as his dream. A transit officer was wounded later," *Los Angeles Times*, April 20, 2013.

149 **Tamerlan Tsarnaev partied with friends at Salem State:** Jacobs, Filipov, and Wen, "The Fall of the House of Tsarnaev." Additional reporting contributed by Jacobs, Filipov, and Wen.

149 **he got his first real police assignment:** Dan Barry and Dina Kraft, "Violent Trail Adds 2 Victims, Officers Linked by Friendship and Dedication," *New York Times*, April 20, 2013.

150 **Collier joined the MIT Outing Club:** Hennessey and Venteicher, "Officer slain"; Carolyn Y. Johnson, David Abel, and Kay Lazar, "MIT's fallen officer built enduring connections," *Boston Globe*, April 20, 2013.

150 **may have crossed paths with Tamerlan:** Jacobs, Filipov, and Wen, "The Fall of the House of Tsarnaev." Additional reporting contributed by Jacobs, Filipov, and Wen.

150 **Collier's dream was to become:** *The Lead with Jake Tapper*, CNN, April 30, 2013; and Johnson, Abel, and Lazar, "MIT's fallen officer."

150 **"You've done a fine job for me":** Farragher, Russell, and *Globe* staff, "102 hours"; interview of John DiFava by Shelley Murphy of the *Globe* staff, April 2013.

150 **On the night of Thursday, April 18:** Farragher, Russell, and *Globe* staff, "102 hours."

151 **Shortly before 10:30 P.M.:** Farragher, Russell, and *Globe* staff, "102 hours"; federal indictment of Dzhokhar Tsarnaev, June 27, 2013.

151 **The two bombing suspects then sought:** Ibid.

151 **The beloved twenty-seven-year-old with big promise:** Cullen, "Officer always."

151 **violent prelude to a violent night:** Davis and Alben interviews.

153 **The man jumped out of his car:** Danny agreed to be interviewed only if he was identified by his American nickname. Details and descriptions of the carjacking and his interactions with the Tsarnaev brothers come from two interviews with Danny, one by Eric Moskowitz of the *Globe* staff in April 2013, and a second by Eric Moskowitz and Scott Helman in July 2013. Many aspects of his story were featured in the following article: Eric Moskowitz, "Carjack victim recounts his harrowing night," *Boston Globe*, April 26, 2013.

159 **Back in Cambridge:** Davis interviews; interviews with law enforcement officials, 2013.

165 **The report crackled across the radio:** Farragher, Russell, and *Globe* staff, "102 hours"; additional details from interviews of Watertown

Police Captain Raymond Dupuis and Police Chief Edward Deveau by Jonathan Saltzman and Thomas Farragher of the *Globe* staff, April 2013; and interviews with other law enforcement officials.

166 **Reynolds swung a U-turn:** *The Last Word with Lawrence O'Donnell*, MSNBC, May 14, 2013.

167 **Peter Kehayias, a sixty-five-year-old restaurant chef:** Interview of neighbors Peter and Loretta Kehayias by Jenn Abelson and Jonathan Saltzman of the *Globe* staff, April 2013.

167 **Dzhokhar helped Tamerlan load a fresh clip:** Farragher, Russell, and *Globe* staff, "102 hours"; interview of neighbor Lizzy Floyd by Jenn Abelson and Jonathan Saltzman, April 2013; interview with law enforcement officials.

168 **Jeff Pugliese, a thirty-three-year veteran:** Farragher, Russell, and *Globe* staff, "102 hours"; Deveau and Dupuis interviews; interview with law enforcement officials.

169 **Tamerlan was not so lucky:** Farragher, Russell, and *Globe* staff, "102 hours"; Deveau and Dupuis interviews; interviews of neighbor Jean MacDonald by Jenn Abelson and Jonathan Saltzman, and of neighbor Rob Mullen by Sean P. Murphy of the *Globe* staff, April 2013; Kevin Cullen, "Valor, devotion brought Watertown drama to end," *Boston Globe*, April 26, 2013.

169 **The alert pierced the silence:** Farragher, Russell, and *Globe* staff, "102 hours"; interviews of Patrick Menton and Jimmy Caruso by Thomas Farragher, April 2013.

169 **"I'm hit!" Donohue yelled:** John Miller, interview with Donohue, CBS Evening News, May 13, 2013, http://www.cbsnews.com/8301-18563_162 -57584300/injured-officer-recounts-shootout-with-boston-suspects.

170 **Donohue's condition deteriorated quickly:** Ibid; Cullen, "Valor, devotion."

170 **Donohue had grown up:** Kay Lazar, Martine Powers, and David Abel, "Wounded T officer known as a devoted father," *Boston Globe*, April 20, 2013; "Wounded Boston transit officer graduated from VMI in 2002," *Richmond Times-Dispatch*, April 20, 2013; Jennifer Brown Bonniwell, "Transit officer remains critical," *Winchester Star*, April 25, 2013; Peter Hermann, "Transit officer was shot in Watertown," *Washington Post*, April 28, 2013.

170 **Donohue had been one of the officers:** John Miller, *CBS This Morning*, May 14, 2013.

170 **He got to the scene:** Brown Bonniwell, "Transit officer."

171 **Behind the wheel in the front:** Cullen, "Valor, devotion."

171 **Tim Menton didn't really know how to drive:** Derek J. Anderson, "MBTA officer hangs tough in recovery from shooting," *Boston Globe*,

May 19, 2013; Erin Ailworth, "MBTA officer's family distraught but proud," *Boston Globe*, April 22, 2013; Farragher, Russell, and *Globe* staff, "102 hours"; Menton and Caruso interviews; Cullen, "Valor, devotion."

171 **Donohue's wife, Kim, was asleep:** Miller, CBS News and *CBS This Morning*; Kim Donohue, e-mail message to author, September 5, 2013.

172 **Just whose bullet it was:** Sean P. Murphy and Todd Wallack, "Witnesses suggest friendly fire felled officer," *Boston Globe*, May 7, 2013.

173 **"It was very, very bad":** Murphy and Wallack, "Witnesses suggest"; interview of Ed Davis by Scott Helman, August 2013.

173 **The police activity around the car:** Davis and Linskey interviews.

174 **Kerman heard the distant gunfire:** Farragher, Russell, and *Globe* staff, "102 hours"; Wayne Drash, "From fear to cheers: The final hours that paralyzed Boston," CNN, April 28, 2013, http://www.cnn.com/2013/04/26/us/boston-manhunt-recap/.

174 **As police chased after him:** Farragher, Russell, and *Globe* staff, "102 hours"; Dupuis and Deveau interviews; Davis interviews.

175 **Scores of police swarmed the neighborhood:** Ibid.

175 **"You're in the middle":** Alben interview.

175 **Police would later recover only a handgun:** federal indictment of Dzhokhar Tsarnaev, June 27, 2013; interview with law enforcement officials.

176 **It had already been a long day:** Farragher, Russell, and *Globe* staff, "102 hours."

176 **Dr. David Schoenfeld was reading:** Liz Kowalczyk, "Beth Israel medical staff tried to revive suspect," *Boston Globe*, April 20, 2013.

180 **Governor Deval Patrick conferred hourly:** Patrick interviews.

180 **But as the governor was on his way:** Patrick interviews; Farragher, Russell, and *Globe* staff, "102 hours."

180 **So Patrick turned to the playbook:** Maria Sacchetti, "Travel ban surprises many, pleases some," *Boston Globe*, February 9, 2013; Patrick interviews.

181 **Patrick went before the TV cameras:** Deval Patrick press conference, *Today*, NBC, April 19, 2013, http://www.today.com/video/today/51594289.

181 **Police drew up a map:** Details on the house-by-house searches come from multiple interviews with Watertown residents and with law enforcement officials, including: Alben interview; interview of Malden SWAT team members by Scott Helman, June 2013; interview of William Evans by Shelley Murphy of the *Globe* staff, April 2013; Davis and Linskey interviews; Deveau and Dupuis interviews; additional details from the following article: Farragher, Russell, and *Globe* staff, "102 hours."

183 **It is a shopping mecca:** Cindy Rodriguez, "Committee has big plans for Arsenal," *Boston Globe*, January 11, 1998; Patrick interviews.

185 **With the whole world looking:** Federal indictment of Dzhokhar Tsarnaev; John Miller, *CBS This Morning*, May 16, 2013; Maria Cramer and Peter Schworm, "Note may offer details on bomb motive," *Boston Globe*, May 16, 2013; Scott Shane and Ellen Barry, "Chechen Refugee Questioned in FBI's Inquiry of Bombing," *New York Times*, May 16, 2013.

190 **They were starving when they arrived:** Patrick interviews.

190 **Less than an hour later:** Farragher, Russell, and *Globe* staff, "102 hours"; Patrick interviews.

193 **David Henneberry had been looking:** Interviews of David Henneberry by Jenna Russell, 2013.

197 **William Evans jumped in his Boston police car:** Evans interview; Farragher, Russell, and *Globe* staff, "102 hours"; Weldon, "One Hell of a Week," 112.

197 **Rich Correale, Mike Powell, and Nick Cox had spent all day:** Details of the boat standoff and aftermath come from numerous sources, including the following: interview of Malden SWAT team members Rich Correale, Mike Powell, and Nick Cox by Scott Helman, June 2013; interview of MBTA SWAT team members Jeff Campbell, Brian Harer, Saro Thompson, and Kenneth Tran by Sean P. Murphy of the *Globe* staff, April 2013; interview of Revere Police chief Joseph Cafarelli by Scott Helman, August 2013; interview of Revere Police officer Mike Trovato by Scott Helman, August 2013; interviews of other law enforcement officials by Scott Helman; Evans interview; Farragher, Russell, and *Globe* staff, "102 hours."

198 **Around this time, an FBI tactical unit:** Interview of law enforcement officials, 2013.

200 **The call came while Deval Patrick:** Patrick interviews; Farragher, Russell, and *Globe* staff, "102 hours."

200 **The principals gathered in a trailer:** Patrick and Menino interviews; interviews with law enforcement officials, 2013; Farragher, Russell, and *Globe* staff, "102 hours."

201 **What was clear was that no one:** Henneberry interviews; Farragher, Russell, and *Globe* staff, "102 hours."

202 **a public plea by his high school wrestling coach:** Reitman, "Jahar's World."

203 **The same mop of dark hair:** Additional details from photographs taken by Massachusetts State Police sergeant Sean Murphy and published by *Boston* magazine, in "Behind the Scenes of The Hunt for

Dzhokhar Tsarnaev," September 2013, http://www.bostonmagazine
.com/news/article/2013/08/27/dzhokhar-tsarnaev-manhunt-photos.

204 **Menino's voice cut in:** Farragher, Russell, and *Globe* staff, "102 hours";
Mark Arsenault, "Second Marathon bombing suspect captured," *Boston Globe*, April 20, 2013.

205 **Dzhokhar was in rough shape:** Travis Andersen, "Dzhokhar Tsarnaev's injuries detailed in documents," *Boston Globe*, August 20, 2013.

206 **At 10:05 P.M., President Obama spoke:** Statement by the president,
10:05 P.M., April 19, 2013, http://www.whitehouse.gov/the-press
-office/2013/04/19/statement-president; Menino and Patrick interviews.

207 **As Krystle Campbell's brother put it:** Arsenault, "Second Marathon
bombing."

212 **Kevin Brown first saw the memorial:** Interviews of Kevin Brown by
Jenna Russell, 2013.

212 **The square, named for the colonial portrait painter:** William A.
Newman and Wilfred E. Holton, *Boston's Back Bay: The Story of
America's Greatest Nineteenth-Century Landfill Project* (Boston:
Northeastern University Press, 2006), vii–xii.

214 **It was hard to explain:** Evan Allen, "Copley Square a place to mourn,
heal after bombings," *Boston Globe*, May 3, 2013.

215 **"Yeah! We're alive!":** Sarah Schweitzer and Evan Allen, "Joining
sorrow—the joy of coming together," *Boston Globe*, April 21, 2013.

216 **Mental health experts voiced concern:** Deborah Kotz, "Mental health
experts worried about 'Boston Strong' slogan," *Boston Globe*, May 13,
2013.

217 **But the IRS was cool:** Menino interviews.

218 **That day, September 11, 2001:** Bob Oakes and Lisa Tobin, "9/11:
Menino on Leading Boston Through Chaos," WBUR, September 7,
2011.

219 **"We're a big city":** Andrew Ryan and John R. Ellement, "Mayor
Menino lunches on Boylston Street; says businesses helping each other
to recover," *Boston Globe*, April 25, 2013, http://www.boston.com
/metrodesk/2013/04/25/mayor-menino-lunches-boylston-street-says
-businesses-helping-each-other-recover/NLmEwVSxjznE1OV2ujWrcN
/story.html.

220 **On the weekend following the attack:** Interviews of McGillivray
and race official Josh Nemzer by Scott Helman, August and September
2013.

220 **"I'm just trying to pull it together":** Jenn Abelson and Casey Ross,
"Back, but in no way business as usual," *Boston Globe*, April 24, 2013.

221 **Sharon Maes returned to her apartment:** Evan Allen and Brian

MacQuarrie, "Residents return to homes forever changed," *Boston Globe*, April 23, 2013.

221 **At 3:35 that morning:** Martine Powers and Evan Allen, "At Copley Square, reopening and reflection," *Boston Globe*, April 24, 2013.

221 **but if you watched closely:** Powers and Allen, "At Copley Square."

222 **a new sign had appeared:** "Marathon memorial to be moved to Copley Sq. Park," WHDH, April 22, 2013, http://www1.whdh.com/news/articles/local/boston/10010432402737/marathon-memorial-to-be-moved-to-copley-sq-park/.

222 **Shane O'Hara had gone back in:** O'Hara interviews.

225 **Heather Abbott had been waiting:** Abbott interviews.

226 **Her friend Jason had been with her:** Geremia interviews.

227 **Medford was the city where he'd grown up:** Interviews of Dave McGillivray, Amy Dominici, and Susan West by Scott Helman, 2013.

227 **In a room near the entrance:** Bryan Marquard, "Hundreds bid goodbye to Campbell," *Boston Globe*, April 23, 2013; interview of Bryan Marquard by Scott Helman, October 2013.

227 **McGillivray was nervous:** McGillivray and Dominici interviews.

228 **With hundreds of mourners:** Interview of Fred Dello Russo by Scott Helman, October 2013.

228 **The skin on her forearm:** Richard A. Oppel Jr., Jess Bidgood, and Katharine Q. Seelye, "Bostonians, Assured That Danger Is Past, Begin Farewells to Victims," *New York Times*, April 22, 2013.

228 **"I'm here because my heart hurts":** Franci Richardson Ellement and Rich Schapiro, "She was so loving," *New York Daily News*, April 22, 2013.

228 **As the first wake or funeral:** Marquard interview.

228 **About two hundred people:** Marquard, "Hundreds bid goodbye."

229 **Dave McGillivray had mowed the grass:** McGillivray and Fechter, *The Last Pick: The Boston Marathon Race Director's Road to Success*, 19.

229 **A hush fell over the gathering:** Marquard, "Hundreds bid goodbye"; Marquard interview.

229 **her friends had trouble leaving her:** Interviews of Tim Getchell, Sean McLaughlin, and Bryan Conway by Scott Helman, August 2013.

229 **Brian Fleming spent the week:** Interview of Brian Fleming by Jenna Russell, September 2013.

231 **Shana Cottone knew she needed some time off:** Cottone interviews.

233 **Celeste was in tears:** Eric Moskowitz, "Marines bring hope to Marathon attack victims," *Boston Globe*, April 23, 2013; "Celeste and Sydney get an inspiring visit from the Marines," posted to YouTube by Alyssa

Carter, April 21, 2013, http://www.youtube.com/watch?feature=player
_embedded&v=hy_LNYR-MiI.

234 **More than 1,500 American soldiers:** David Wood, "US Wounded in
Iraq, Afghanistan, includes more than 1,500 amputees," *Huffington
Post*, November 7, 2012; Gregg Zoroya, "Some wounded troops choose
amputation," *USA Today*, April 19, 2011.

237 **What was clear, within minutes:** FBI, "Updates on Investigation Into
Multiple Explosions in Boston," accessed September 8, 2013, http://
www.fbi.gov/news/updates-on-investigation-into-multiple-explosions-in
-boston; Michael Kranish, Bryan Bender, Sean P. Murphy, and Noah
Bierman, "Data-sharing troubles raise questions in Marathon case,"
Boston Globe, April 25, 2013.

238 **In March of 2011:** Kathy Lally, "Russian FSB describes its Tsarnaev
letter to FBI," *Washington Post*, May 31, 2013.

238 **The Russians reported that Tamerlan:** The contents of the letter, as
read by a translator, were recounted by US Representative Bill Keating
in an interview by Walter Alarkon, September 2013.

238 **The Russians' concerns:** Siobhan Gorman, Evan Perez, and Alan
Cullison, "U.S.: Russia Withheld Intel on Boston Bomb Suspect," *Wall
Street Journal*, May 10, 2013.

238 **two years before the Boston bombing:** Kranish, Bender, Murphy, and
Bierman, "Data-sharing troubles."

238 **Under its own guidelines:** Major Garrett, "Was the Ball Dropped in
the Tsarnaev Questioning?" *National Journal*, April 24, 2013.

238 **The FBI reported its inconclusive findings:** Eric Schmitt and Michael
S. Schmidt, "2 U.S. Agencies Added Boston Bomb Suspect to Watch
Lists," *New York Times*, April 24, 2013.

238 **In September 2011, they went to the CIA:** Schmitt and Schmidt, "2
U.S. Agencies."

239 **the TIDE database didn't flag him:** Ibid.

239 **"My fear is that the Boston bombers":** Transcript of House Homeland
Security Committee Hearing, May 9, 2013.

240 **"If there is information that comes":** Transcript of Senate Homeland
Security and Governmental Affairs Committee Hearing, July 10, 2013.

240 **US officials apparently never informed:** Noah Bierman, "FBI director
admits to lapse before Marathon bombing," *Boston Globe*, June 14,
2013.

240 **In a May 2013 meeting:** Keating interview.

240 **In August 2013, the *New York Times*:** Michael S. Schmidt, "FBI Said
to Find It Could Not Have Averted Boston Attack," *New York Times*,
August 1, 2013.

241 **McCaul said that US officials:** Interview of Michael McCaul by Walter Alarkon, October 2013.

241 **They were found the next morning:** Michael Rezendes, "Bombing case casts shadow over Waltham triple murder," *Boston Globe*, June 8, 2013.

241 **Then, in the wake of the marathon bombing:** Serge F. Kovaleski and Richard A. Oppel Jr., "In 2011 Murder Inquiry, Hints of Missed Chance to Avert Boston Bombing," *New York Times*, July 10, 2013.

242 **More troubling:** Rezendes, "Bombing case casts shadow."

242 **"He laughed off the fact":** Kovaleski and Oppel, "In 2011 Murder Inquiry."

242 **whose phone number the FBI had obtained:** McCaul interview.

242 **"He's got a bad temper":** Kovaleski and Oppel, "In 2011 Murder Inquiry."

242 **He had come to the United States in 2008:** Maria Sacchetti, "After FBI probes, questions on granting of asylum," *Boston Globe*, July 5, 2013.

242 **In April and May 2013:** Maria Sacchetti, "Potential witness must be jailed until leaving US," *Boston Globe*, June 29, 2013.

243 **Todashev sat down for a fourth interview:** Michael S. Schmidt and Ellen Barry, "Man Tied to Boston Suspect Is Said to Have Attacked Agent Before Being Shot," *New York Times*, May 30, 2013; Milton J. Valencia, Michael Rezendes, and Martin Finucane, "Todashev implicated Tsarnaev in murders, prosecutors reveal," *Boston Globe*, October 23, 2013.

243 **The bureau even told the Florida medical examiner:** Maria Sacchetti, "FBI bars Fla. from releasing Todashev autopsy," *Boston Globe*, July 16, 2013.

244 **the agents began to pepper him:** Eric Schmitt, Mark Mazzetti, Michael S. Schmidt, and Scott Shane, "Boston Plotters Said to Initially Target July 4 for Attack," *New York Times*, May 2, 2013; Richard A. Serrano, Melanie Mason, and Ken Dilanian, "Boston suspect says no outside role in blasts, " *Los Angeles Times*, April 24, 2013.

244 **he and his brother had considered other schemes:** Brian MacQuarrie, Maria Sacchetti, and David Filipov, "Brothers first planned July 4 attack, officials say," *Boston Globe*, May 3, 2013; Schmitt, Mazzetti, Schmidt, and Shane, "Boston Plotters"; Serrano, Mason, and Dilanian, "Boston suspect."

245 **In mining Dzhokhar's laptop:** Federal indictment against Dzhokhar Tsarnaev.

245 **an apparent source of inspiration:** Paul Cruickshank and Tim Lister, "From the grave, the cleric inspiring a new generation of terrorists,"

CNN, April 24, 2013; Margaret Coker, "Cleric Cited by Tsarnaev Lives On—Online," *Wall Street Journal*, May 5, 2013.

245 **after a British student:** Vikram Dodd, "Roshonara Choudhry: I wanted to die . . . I wanted to be a martyr," *Guardian*, November 3, 2010.

245 **US officials viewed Awlaki:** Mark Mazzetti, Eric Schmitt, and Robert F. Worth, "Two-Year Manhunt Led to Killing of Awlaki in Yemen," *New York Times,* September 30, 2011.

246 **these smaller, self-contained terror plots:** Greg Myre, "Boston Bombings Point to Growing Threat of Homegrown Terrorism," NPR, April 20, 2013.

246 **"These extremists have no formal relationship":** Matthew Olsen, Remarks at the Intelligence and Information Sharing to Protect the Homeland Conference, June 26, 2011, http://csis.org/files /attachments/120626_InfoSharing_TRANSCRIPT.pdf.

246 **"The number of individuals remains limited":** "Empowering Local Partners to Prevent Violent Extremism in the United States," *The White House*, August 2011, http://www.whitehouse.gov/sites/default/files /empowering_local_partners.pdf.

247 **The three friends were among:** Maria Sacchetti and Matt Carroll, "Portrait emerges of immigrants' friendship with bombing suspect," *Boston Globe*, May 1, 2013.

247 **shared a black BMW:** Jennifer Levitz and Paul Sonne, "Heritage Linked Suspect, Students," *Wall Street Journal,* May 3, 2013.

247 **The car had a fake license plate:** David Filipov, "Kazakh students drove BMW with license plate reading 'Terrorista #1'" *Boston Globe*, May 3, 2013.

247 **Tazhayakov's father would explain:** Richard Weir, "Dad of suspect: 'We are not terrorists,'" *Boston Herald*, May 17, 2013.

247 **"Terrorista #1 doesn't mean Osama bin Laden":** MacQuarrie, Sacchetti, and Filipov, "Brothers first planned."

247 **two days after the bombing:** Accounts of the alleged actions of Kadyrbayev, Tazhayakov, and Phillipos after the bombing come from the following sources: Evan Perez, Jennifer Levitz, and Jon Kamp, "U.S. Charges Three More in Boston Marathon Case," *Wall Street Journal*, May 1, 2013; Allen G. Breed, "Bomb Suspect's Friends' Road To Arrest," Associated Press, May 1, 2013; Michael Wines and Katharine Q. Seelye, "After Boston Attack, 3 Friends Covered It Up, Prosecutors Say," *New York Times*, May 1, 2013; Brian MacQuarrie and Todd Wallack, "Three accused of obstructing bombing investigation," *Boston Globe*, May 2, 2013; and the federal indictment of Kadyrbayev and Tazhayakov, August 8, 2013.

248 **Kadyrbayev's lawyer contended:** Maria Sacchetti, "Third college

friend of Dzhokhar Tsarnaev indicted," *Boston Globe*, August 29, 2013; MacQuarrie and Wallack, "Three accused."

249 **After hours of searching:** Federal indictment of Kadyrbayev and Tazhayakov.

249 **An opinion writer:** Alexandra Petri, "Uncle Ruslan's inspiring words —a moment we needed," *Washington Post*, April 19, 2013, http://www .washingtonpost.com/blogs/compost/wp/2013/04/19/uncle-ruslans -inspiring-words-a-moment-we-needed/.

250 **The *New Yorker* said:** Nicholas Thompson, "The Suspects' Uncle," *New Yorker*, April 19, 2013, http://www.newyorker.com/online/blogs /newsdesk/2013/04/the-suspects-uncle.html.

250 **"I'm suspicious that this was staged":** Transcript of Maret Tsarnaeva press conference, CNN, April 19, 2013, http://transcripts.cnn.com /TRANSCRIPTS/1304/19/cnr.09.html.

250 **he wasn't an extremist:** Kirit Radia, "Tamerlan Tsarnaev's Aunt, Uncle: Nephew Was Deeply Religious but Not an Extremist," *ABC News*, April 22, 2013.

250 **"A man who takes Islam":** Miriam Elder, "Tsarnaev aunt reveals further details about visit to Dagestan," *Guardian*, April 21, 2013.

250 **it was all "lies and hypocrisy":** David Caruso, Michael Kunzelman, and Max Seddon, "Mother of bomb suspects insists sons are innocent," Associated Press, April 29, 2013.

251 **the bombing had complicated things:** McGillivray interviews.

252 **they prepared to set off:** Nemzer interviews.

252 **Jacobs picked up on it:** Interview of Ed Jacobs by Scott Helman, October 2013; McGillivray interviews.

254 **"Goddamn it, I'm not going to let":** Sagal interview.

254 **More than one political leader promised:** Michael Muskal and Molly Hennessy-Fiske, "Pressure-cooker lid, other pieces tied to Boston marathon bombing found," *Los Angeles Times*, April 17, 2013; "Kerry: Boston Marathon will return, 'bigger and better' than ever," *CBS News*, April 18, 2013.

254 **it was clear immediately:** Interviews of McGillivray and Tom Grilk by Scott Helman, September 2013.

254 **One of the first things:** Matt Pepin, "Non-finishers can run in 2014," *Boston Globe*, May 17, 2013.

255 **The BAA ultimately announced:** Grilk and McGillivray interviews.

255 **limited number of nonelite runners:** Boston Athletic Association, "Important Information Regarding Submissions Requesting Invitational Entries by those impacted by the events of April 15, 2013," November 18, 2013, http://www.baa.org/news-and-press/news-listing/2013 /november/2014-boston-marathon-limited-invitational-entries.aspx.

257 **Before they turned to 2014:** McGillivray interviews; "Fresh Finish," *Runner's World*, June 4, 2013, http://www.runnersworld.com/races /fresh-finish.

258 **she had promised him the trip:** Lamarche interviews.

258 **Peter Sagal was moved:** Sagal interview.

259 **Heather Abbott was back at Fenway Park:** This chapter is based on interviews of and reporting on Heather Abbott by Jenna Russell, in 2013, as well as interviews of Geremia, Matt Albuquerque, and Bert Reid; and the following additional sources: Kay Lazar, "Caregivers become confidantes as marathon victims heal," *Boston Globe*, June 9, 2013; "Heather Abbott throwing out the first pitch at Fenway Park," posted by dayocreative on YouTube, May 12, 2013, http://www.youtube .com/watch?v=ZsHs86XodP0.

271 **For Shane O'Hara and his staff:** O'Hara interviews.

273 **The celebration carried into Thursday:** David Filipov, Billy Baker, and Martine Powers, "Red Sox fans flock to Fenway, Marathon finish line," *Boston Globe*, October 31, 2013.

273 **Two days later:** Bryan Marquard, "Fans throng the city for World Series victory celebration," *Boston Globe*, November 3, 2013; David Filipov, "A pause to pay tribute, to weep at Marathon finish line," *Boston Globe*, November 3, 2013; O'Hara interviews.

274 **After Dzhokhar:** Henneberry interviews.

275 **Danny didn't tell his parents a thing:** Danny interviews.

276 **It started before:** Wall interviews.

278 **More than a few citizens:** Kevin Cullen, "The Red Sox as America's Team?" *Boston Globe*, October 25, 2013; Michael Walsh, "Red Sox game sees Boston Marathon victim, seven, sing national anthem," *New York Daily News*, October 14, 2013.

278 **"we are making progress":** *Richard Family Updates*, accessed October 2013, http://richardfamilyboston.tumblr.com.

278 **One thing she loved:** Tenley Woodman, "Big (Irish) step to her new life," *Boston Herald*, August 16, 2013; Zachary T. Sampson, "Young step-dancers perform to honor Jane Richard, injured in Boston Marathon bombings," *Boston Globe*, April 27, 2013, http://www.boston.com /metrodesk/2013/04/27/young-stepdancers-stepdancers-perform -honor-jane-richards-injured-boston-marathon-bombings /FphVyr6dZQm6sqqq6X2iTM/story.html; *Richard Family Updates*.

278 **US marshals had quietly transferred him:** Brian MacQuarrie and Liz Kowalczyk, "Bombing suspect moved to Devens," *Boston Globe*, April 27, 2013; Milton J. Valencia, "Tsarnaev restrictions spark legal debate," *Boston Globe*, October 6, 2013.

279 **In announcing the indictment:** Press conference unveiling the federal

indictment against Dzhokhar Tsarnaev, June 27, 2013; David Abel and Martin Finucane, "Tsarnaev indicted on 30 counts," *Boston Globe*, June 28, 2013.

279 **he decided he had a message to send:** Jacobs, Filipov, and Wen, "The Fall of the House of Tsarnaev." Additional reporting contributed by Jacobs, Filipov, and Wen.

279 **he came into the courtroom:** David Abel and Eric Moskowitz, "As kin, survivors watch, Tsarnaev pleads not guilty," *Boston Globe*, July 11, 2013; Richard A. Serrano, "Tsarnaev denies bombing charges in court," *Los Angeles Times*, July 11, 2013.

280 **the body of his brother Tamerlan:** Lauren Dezenski, Milton J. Valencia, and John R. Ellement, "Tamerlan Tsarnaev's body is in Worcester funeral home where services are being planned," *Boston Globe*, May 3, 2013, http://www.boston.com/metrodesk/2013/05/03/tamelan-tsarnaev -body-longer-north-attleboro-funeral-home-company-says/v6NAWyt Pxh5SR4p7q2hMxM/story.html; "Marathon suspect's in-laws testify at grand jury," Associated Press, September 13, 2013.

280 **wanted to bring her son's body:** Wesley Lowery and David Filipov, "Activist: Parents of Marathon bombing suspect have 'made their peace' with his burial," *Boston Globe*, May 9, 2013.

280 **Tamerlan wouldn't be laid to rest in Cambridge:** Brian MacQuarrie and Wesley Lowery, "Question of site for burial goes on," *Boston Globe*, May 9, 2013.

280 **Martha Mullen stepped in:** Wesley Lowery, "Virginia woman who co-ordinated Tamerlan Tsarnaev's burial says protests showed 'America at its worst,'" *Boston Globe*, May 10, 2013, http://www.boston.com /metrodesk/2013/05/10/virginia-woman-who-coordinated-tamerlan -tsarnaev-burial-says-protests-showed-america-its-worst/MUVSIfHs GMxp23XC1tJOCN/story.html#sthash.8Qtame2P.dpuf; Wesley Lowery and Matt Viser, "Marathon bombing suspect buried in Virginia," *Boston Globe*, May 11, 2013.

281 **They parked his truck:** Brian Ballou, "Police, governor also honor slain MIT officer," *Boston Globe*, April 23, 2013.

281 **Collier acquired the municipal badge:** Jarret Bencks, "Sean Collier posthumously receives Somerville badge," *Boston Globe*, August 23, 2013.

281 **That same spirit drove:** Eric Moskowitz, "A long night's journey with One Run for Boston," *Boston Globe*, June 30, 2013.

282 **capped off the benefit run:** Bella English, "With grit, determination Odoms adjust to a new life," *Boston Globe*, July 9, 2013.

282 **Allison Byrne was among thousands:** Interview of Alain Ferry by

Scott Helman, June 2013; Peter Schworm, "With memories and spirits strong, runners to take to the line again," *Boston Globe*, May 24, 2013.

282 **She was nervous about participating:** Byrne interviews; Ferry interview; Jackie Bruno, "Taking back the Boston Marathon finish line," *NECN*, May 24, 2013, http://www.necn.com/05/24/13/Taking-back -the-Boston-Marathon-finish-l/landing.html?blockID=841977.

282 **The trauma surgeon stepped onstage:** King interviews.

283 **Her friends weren't wild about the idea:** Abbott interviews.

284 **There was even a brazen imposter:** Interviews of Boston city officials by Jenna Russell, 2013; Derek J. Anderson, "Brothers plead not guilty to attempting to defraud One Fund," *Boston Globe*, September 12, 2013.

284 **At dawn the next morning:** David Abel, "Boston Marathon bombing memorial is dismantled," *Boston Globe*, June 25, 2013.

285 **It was their first visit to the memorial:** Patty Campbell remarks at the memorial dismantling, June 25, 2013; interview of Billy Campbell by Scott Helman, September 2013.

287 **Shana Cottone didn't recognize the feeling:** Cottone interviews.

289 **He'd done this hundreds of times:** McGillivray interviews.

291 **David King hadn't written a speech:** King interviews.

293 **"You have to smile, babe":** Campbell interviews.

296 **The October weekend had been busy:** Abbott interviews.

299 **A heavy spring rain fell:** Jenna Russell, "On anniversary, much to embrace," *Boston Globe*, April 16, 2014.

300 **All across the city:** Peter Schworm, "Around the city, a pause to remember and honor," *Boston Globe*, April 16, 2014.

301 **On Franklin Street in Watertown:** Interview of David Henneberry by Jenna Russell, March 2014.

301 **the organization announced:** Martin Finucane and Travis Andersen, "One Fund plans to distribute final $18.5 million to victims," *Boston Globe*, September 3, 2014; Travis Andersen, "Marathon victims' advocates praise new One Fund criteria," *Boston Globe*, June 28, 2014.

302 **In November 2014:** Eric Moskowitz, "Long after marathon bombings, survivor loses leg," *Boston Globe*, November 11, 2014.

302 **a federal judge in Boston:** Milton J. Valencia, "Court will cast wide net to impanel a jury for Marathon bombing trial," *Boston Globe*, November 6, 2014.

302 **"My life would have been":** John Powers, "The time of his life; Win in Boston leaves Keflezighi appreciative," *Boston Globe*, April 23, 2014; Kelly Whiteside, "'Tears of joy' in Boston; Running with pride and purpose, Keflezighi ends 31-year U.S. drought," *USA Today*, April 22, 2014.

303 **he was getting up there in age:** Peter May, "A Year Later, It's Old Glory in Boston Race," *New York Times*, April 22, 2014; John Powers, "Memories propel first US men's winner since '83," *Boston Globe*, April 22, 2014.

303 **The morning of the race:** McGillivray interview; Laura Crimaldi, Eric Moskowitz, John R. Ellement and Martin Finucane, "With 2014 Boston Marathon, Boston moves forward," *Boston Globe*, April 21, 2014.

303 **McGillivray tried to focus:** McGillivray interview.

304 **David King was out there:** Interview of David King by Jenna Russell, April 2014.

304 **Shana Cottone was among those:** Interview of Shana Cottone by Jenna Russell, April 2014.

304 **Heather Abbott had always known:** Interviews of Heather Abbott by Jenna Russell, March and April 2014.

305 **he was almost a full minute:** John Powers, "American made; Keflezighi's win was a team effort," *Boston Globe*, April 27, 2014; Powers, "Memories propel"; Powers, "The time of his life"; McGillivray interview.

306 **"This is it":** Powers, "Memories propel."

306 **"I wanted and needed":** Interview of Andrew Thomas by Scott Helman, April 2014.

306 **After crossing the finish line:** Powers, "Memories propel"; Whiteside, "'Tears of joy' in Boston"; WBZ-TV live coverage of the 2014 Boston Marathon.

Index

INDEX

INDEX

INDEX

INDEX

Photo © Dina Rudick/*The Boston Globe* Staff

Scott Helman is a staff writer at the *Boston Globe Magazine* and coauthor of *The Real Romney*.

Jenna Russell was one of the reporters at the forefront of the *Globe*'s coverage of the bombing and is a coauthor of the *New York Times* bestseller *Last Lion*. Both authors live near Boston.

CONNECT ONLINE

jennaleerussell.com
twitter.com/jrussglobe
scotthelman.com
twitter.com/swhelman
bostonglobe.com